All too often it is said that common-sense philosophers fail to justify their appeal to common sense as a philosophical standard, and that they merely repeat one another in the glorification of philosophical trivialities. This book challenges these and other widespread assumptions about common-sense philosophies and provides a major reassessment of an influential segment of the history of ideas.

Claude Buffier (1661–1737) was a French Jesuit whose philosophy earned Voltaire's praise. Thomas Reid (1710–96) was the one Scottish philosopher whose response to David Hume is still taken seriously. In this comparative study Professor Marcil-Lacoste not only refutes common assumptions, but also shows that, despite their similar concerns and the unfounded charge that Reid plagiarized from Buffier, a comparison of Reid and Buffier illuminates a range of significant epistemological issues. Further, she demonstrates that common-sense philosophies can be varied, subtle, and original.

This book also includes an edited and annotated version of Reid's hitherto unpublished *curâ primâ* on common sense prepared by David Fate Norton.

Louise Marcil-Lacoste is an associate professor of philosophy at the Université de Montréal.

McGILL-QUEEN'S STUDIES IN THE HISTORY OF IDEAS

Richard H. Popkin, Editor

3

CLAUDE BUFFIER AND THOMAS REID
Two Common-Sense Philosophers

Louise Marcil-Lacoste

McGill-Queen's University Press
Kingston and Montreal

© McGill-Queen's University Press 1982
ISBN 0-7735-1003-6
Legal deposit 3rd quarter 1982
Bibliothèque nationale du Québec

Printed in Canada

Much of the work for this book was made possible by a post-doctoral
fellowship under the auspices of the Department of Philosophy,
McGill University, and the FCAC Program of the Ministry of Education,
Province of Quebec.

Thomas Reid's *curâ primâ* on common sense is published
with the permission of King's College Library, University of Aberdeen.

This book has been published with the help of a grant from the Canadian
Federation for the Humanities, using funds provided by the Social Sciences
and Humanities Research Council of Canada.

Canadian Cataloguing in Publication Data

Marcil-Lacoste, Louise, 1943-
Claude Buffier and Thomas Reid

(McGill-Queen's studies in the history of ideas, ISSN 0711-0995; 3)
Includes text of a speech given by Thomas Reid to the Literary Society of
Glasgow, Feb. 10, 1769?, and currently held in the Birkwood Collection
(Item 2/III/7, Ms. 2131) of King's College, University of Aberdeen.
Bibliography: p.
Includes index.
ISBN 0-7735-1003-6
1. Buffier, Claude, 1661-1737.   2. Reid, Thomas, 1710-1796. I. Reid,
Thomas, 1710-1796. II. Title. III. Series.
B1959.B7M37   192   c82-094369-x

Contents

I General Introduction   1

II Claude Buffier   11
  1. The Context of Buffier's Doctrine of
      Common Sense   11
  2. The Problem of Asserting the Core of
      Buffier's Philosophy of Common Sense   15
  3. The Problem of Defining Common Sense as
      Buffier Sees It   16
  4. What Common Sense Is Not   21
  5. What Common Sense Is   32
  6. Buffier's Justification of the Appeal to
      Common Sense   43
  7. Conclusion   65

III Thomas Reid   73
  1. Difficulties in Assessing the Core of Reid's Doctrine   73
  2. Reid's Methodological Rules Concerning the
      Intellectual Powers of Man   79
  3. The Importance of Reid's Decision to Elucidate
      the Meaning of Common Sense in His "Essay on
      Judgment"   82
  4. Reid's Elucidation of the Proper Meaning of
      Common Sense   88
  5. Reid's Analysis of Philosophical Objections to the
      Common Meaning of Common Sense   94
  6. Reid's Analysis of the Problem of First Principles   97
  7. Reid's Alternative Model in the Treatment of
      Self-evident Propositions   100

8. The Background of Reid's Alternative   107
9. Reid's Codification of Self-evident Propositions   111
10. Reid's Justification of the Appeal to Common Sense 119
11. Reid's Understanding of Newton's
    Methodological Rules   124
12. Reid's Understanding of Francis Bacon's
    Methodological Advice   131
13. The Impact of Reid's Method on His General
    Doctrine of First Principles   140
14. Conclusion   143

IV General Conclusion   153
1. The Different Views of Buffier and Reid
   on Introspection   156
2. The Views of Buffier and Reid on the Most
   Important Features of the Human Mind   159
3. The Different Common-Sense Doctrines of Buffier
   and Reid   164
4. Two Counterexamples to the Caricatures of
   Common-Sense Doctrines   169

Appendix: Thomas Reid's *Curâ Primâ* on Common Sense   179
   Edited by David Fate Norton

Bibliography   209

Index   221

I

General Introduction

IN THIS BOOK, I want to show that common-sense philosophy is an important segment of the history of ideas and should be reevaluated by philosophers. My general claim is that common-sense philosophy is not taken seriously because of incorrect presuppositions about what it is. In order to substantiate this claim, I shall compare the doctrines of Claude Buffier and Thomas Reid. I chose these philosophers not only because they are important in a history of the doctrines of common sense, but also because their respective views present interesting counterexamples to the general misconceptions about this philosophy.

Common-sense philosophy has often been dismissed as philosophically irrelevant on the grounds that it merely states that men believe certain propositions to be true and that they act in accordance with these propositions. According to this interpretation, common-sense philosophers answer all philosophically important questions in the same way that Diogenes or Dr. Johnson refuted skeptical theories: by appeal to the alleged absurdity of the questions. To appeal to common sense would thus be a matter of repeating something like Diogenes' argument that we refute Zeno's arguments against the possibility of motion by *walking*— or something like Dr. Johnson's argument that *kicking a stone* could refute Berkeley's arguments against the possibility of a material world.

This view of common sense assumes that whenever common-sense philosophers argue, they make use of a very weak form of the *reductio ad absurdum*, the argument *ad risum*. Thus common-sense philosophers would consider a philosophical question adequately answered when they have provoked laughter at the absurdities of statements they reject as too ridiculous to deserve philosophical analysis.

This standard view is really a caricature, which is presented with greater or lesser degrees of sophistication. It has been argued that common-sense philosophers stop (they conclude) where philosophy must begin (it wonders, it questions, it doubts). Some critics have admitted that common-sense philosophies offer interesting arguments against skeptical systems, but have maintained that the function of these arguments is merely negative: they offer nothing by way of alternatives. Other critics have even admitted the soundness of common-sense claims, but they have argued that the appeal to common sense gives too much status to what are merely beliefs accepted without adequate philosophical arguments; at most, philosophy can only start with common sense. For those who feel that I overemphasize these misinterpretations, I shall quote some passages from a classic, Kant's *Prolegomena to Any Future Metaphysics*.

To appeal to common sense . . . is one of the subtile discoveries of modern times, by means of which the most superficial ranter can safely enter the lists with the most thorough thinker and hold his own.

It is a common subterfuge of those false friends of common sense . . . to say that there must surely be at all events some propositions which are immediately certain and of which there is no occasion to give any proof, . . . But if we except the principle of contradiction . . . they can never adduce, in proof of this privilege, anything else indubitable which they can immediately ascribe to common sense, except mathematical propositions, such as twice two make four . . .

. . . [the adept of common sense] gives by his popular language a color to his groundless pretensions . . .

. . . [the adepts of common sense] must grant that they are not allowed even to conjecture, far less to know . . . but only to assume (not for speculative use, which they must abandon, but for practical use only) the existence of something possible and even indispensable for the guidance of the understanding and of the will in life.[1]

However sophisticated this last account, I think it shares the mistaken assumption that all common-sense philosophers are silent about the justification of human beliefs. Common-sense philosophers are held to *evade* the question of the grounds of men's judgments. The basis for their (alleged) reliance on the argument *ad risum* and their

---

1. See Kant, [106], pp. 6–7, 25, 61, 119.

(alleged) inability to understand the point of skeptical arguments would ultimately rest on an (alleged) confusion between theoretical and practical issues and the subsequent subordination of the former to the latter.

I think that this view of common-sense philosophy, although widely held, is false. The central question of this book may thus be summarized as follows: Is it true to say that common-sense doctrines are interchangeable in that they are all silent about the philosophical justification of the appeal to common sense in philosophy? If we could show that two of the foremost spokesmen for common sense do provide philosophical justification for their doctrines and if we could show further that their justifications are not identical, then, I think, we should have a basis for concluding that other common-sense doctrines need reevaluation.[2]

Let me add that the absence of an accurate history of common-sense doctrines is even more amazing because such philosophies have been quite important and influential—even becoming the institutionalized philosophy in Scotland, France, Spain, Italy, and the United States.[3] Once the actual writings of common-sense philosophers are considered, the tendency to represent all common-sense philosophies by the same caricature is difficult to understand. A brief survey of the claims made on behalf of common sense immediately suggests various and different views of the nature of human knowledge. Shall we say, with Descartes, that common sense is of all things the most equally distributed or, with d'Holbach, that there is nothing more uncommon in the world than common sense? Shall we admit, with Shaftesbury, that it is easier to imagine half mankind run mad and joined precisely in the same species of folly than to reject the truth of common sense? Shall we, like Hume, base our approach to common sense on the awareness of both the obstinacy and the corrigibility of man's "natural" beliefs.

The point is that from Descartes to d'Holbach, from Shaftesbury to Hume, various different postulates about the nature of human

2. For the kinds of issues I have in mind concerning the question of justification, see "Démonstration, vérification, justification," [117].

3. E. Gilson, [77], p. 18, says that we need a history of such doctrines. Working on these lines, see D. F. Norton, [148], and his article in [150]; E. de Angelis, [5]; R. G. Mayor, [138]; E. Pust, [166]. For the influence of common-sense doctrines in French Canada, see my essay, [127].

knowledge have been made on behalf of common sense, and the question whether common-sense philosophers *did* offer a justification for their basic position can be answered only by an analysis of specific common-sense philosophies. In comparing the doctrines of Claude Buffier (1661–1737) and of Thomas Reid (1710–1796), I shall attempt to show the extent to which they take the question of the conditions for a valid claim to knowledge seriously; the extent to which their views on such conditions offer substantial differences; and the sense in which they have much more to offer than the "kicking-the-stone" argument.

Before I begin the comparison between Buffier and Reid, a few remarks are in order concerning the ways in which their specific doctrines have been inadequately treated. Buffier and Reid cannot be presented as "forgotten" philosophers. On the contrary, there are many writings on their doctrines and almost all philosophical dictionaries and most histories of philosophy mention their appeal to common sense.[4]

However, many previous surveys of the works of Buffier and Reid ignore their actual doctrines and focus on a very different question: the extent to which it is possible to make these doctrines fit the models and issues of other philosophical systems. Indeed, because it is assumed that Buffier and Reid were merely writing in reaction to other philosophers, accounts of their philosophies concentrate on how they understood and above all misunderstood Descartes, Locke, Hume, and others. These attempts are confusing not only because any rigorous assessment of these philosophers' *original* views is generally missing, but also because they fail to take into account the complex historical contexts of the doctrines of Buffier and Reid.

Buffier and Reid are thinkers who belong to different milieus and philosophical traditions: Claude Buffier, a French Jesuit of the early

---

4. More detailed accounts of the writings on Buffier and Reid will be given in the following chapters on each thinker. There are a few books on Buffier's works and a much larger number of books on Reid. We have only a few analyses of certain topics related to both thinkers: J. Strasser related Buffier and Reid to Descartes ([195], pp. 177–198). S. A. Grave thinks that Buffier and Reid have the same reaction against philosophical paradoxes and skepticism ([80], pp. 81ff.). G. Ardley sees a new-Cartesian (and anti-Humean) basis in the common sense of Buffier and Reid ([6], pp. 98–101). J. R. Armogathe shows the concern of Buffier and Reid with "egoism," either metaphysical or moral ([8], pp. 131–138, 152–156).

eighteenth century, was presumably influenced by Cartesian-Male-branchian rationalism; Thomas Reid, a Scottish Presbyterian, late eighteenth century, was presumably influenced by Lockean-Humean empiricism and the moral sense of Shaftesbury and Hutcheson. However, the doctrines of Buffier and Reid cannot be explained merely by reference to the prevailing theories of their time and country. For example, we know that Buffier knew and highly praised Locke's *Essay concerning Human Understanding* and that Reid read Descartes, Malebranche, Arnauld, and other continental philosophers very carefully. Furthermore, although they belonged to different traditions, both Buffier and Reid reacted against the extreme positions of the received philosophies of their countries.[5]

I take this historical complexity and the failure of philosophers to analyze accurately the writings of Reid and Buffier to account for the series of incompatible epithets applied to the views of both. Thus Buffier and Reid are considered by different authors to be both Cartesian and anti-Cartesian, Lockean and anti-Lockean, Humean and anti-Humean, realist and mystic, irrationalist, Aristotelian, Pascalian, Augustinian, Lamennaisian—not to mention the fact that they are said to be more or less enlightened in an age of Enlightenment. Such confusion invites, even demands, an analysis that will provide a more accurate understanding of common sense in this complex period, as well as a better understanding of the actual common-sense philosophies of Buffier and Reid. The important point, however, is that there is little hope of better understanding if we merely try to show the extent to which these common-sense philosophers have misunderstood Descartes, Locke, Aristotle, Hume—or anticipated Lamennais, Cousin, Peirce, Moore.[6]

5. Of course, part of the problem is, for example, that we have little knowledge of the Jesuits' philosophical role during the Enlightenment. See E. Allard [3]; B. Jansen [97]; [98]; P. A. Alletz [4]; A. R. Désautels [60], G. Dumas [65]; A. Monod [141]; B. T. Morgan [146]; Comte de Montbas [142]; J. Pappas [153]; R. R. Palmer, [151], [152]; G. Sortais [191]; L. Marcil-Lacoste [123]. See also D'Alembert [2]; Diderot [63]; and the anonymous [62], [99], [100], [101], [102], [174].

6. To give an example of the difficulties in treating the common-sense doctrines by reference to external evidence, we can compare L. M. Marsak's statement to that of E. Bréhier. For Marsak, the examples of Fontenelle and Buffier "should serve to indicate that even in the height of the Cartesian-Newtonian controversy, in France, the real issue had nothing to do with empiricism vs rationalism" (see [133], p. 32). Bréhier says: "Empiriste et déductif presque tout le monde l'est au 18ème siècle: chacun cherche en chaque science le fait fondamental d'où tout le reste pourra se déduire" (in [23], 2:436).

In the case of Buffier and Reid, my claim that certain preconceptions have impeded attempts to understand their doctrines can be further illustrated by another revealing fact. In 1780, an anonymous author attacked Thomas Reid and charged that Reid had plagiarized Buffier's treatise on common sense published in 1724. The charge made against Reid did not lack vigor. As the author says in explaining his denunciation of "plagiarism, concealment and ingratitude":

whoever will attentively consider his work, and compare it to that of Père Buffier, will certainly find that Reid has the greatest obligations to the learned Jesuit; that he has exerted much art in concealing what he has stolen, and afforded no satisfactory, or even any explanation of his ideas, concerning the principles of common sense.[7]

This attack raised serious questions about the originality of Reid's doctrine of common sense, questions that are still *unanswered* despite work by several historians of ideas. Indeed, as Aguilar has recently shown, the different approaches used in the history of philosophy, either to attack or to defend Reid on this question, have not yet produced any direct or substantial answer based on *internal* evidence.[8]

Whether we consider the lines of defenses used in the nineteenth century by D. Stewart[9] and F. Bouillier[10] or the historical approaches

---

7. The quotation is from p. xii of the English translation (London: J. Johnson, 1780) of Buffier's *Traité des premières véritez et de la source de nos jugements où l'on examine le sentiment des philosophes sur les premières notions des choses* (Paris, 1724). Hereafter referred to as *Traité*.

8. Juan A. Ventosa Aguilar, *El Sentido Commun en las Obras Filosoficas del P. Claude Buffier* (Barcelona: Seminario Conciliar, 1957). To Aguiliar's summary we must add more recent writings on this question: Johano Strasser's article, [195]; B. A. Brody's introduction to his reprint of Reid's works, [169]; K. S. Wilkins's book on Buffier, [203]; and H. M. Bracken's introduction to another recent edition of Reid's works [171]. Strasser only alludes to the question of plagiarism as an already settled question, and Brody straightforwardly affirms that Reid knew Buffier's works *after* he had developed his own ideas ([169], p. xxiii). The conclusions of Wilkins and of Bracken are more accurate: both argue that the question of Reid's originality is an open question that needs reexamination (see Wilkins [203], pp. 12, 112–14; Bracken [171], 1: xxix).

9. D. Stewart, *Elements of the Philosophy of the Mind*, pp. 60–69, in [194], vol. 3; see also Aguilar, [1], pp. 104–7. Stewart's analysis refers to Reid's *Inquiry* only and it concentrates on criteria by which one would distinguish Reid's first principles from Baconian *idolatribus*. Stewart concludes that Buffier's views are superior to that of Reid, and that Reid's acknowledgment of Buffier's *Traité* in his later works shows that the absence of a reference to it in the *Inquiry* proceeds from ignorance.

10. [133], pp. xxxii–xiv. Bouillier does not mention the charge of plagiarism. How-

used by W. Hamilton[11] and J. McCosh,[12] whether we consider the arguments used by twentieth-century writers such as F. K. Montgo-

---

ever, concerning Buffier's list of first principles, which he compares to Reid's list of first principles of contingent truths, he says: "Ces analogies sont si grandes qu'il est difficile de ne pas croire qu'il [Reid] en a pris l'idée et l'exemple dans le *Traité des Vérités premières*" (p. xix). "Je trouve en germe, dans le P. Buffier, presque tous les arguments développés par Reid en faveur de la certitude du témoignage des sens" (p. xxxii). Bouillier concludes: "La France aussi peut se vanter d'avoir eu sa philosophie écossaise" (p. xlvi). Concerning a similar rejection of representative ideas, see pp. xxv ff. See also Aguilar, [1], pp. 108–9. According to Aguilar, a Sulpician named Manier (1843) was also interested in the question of Reid's originality in the nineteenth century. He insists on Reid's sincerity as an unquestionable fact. Also Louis Peisse (1840), who translated Hamilton's works into French, affirms the similarity of the two doctrines (see Aguilar [1], pp. 107–8). According to H. Valroger, Manier would have been the editor of Buffier's treatise: *Traité des Premières Vérités et de la source de nos judgements*, nouvelle édition augmentée d'une notice et de notes critiques par un Professeur de philosophie (Paris-Lyon: Adolphe Delahay, 1843). See Aguilar, [1], p. 107, n. 36. Louis Peisse denies that the Scottish philosophy could be called Kantian: "C'est dans les écrits si injustement négligés du P. Buffier qu'on peut trouver une véritable conformité avec les principes de l'école écossaise. Cette conformité est si frappante qu'on ne peut s'empêcher de croire que c'est à cet auteur que Reid a directement emprunté sa méthode, ses vues les plus générales et jusqu'à certaines formes de langage. On peut ajouter à notre honte que cet excellent philosophe serait encore absolument inconnu en France, si Reid lui-même n'avait signalé son mérite. Cette citation de Reid, une mention de M. Destutt de Tracy (Logique, discours préliminaire), deux lignes de Voltaire (Siècle de Louis XIV) composent à peu près toute l'histoire du P. Buffier. Il est surprenant surtout que les disciples de l'école écossaise en France n'aient pas songé, malgré l'indication de Reid, à établir cette filiation" (in Sir W. Hamilton [86], p. xxii).

11. Thomas Reid, *Philosophical Works*, with notes and supplementary dissertations by Sir William Hamilton, introduction by H. M. Bracken. 2 vols. (Hildesheim; Georg Olms, 1967), 2: 788a–789b. Hereafter cited as *Works*. (Note A: On the philosophy of common sense or our primary beliefs considered as the ultimate criterion of truth; see also Aguilar, [1], pp. 109–12.) Hamilton who wants to put down the imputation of plagiarism "once and for ever" argues that there is a tradition of appeal to common sense that goes back to Hesiod, Heraclitus, and Aristotle. Hamilton lists more than one hundred testimonies and concludes that it would be "the apex of absurdity" to presume that none but Buffier could have suggested to Reid either the principle or its designation.

12. James McCosh, [138], pp. 220–23. See also Aguilar, [1], p. 112. For McCosh also there was a tradition of appeal to common sense and he refers to Shaftesbury, Hutcheson, and Turnbull.

mery,[13] T. Segerstedt,[14] and J. F. McCormick,[15] we shall not find any solution to the question of plagiarism based on what Buffier and Reid actually say about common sense. In general, rather than comparing the definitions and the arguments offered by Buffier and Reid, the conclusions concerning Reid's originality rest on decisions about the moment when he could have read Buffier's treatise.[16] Thus we have conflicting divisions of Reid's works into "before/after" he read the French defender of common sense, and the evidence is not convincing: whatever the precise moment, the central question is the extent to which the two doctrines duplicate each other. Accordingly, the conclusions concerning the originality of Reid's doctrine are remarkably vague.[17]

But if the question of Reid's originality is still an open one, the view that the doctrines of Buffier and Reid are very similar is a matter of growing unanimity. For example, P. Hazard, E. Gilson, M. F. Sciacca, A. N. Foxe, E. Bréhier, J. Maréchal, A. Bertrand, and P. Bernard echo F. Ueberweg, P. P. Royer-Collard, A. Sicard, and N. J. Laforêt—

13. Francis K. Montgomery, [144], p. 142; see also Aguilar, [1], p. 113. Montgomery defends Reid's originality in a straightforward appeal to the fact that Reid says, before Buffier, that it is a desideratum of logic that we delineate first principles of common sense.

14. Torgny T. Segerstedt, [183], pp. 5–8, 21, 44–45, 18; see also Aguilar, [1], pp. 113–14. Segerstedt thinks that we can defend the originality of at least Reid's *Inquiry*, where he finds a Baconian influence upon Reid's "empirical" common sense and the Cambridge Platonists' influence upon Reid's "rationalistic" common sense.

15. John F. McCormick, [135], pp. 299–317, esp. pp. 315–16; see also Aguilar, [1], pp. 114–15. McCormick argues that the similarities between the two doctrines are "too pat to be entirely accidental" and concludes that even Reid's *Inquiry* can hardly be said to be original.

16. Reid *Works*, 2: 713b. According to Hamilton, the most probable date is 1767, i.e., when Reid wrote an account of Aristotle's *Logic* in which we find his first mention of Buffier (see 2: 681a, note). Notice also that Reid refers to Buffier three times in his *Intellectual Powers*. See, in particular, Reid, *Works*, 2: 468a–b.

17. Notice that such external criteria also include nationalistic reactions. For example, M. Chastaing is surprised that common-sense philosophy is identified as "Scottish" when it has been defined by a French thinker; on the other hand, Urquhart thinks that "metaphysical Scotland" obviously has an advantage over French philosophy (see Maxime Chastaing, [42], pp. 352–99, esp. p. 356, n. 2; Sir T. Urquhart, "Discovery of a Most Exquisite Jewel," quoted in J. McCosh, [136], p. 25). For references to Descartes, see, e.g., Bouillier, [33]; Strasser, [195]; for references to Bacon, see Stewart, [194]; Segerstedt, [183]; for reference to Thomas Aquinas, see McCormick, [135]; and for references to Hume, see almost all of Reid's commentators.

all see Reid as bringing back and developing Buffier's doctrine of common sense.[18] Apparently, because both philosophers appeal to common sense, it has been assumed that their doctrines must be similar in all philosophically relevant aspects. Thus, if in my analysis of the views of Buffier and Reid I can show that their views are different, it should be possible to provide some answers to the question of the extent of Reid's originality.

Let me add that this situation concerning the cases of Buffier and Reid is more than a historical accident. As I said earlier, there are preconceptions concerning what common-sense philosophy is. Indeed, the peripheral ways in which the question of plagiarism has been approached and the absence of a comparative study of the content of these two doctrines are illustrations of the fact that common-sense philosophies have not received accurate treatment *as philosophies.* It is tempting to see the lack of concern with what these philosophers actually say as a result of the caricatures that are held concerning common-sense doctrines. In any case, it is surely meaningful to realize that the *substantial* answer to the question of plagiarism could only be found precisely where common-sense philosophers are assumed to be silent: in the justification of the appeal to common sense in philosophy.

18. P. Hazard, [88], 1: 117. E. Gilson, [77], p. 16. M. F. Sciacca, [182], pp. 67 (n. 95), 79, 103. A. N. Foxe, [72], p. 134. E. Bréhier, [23], vol. 2, fasc. 2, J. Maréchal, [132], 1: 89. A. Bertrand, [17], p. 371. P. Bernard, [16], p. 1168. F. Ueberweg, [197], 2: 396. P. P. Royer-Collard, in E. Boutroux [19], p. 20. A. Sicard, [184], p. 374. N. J. Laforêt, [110], pp. 67–70.

II

Claude Buffier

1. THE CONTEXT OF BUFFIER'S DOCTRINE OF COMMON SENSE

VOLTAIRE WAS ONE of the first to praise Buffier's philosophy. In *Le siècle de Louis XIV*, he included Buffier in his "Catalogue de la plupart des écrivains" and wrote: "Il y a dans ses traités de métaphysique des morceaux que Locke n'aurait pas désavoués; et c'est le seul jésuite qui ait mis une philosophie raisonnable dans ses ouvrages." Despite Voltaire's praise, Buffier's philosophy is still little known. This "shameful neglect," as Louis Peisse once called it, may derive from the fact that Buffier's doctrine of common sense is part of a far-ranging intellectual activity. A brief survey of his publications reveals indeed that this French Jesuit was interested in the intellectual issues of his time and much concerned with systematizing his views on many topics. His attempt to understand all sciences and ideas in their historical development and to present these in a form that would be understandable to the general public can be related to his particular function in the Society of Jesus. From 1699 until his death, Buffier was a "scriptor" at the Collège Louis-le-Grand. Having no teaching responsibilities and being primarily assigned to the writing of educational and literary works, he wrote copiously, to become the author of nearly fifty books. Buffier was also one of the principal authors of the *Dictionnaire de Trévoux*, as well as an active writer for the *Mémoires de Trévoux* from 1701 until his death in 1737.[1]

---

1. For L. Peisse's statement, see Hamilton, [86], p. xxii. For more details on Buffier's literary activities and its context, see Jean M. Faux, [69], pp. 131–51, esp. p. 147;

His work reaches its peak in 1732 with the publication of *Cours de sciences, sur des principes nouveaux et simples; pour former le langage, l'esprit et le coeur, dans l'usage ordinaire de la vie.*[2] This enormous book includes

---

H. Bernard, [15], pp. 176–81; C. Sommervogel, "Essai historique sur les Mémoires de Trévoux" in [189]: Sommervogel is not sure that Buffier was among the first writers of the *Mémoires de Trévoux* (see 1: 8–11; also Jean M. Faux, [69], p. 134; René Pomeau, [162], p. 49; L. M. Marsak, [133], p. 15; Jean Molino, [140], pp. 794 ff.; *Mémoires de Trévoux* (July 1732), p. 1161). It is never mentioned that one of Buffier's works has been subject to censorship. His *Pratique de la mémoire artificielle pour apprendre et pour retenir aisément la Chronologie, et l'histoire universelle* was published in 1705 in Paris (Nicolas le Cler, Edme Couterot, and M. Brunet) with the approbation of the king. But this book was prohibited a year later, after the detection of a passage was said to be false, injurious, prejudicial, and in opposition to the doctrine of Gallicanism. The (anonymous) author of this censorship charges that the first censor, M. Pouchard, inadvertently approved the publication of Buffier's book because he wrongly assumed that all priests are orthodox. For the prohibition, see the bottom page of this edition. The passage in question (pp. 145–46) refers to Pope Innocent XI, who refused to grant bulls to French bishops because, says Buffier, the French clergy had not yet withdrawn from the Assemblée of 1681. The censor notices that the passage implies that the French clergy did afterwards withdraw and therefore it is injurious to the theory and practice of Gallicanism. Because of this criticism, Buffier's rights to publish this book were withdrawn. This censorship does not seem to have greatly affected Buffier's literary works, even though his *Pratique de la mémoire artificielle* had a new complete edition only in the nineteenth century. Apparently Buffier moved the ecclesiastical section of his *Pratique de la mémoire* into the edition of his history announced in 1714. See at the end of *Les Principes du raisonnement* (Paris: Pierre Witte, 1717). Buffier had already attacked the practice of the law of censorship in *Préjugés*, nos. 326–66, pp. 455–69. On the question of censorship, see F. T. Perrens, [159]; A. Bachman, [9]; I. O. Wade, [199].

2. Hereafter referred to as *Cours de sciences*. Published in Paris by Guillaume Cavalier and P. F. Giffard, in 1732. The references to Buffier's works are from Carlos Sommervogel, [188], pp. 342 ff.

In the *Cours de sciences*, we have the following: "Grammaire françoise sur un plan nouveau," pp. 1–292 (hereafter referred to as *Grammaire*). "Traité philosophique et pratique d'éloquence," pp. 293–420. "Traité philosophique et pratique de poésie," pp. 421–552. "Traité des premières véritez et de la source de nos jugements," pp. 553–744 (referred to as *Traité*). "Traité des véritez de conséquence; ou les principes du raisonnement," pp. 745–892 (hereafter referred to as *Raisonnement*). "Elemens de métaphysique, a la portée de tout le monde," pp. 893–936 (hereafter referred to as *Métaphysique*). "Examen des préjugez vulgaires; Pour disposer l'esprit à juger sainement et précisément de tout," pp. 937–1060 (hereafter referred to as *Préjugés*). "Traité de la société civile, et du moyen de se rendre heureux en contribuant au bonheur des personnes avec qui l'on vit," pp. 1061–1256 (hereafter referred to as *Société civile*). "Exposition des preuves les plus sensibles de la véritable Religion; avec une analise succincte et suivie," pp. 1423–70 (hereafter referred to as *Exposition*). "Eclaircissements des dificultez, proposées sur divers traitez de ce cours de science" (hereafter referred

many new editions of already published works. It puts together Buffier's views on grammar, eloquence, poetry, philosophy, society and morality, and religion; it also includes a discourse on the study and method of sciences.

Buffier's works were quite popular in Europe, especially in France. In fact, his *Cours de sciences* illustrates many of the features of what was later to be called the Encyclopedist movement. Many of Buffier's ideas are recognizable, even in detail, in the *Encyclopédie* itself: there one finds not only his celebrated distinction between internal and external truths, but also his notions regarding first principles, common sense, reasoning, internal sentiment, society, freedom—about twenty such items in all.³

However varied Buffier's intellectual interests were, most of the attention that his writings have attracted was the result of his "new," "peculiar," "audacious" doctrine of common sense, a doctrine first presented in his *Traité des premières vérités et de la source de nos jugements où l'on examine le sentiment des philosophes sur les premières notions des choses* (1724).⁴ This doctrine remains remarkably articulate and consistent throughout Buffier's many books. For example, he almost never uses

---

to as *Eclaircissements*). "Discours sur l'étude et sur la méthode des sciences," pp. 1471–96. "Dissertations sur divers sujets, Par raport au Cours des Sciences," pp. 1497–1560. For more details on Buffier's writings, see Montgomery, [144], pp. 10–55; Wilkins, [203], pp. 15–65; René Pomeau, [162], pp. 39, 64–65, 49; Georges Snyders, [187], pp. 86–88, 103; Gabriel Compayré [48], vol. 1, bk. 6, chap. 1; see also A. L. C. Destutt de Tracy, [61], part. 3, p. 135.

3. The articles "Common sense" and "Internal sentiment" are literally the same in the *Encyclopédie* and in Buffier's *Traité*, except perhaps a few commas or a definite or indefinite article. For more details on the articles of the *Encyclopédie* and their corresponding passages in Buffier's works, see Wilkins, [203], pp. 102–3, and appendix. She mentions: agir, appréhension, connaissance, liberté, logique, premiers principes, propriété, raisonnement, sens, sens commun, sentiment intime, vérité, vraisemblable. In a letter (June 17, 1973) she mentions also: division, identité, naturel, as further examples of the reproduction of Buffier's passages. See also Montgomery, [144], pp. 190–95 for a similar list, and Pierre Hermand, [91], pp. 231–32. Notice that at Buffier's time there were 612 collèges, 197 "pensionnats," and many universities belonging to the Jesuits. See A. Sicard, [184], p. 373; C. Rochemonteix, [176], 2 vols.; and M. G. Dupont-Ferrier, [66].

4. In Buffier's lifetime the *Traité* was published in the following editions: Paris: Veuve Mongé, 1724; Paris: Jean Luc Nyon, 1724; Paris: François Flahant, 1724; Paris: Chez François Didot, 1724; also in *Cours de sciences* (1732), pp. 553–744.

the expression "common sense" in any but the philosophical sense his *Traité* is meant to establish and defend.

Although the most articulate statement of the doctrine of common sense is to be found in the *Traité*, Buffier's views are also expressed in three other books: the *Examen des préjugez vulgaires; Pour disposer l'esprit à juger sainement et précisément de tout* (1704), where one finds a logical analysis of twelve prejudices and a plea for paradoxes contrary to vulgar opinions; *Les principes du raisonnement exposés en deux Logiques nouvelles. Avec des remarques sur les Logiques qui ont eu le plus de réputation de notre temps* (1714), which provides an epistemological analysis of the many meanings of the notion of truth and a plea for enlarging the scope of the modern criteria of truth; and his *Elémens de métaphysique à la portée de tout le monde* (1725), which is a defense of the subtlety, the utility, and the soundness of metaphysics.[5]

In order to understand Buffier's doctrine, it is thus necessary to analyze not only his *Traité*, but also his other philosophical writings. This has not been done yet, which is all the more deplorable given Buffier's claim that his doctrine of common sense is central to an understanding of the relationships between his logical, metaphysical, epistemological, and practical views:

First truths, or those which are to be drawn from the inmost recesses and most immediate operations of the human mind, belong to that more extensive science which forms the subject of this treatise. If it shall be considered by some as truly metaphysical, they will not perhaps be mistaken; but, whatever it may be it must so closely accompany, precede or follow logic, that they mutually lend a necessary support to each other. Logic therefore remains in some measure incomplete, until it be joined to this, which likewise, in various places, supposes the former; but those two articles, being united, furnish everything that relates to the science of the human understanding, and teach

---

5. *Préjugés*, Paris: Mariette, 1704; also in *Cours de sciences*, pp. 937–1060. *Raisonnement*, Paris: Pierre Witte, 1717; also in *Cours de sciences*, pp. 745–892. *Métaphysique*, Paris: Pierre François Giffart, 1725 (also, in 1750, new ed.); Paris: La Veuve Mongé, 1725; also in *Cours de sciences*. The *Préjuges* was republished in 1725 with the following new title: *Examen des préjugez vulgaires, pour disposer l'esprit à juger sainement et précisément de tout, nouvelle édition considérablement augmentée avec l'Analise et l'Usage Moral ou Litéraire de chaque sujet*, imprimé à Evreux, Paris: Chez Pierre François Giffart et La Veuve Mongé, 1725. The *Principes du raisonnement*, republished in 1724, has the following new title: *Suites du Traité des premières véritez, ou des véritez de conséquence*. Paris: Chez François Didot, 1724.

us to form thence the true art of thinking justly, and with precision;—the object most deserving the attention of man; the most solid fruit of science.[6]

Buffier's views on common sense also question the usual distinction between academic and nonacademic topics. For example, he claims that an analysis of vulgar prejudices is necessary in determining the first principles of common sense because our problem is to make sure we do not mistake these principles for mere stubbornness in opinion. As he puts it, "too much good sense can do harm to mankind," hinting at his permanent target, dogmatism.[7] This concern with ordinary opinions does not imply a neglect of philosophical theory. On the contrary, Buffier sees his doctrine of common sense as an attempt to defend the plausibility and the importance of metaphysics itself.

2. THE PROBLEM OF ASSERTING THE CORE OF BUFFIER'S PHILOSOPHY OF COMMON SENSE

Given Buffier's attempt to avoid static categories, it is not easy to pinpoint the essentials of his doctrine of common sense. What I propose is an analysis of Buffier's notion of common sense (1) as a disposition, (2) as a set of first principles, (3) as a philosophical doctrine. My claim is that the relationships between these three levels of analyses of common sense give Buffier's philosophy its originality.

In analyzing Buffier's notions of common sense, I shall rely mainly on the *Traité des vérités premières*, a book which, according to Sir William Hamilton, offers "the most formal and the most articulate presentation of common sense after Lord Cherbury's *De Veritate* (1624)."[8] I shall, however, supplement my discussion of Buffier's views by an analysis of crucial ideas and arguments more fully developed in the three books I mentioned earlier, his *Examen des préjugez vulgaires*, his

---

6. *Traité*, no. 2, p. 3/p. 2. Unless otherwise indicated, all references to the *Préjugés* and to *Métaphysique* are to the number (no.) in the edition of the *Cours de sciences* followed by the corresponding page (p.) in Bouillier's ed., [33]. The same pattern holds for the *Traité*, with an addition of the corresponding page (/p.) in the English edition of 1780, [30]. The references to the *Raisonnement* are to the number (no.) of the edition of the *Cours de sciences* followed by the corresponding page (p.) in the edition of 1714, [32].

7. *Préjugés*, no. 365, p. 469.

8. Hamilton says: "If we except Lord Herbert of Cherbury, Buffier was the first regular and comprehensive attempt to found philosophy on certain primary truths given in certain primary sentiments and feelings" (in Reid, *Works*, 2: 786–89).

Principes du raisonnement, and his *Eléments de métaphysique*. This will not only help to provide a more systematic understanding of Buffier's philosophy, but also to eliminate some misunderstandings, in particular the view that common-sense philosophers are unaware of the problem of defining common sense.

3. THE PROBLEM OF DEFINING COMMON SENSE AS BUFFIER SEES IT

In the very beginning of his attempt to defend common sense, Buffier makes it clear that the issue is to define the notion in philosophical terms and to provide a justification for the beliefs that his definition involves. In the *Traité*, his goal is to show that there are truths—first principles—which are epistemologically prior to any other truths. The truth of such principles is guaranteed by their being shown to proceed from the most natural, immediate, and "internal" operations of the human mind. In other words, the attempt is to demonstrate the existence of self-evident truths, which provide the ground of human beliefs, and to show the validity of such grounds.

Delineating first principles is a problem because, according to Buffier, there is a limit to the possibility of *demonstrating* the truth of human judgments. For him, the human mind perceives propositions that are "so clear, so obvious, that they can neither be proved, nor refuted by other propositions of greater perspicuity."[9] However, philosophers pay little attention to such truths and their implications, while ordinary men—Buffier expects—will find this subject very difficult:

If the subject of this book be interesting to the Reader, how very formidable must it appear to the author! The researches it necessarily implies demand reflections that are frequently abstruse; and, whatever care may be taken to explain in the clearest manner, they are little relished, and frequently as little understood, by men of ordinary capacity. I have in this work endeavoured to found them on common sense; but common sense itself is not always easily conceived, or precisely understood, by those who have not made themselves familiar with objects above the capacity and notions of the vulgar.

It would be some consolation could we securely hope for the approbation of the learned; but this is another difficulty we have to encounter.[10]

---

9. *Traité*, no. 8, pp. 5–6/p. 6.

10. *Traité*, nos. 3–5, pp. 3–5/pp. 3–5. Buffier's point is that apparently philosophers and logicians prefer abstruse treatises, as if what is unintelligible were sound and what is intelligible could not be.

In order to eliminate the problems created by the inaccurate use of philosophical terms related to common sense and in order to evaluate the truth of the propositions that are said to be self-evident, Buffier's general strategy will thus be an attempt to make his endeavor to define common sense clearly in philosophical terms part of his justification of the appeal to common sense.[11]

Far from holding that common sense is a ready-made notion, Buffier insists that there are serious difficulties in the attempt to define this term. As he remarks, common sense is not very common: philosophers do not agree on what it is and what it means in philosophy, while the common man does not seem to realize that the question of its justification is a serious one. These difficulties, however, derive from a more fundamental problem: the problem of designation and language. Buffier's view on the last issue has not been taken into account when evaluating his definition of common sense. This has created misunderstandings. Indeed, Buffier's main thesis on designations and language indicates that we should *not* assume that a common-sense philosopher cannot defend a skeptical position, in particular on the issue of metaphysical realism.

Buffier notes that it is easy to define a word by using other words. But verbal designation alone does not allow us to reach understanding because, while "men do not differ much as to sentiment, . . . they differ in the words adopted by each sect and to which they are severally attached which produces confusion in discourse and afterwards in thought."[12] Our use of terms if often arbitrary and, for Buffier, one essential part of true logic is an attempt to protect men from the "contagion of words," which is the most dangerous and fruitful source of all errors. Many of our misunderstandings are, properly speaking, mere "querelles de mots," a problem that "verbiage," the habit of using words without attention to their significance, simply reinforces.

While referring to custom in matters of designation, it is important to notice that Buffier does not want to argue that common usage must be used as a standard of philosophical definitions. He is willing to admit that certain distinctions that are made in ordinary language could be relevant to philosophical issues, at least inasmuch as the

11. On the importance and difficulty of the task, see *Préjugés*, no. 356, p. 465; *Métaphysique*, nos. 65–69, pp. 295–97.

12. *Traité*, no. 555, p. 226/pp. 399–400. Here Buffier quotes Locke.

problem is to avoid confusion. However, he holds that (in general) the customary use of words does not provide a clear standard of meaning. Besides, the "general idea" we have of the ordinary use of *some* terms is usually far from the precision required by philosophy.[13] In brief, the possibility of clear and distinct definition relies on the possibility of clear and distinct ideas and is the chief work of logic-grammar. Thus Buffier's major rule for definition is the following: "In all those metaphysical researches that appear so intricate, all that we have to do is to *distinguish* the most simple ideas we have in our minds, and the names affixed to them by custom, in order to discover what we should hold as first truths with regard to them."[14] In Buffier's view, the analysis of the meaning of our terms requires a metaphysics that permits careful attention to ideas, their minute differences and their points of similarity.

It is in Buffier's view of defining as a philosophical activity that we find the roots of his skeptical attitude toward the possibility of knowing the intrinsic nature of things. He indeed holds that philosophers should not confuse the definition of a word with what they call a definition of the thing. The former is the explanation of a word of established use that agrees with the ideas mankind has been pleased to affix to it; but the latter is no more than the result of affixing to a word the number and quality of ideas that we declare to have actually in mind when we use it.[15] As a matter of fact, Buffier's view of definition is part of his qualified acceptance of Locke's thesis that we do not know the metaphysical essence of things. What we call the metaphysical essence, Buffier insists, is actually no more than the represented essence, to wit, a representation of what we judge to be the most particular, internal features of external things. This limitation on human knowledge has one negative consequence: there are no means to be sure that what we think *is* really true of the thing in itself. No de-

---

13. *Traité*, no. 32, p. 15-p. 21; *Raisonnement*, nos. 45–48, pp. 59–73. It is interesting to compare the similarity of Buffier's views on the vagueness of "common" sense and on the "common" use of terms (see *Grammaire*, nos. 26–43; 182; see also *Préjugés*, no. 193, p. 394; nos. 220–22, pp. 406–7; no. 232, p. 411; *Cours de sciences*, pp. xix–xx; *Raisonnement*, no. 152, pp. 197–198).

14. *Traité*, no. 374, p. 159/p. 259. The English translation says "consider" ideas and words, while in the French text it is clear that Buffier says and means "to distinguish" them; see also *Raisonnement*, no. 208, p. 255; nos. 209–40, pp. 256–98.

15. *Traité*, no. 222, p. 94/ p. 150; nos. 221–26, pp. 93–95/pp. 149–53.

duction, however valid (which Buffier calls "geometrically derived"), could reach further than our ideas: "The truths which we can geometrically derive from our definitions have no other foundations but those imaginary natures arbitrarily formed by the mind, and do not therefore demonstrate or teach us the actual and true nature of things."[16] In the strict sense of the word, we can only "imagine" that our ideas are knowledge of things in themselves, for what we call "truth" refers to certain particularities of our thought.

The limitation on human knowledge concerning the metaphysical essence of things nonetheless has, for Buffier, one positive consequence. Following what he takes to be a crucial contribution of Descartes to philosophy, Buffier argues that because our ideas are internal, they are clearer to us than the nature of things we think about. It follows that, in our definitions, we can be clear about the ideas we have and about the impressions of truth they produce upon our minds, even though we may ignore the nature of what has produced these ideas. It is thus possible to judge of represented essences, to be clear and distinct about our ideas when we use words. Our definitions reach no further than our ideas, and their clarity and precision reach no further than our capacity to distinguish even minute differences between our ideas. Yet our definitions can reach that far, provided we never state absolutely and without qualification anything about a complex object of thought, and provided we are as neat and clear as possible about our own ideas when we define.[17]

The last advice, let us notice, is given as a warning for philosophers when they attempt to provide a clear definition of ideas involved in perceptions. For example, philosophers should not implicitly follow Horace's maxim that "what is clearly understood is clearly expressed." This maxim, Buffier notes, is (paradoxically) a good example of the fact that the *ordinary* sense we affix to our words cannot serve where *philosophical* precision is required.[18] If this maxim were true in all cases, argues Buffier, it would mean that perceptions such as pain, fear, desire, and hope are not clear to our minds because of our difficulty

---

16. *Traité*, no. 225, p. 95/p. 152; *Métaphysique*, nos. 38–42, pp. 278–79; *Raisonnement*, nos. 133–38, pp. 172–77.

17. *Raisonnement*, no. 345–85, pp. 428–43; no. 57, p. 71; no. 286, p. 349.

18. *Métaphysique*, no. 28, p. 271; *Raisonnement*, nos. 149–56, pp. 192–202, and no. 152, pp. 197–98.

in expressing these perceptions in language. But the number and quality of our ideas and perceptions cannot be reduced to the number and quality of available words. A man who has perfectly mastered a language, including both the ordinary and the technical or scientific meanings of available terms, could still be unable to express clearly all that he clearly perceives—as the business of translation suggests. In fact, our *perceptions* reach further than our words, their clearness and distinctness further than our language. We do not know the intrinsic nature of things and we ignore the intrinsic nature of what produces our impressions of truth. Nonetheless, we can distinguish the strong *impressions* certain judgments make upon our mind from the ambiguity or ambivalence other judgments leave in our mind.

In attempting to define common sense, concludes Buffier, we should not despair, for

as there are none of my Readers who are not sensible of every thing that passes within them, with a little attention they may know, or even they already know, as much from their own reflections, as any explanation of mine can possibly convey; and scarcely any thing remains to me to do, but to point out the names suitable to the faculties and sensations of which they daily experience the effects, in order to enable them by that means to avoid confusion in their argument and expressions on a subject of so great importance.[19]

The sense in which philosophy has a genuine role lies in this attempt to improve the operations of faculties common to all men by the discovery, through adequate definitions, of the first principles of reason. These principles refer to what is most immediate in men's thought, and in this sense most common in mankind's judgments. They refer to certain ideas that are understood better than any definition or explanation; certain propositions that are clearer than any proof or disproof. Thus philosophy must recognize truths that are already in men's mind, distinguish these from words and definitions which obscure their truth, and insist that all philosophers rely upon these truths in their geometrical (i.e., logical) reasoning.[20]

19. *Traité*, no. 411, p. 169/p. 279. Buffier agrees with Descartes that philosophers should not attempt to make a thing "more clear" by a definition when it is clearer than any definition; his example is a sentiment (see *Traité*, no. 532, p. 219/p. 381).

20. *Métaphysique*, nos. 6–9, pp. 258–59, and nos. 25–27, pp. 268–70; *Raisonnement*, no. 19, p. 23.

4. WHAT COMMON SENSE IS NOT

Given the basic problem of the ambiguity in mankind's use of words, it is not surprising that Buffier's discussion concerning the meaning of common sense includes a great many remarks on what this term is *not* meant to suggest. "Though no expression is more frequently heard than that of common sense, yet nothing is less generally known than the precise idea which those words would convey; for they may be taken in various senses, which form so many different ideas."[21] Nor is it surprising that Buffier's attempt at definition includes so many arguments and refutations: to define common sense and to justify the appeal to it go hand in hand.

Buffier's discussion is meant to justify his final definition of common sense:

What is here meant by common sense is that disposition or quality which Nature has placed in all men, or evidently in the far greater number of them, in order to enable them all, when they have arrived at the age and the use of reason, to form a common and uniform judgment with respect to objects different from the internal sentiment of their own perception, and which judgment is not the consequence of any anterior principle.[22]

According to Buffier, we should not confuse the notion of common sense with the Aristotelian *sensorium comune,* a new faculty, an innate idea, a feeling, a series of vulgar prejudices, and a set of strictly identical judgments. In going through Buffier's critical assessment on such issues, we shall have an opportunity to avoid important misunderstandings, and in particular the groundless view that Buffier's common sense is the first presentation of what Lamennais was to call the principle of "autorité générale."

Buffier's common sense must not be confused with the Aristotelian faculty, which is said to unite sensible data. On Buffier's view, it is common sense that assures us of the existence of other beings and bodies, and therefore the rules governing the validity of sense testimony are epistemologically subordinate and subsidiary to first prin-

---

21. *Raisonnement,* nos. 45–48, pp. 59–73.
22. *Traité,* no. 33, p. 15/p. 21.

ciples of common sense. How can we be assured that our sensory perceptions are trustworthy if we have no certainty that there *is* something perceived in such and such a manner? The question itself, says Buffier, would become irrelevant.

But if common sense is not the Aristotelian faculty, does this imply that it is a new ("more spiritual") faculty? For Buffier, the answer is not clear but in general it is negative. He talks of such faculties as intelligence, will, memory, imagination, senses: he is even willing to use specific designations in order to avoid a confusion between many operations of the mind. But he refuses to claim the existence of a special faculty whenever we have a clear notion of a particular function of the mind. To do so would lead to numberless faculties and confuse the issue. While Buffier holds that we should distinguish several ideas and operations of the mind in order to avoid confusion in discussions, he also wants to emphasize the complexity of rational operations and assert their relationships. In brief, Buffier feels it is more important to identify the most essential dispositions of human reason than to discuss or amend the Scholastic division of faculties.[23]

Buffier also says that we should not confuse his common sense with a set of innate ideas. In the chapter on the definition of common sense, he is laconic, simply refusing to identify his notion of common sense, concerned with *judgment*, with (innate) *ideas*, the mere representations of things. Elsewhere, however, we find a qualified acceptance of the term "innate." For example, Buffier would accept, in his principles of common sense, two meanings given to the term "innate": if "innate ideas" means the imperceptible *judgment* involved in the representation of certain ideas—rather than mere ideas—or if "innate ideas" means a disposition to think in a certain (*stable*) manner—rather than a thought always actual—he would not refuse to call his common sense "innate."

Buffier thinks, however, that the designation "innate ideas" is misleading when—as is often the case—it refers to the strong necessity

---

23. *Traité*, no. 32, p. 14/p. 22. The English translator adds to the passage to which I refer here (i.e., common sense is more essential to man than the Aristotelian faculty) "and [common sense] may be possessed by him though he should be deprived of one or more of the senses." This could have been Buffier's point, provided the individual is not deprived of all his senses. Indeed, this question is raised in relation to innate ideas (see the next section). For the rules of sense testimony, see *Traité*, nos. 104–39, pp. 49–61/pp. 75–95.

we feel to assent to certain propositions. At this point, he shares Locke's reluctance to use "innate" in order to designate and emphasize the high evidential status of any proposition. For one thing, such a definition of innateness would apply to any demonstrated truth— evident in its deduction from first principles—whereas Buffier's main concern is to distinguish first principles from subordinate ones.[24]

In fact, in his attempt to distinguish common-sense principles from a set of innate ideas, Buffier wants to avoid being caught in the problem of the origin of ideas. He holds that we *cannot* find a satisfactory answer to the question whether man can form any idea that *no* sensitive occasion does or did produce, however remotely. As he says, if we define our soul as "spiritual," it is possible to argue, on the basis of this definition, that thoughts arise without sensitive occasions. But, he argues, there is no contradiction in thinking that our most spiritual ideas arise on sensitive occasions.

For him, the real question is: Do men actually form ideas without the occasion of sensation? The answer, he argues, would require the existence of a man without sensation. At this point, he refers the question to physics, from which he expects a science of so low probabilities that he thinks one can describe it as "a sort of Pyrrhonism."[25] In brief, if all that is meant by "innate ideas" is a rational disposition to judge in certain ways, Buffier would not cavil to say that common-sense principles are innate, but his considered view is that it is better to separate his common-sense doctrine from the doctrine of innate ideas.

Buffier calls his common sense a "sentiment" of reasonable creatures. What must be clear, however, is that he does not mean, by sentiment, a mere feeling. In his *Principes du raisonnement*, he had explained his use of the term "sentiment," suggesting that, for what he has in mind, the term "perception" could also be used.[26] However,

---

24. *Traité*, nos. 40–42, p. 18/pp. 26–27; no. 557, p. 227/pp. 401–2; *Raisonnement*, no. 8, pp. 8–10, and nos. 112–20, pp. 149–57. For example, Buffier thinks that one does not need to claim the idea of God innate in order to defend it (see *Traité*, no. 46, p. 20/p. 29). For the rest of the discussion on innate ideas, see *Raisonnement*, nos. 267–80, pp. 333–46; no. 325, p. 393; no. 139, pp. 179–80; see also *Traité* in Bouillier's ed., p. 238; cf., e.g., J. Denyse, [59]; Abbé Genest, [76].

25. *Traité*, English ed., pp. 353–54. Bouillier's edition of the *Traité* does not include this skeptical section on natural philosophy, but see nos. 500–507, pp. 207–9, on physic.

26. *Raisonnement*, nos. 112–20, pp. 149–57.

when a perception does not refer merely to our ideas but also to certain immediate judgments, Buffier prefers the term "sentiment" over that of "perception." Certain judgments are present, although often almost imperceptible, in the formation or the use of certain ideas. This, explains Buffier, is the reason why we say that certain of our ideas are true or false, contrary to the teachings of logic, which hold that truth and falsity pertain to judgment and not to ideas. Certain impressions are produced in our minds by certain ideas and judgments. These impressions, impressions of truth of a rational nature, can be called "sentiments." They are clear and pure. In Buffier's view, the purest *sentiment* of a rational nature is that of reflection.[27]

Sentiment, as defined by Buffier, has an important epistemological function related to his distinction between kinds of judgment according to the way we arrive at them. We judge in two ways: by way of principle and by way of consequence.[28] In the former case, we have an *immediate* knowledge originating, as Buffier puts it, with the object of thought itself without any anterior knowledge from which it could be deduced. Such immediacy provides the best *evidence* of truth and we ought to take our immediate judgments as the first steps in our reasoning. To know by way of principle is to discern the immediacy of man's rational sentiments or impressions of truth. Thus we all assent immediately to self-evident propositions (direct discernment) although we do not all reflect upon our ideas and their features (reflexive discernment). One example of direct discernment is the perception one has of one's own existence and of one's own thought, a perception Buffier calls the "internal sentiment."

When we judge by way of consequence, we deduce new knowledge from our truths of principle by an act of the mind acting upon *itself*. Truths of consequence are thereby always internal, evident, and inevitable, for they are the operations of our own mind upon its most internal operations and ideas. Such truths are also called "logical" truths because it is the proper object of logic to analyze the rules of their associations. Logical reasoning is exemplified in all sciences, for in all of them we must reason according to the rules of thought. In

27. *Raisonnement*, nos. 157–61, pp. 203–7; p. 205 (this passage is not in the edition of the *Cours de sciences*); *Traité*, no. 79, p. 37/p. 56.

28. *Raisonnement*, nos. 133–38, pp. 172–77.

fact, logical rules are the same, regardless of the content of our reasonings.[29]

The distinction between judgment by principle and by consequence leads Buffier to say that a truth arrived at by way of sentiment or principle is "plausible," while truths of consequence are "demonstrated." The nature of this plausibility should not be misunderstood: what we know by way of sentiment determines the status of the object of thought upon which we can later reason. For example, we know by means of sentiment whether we reason about an object which exists. Buffier holds that it is more difficult to ascertain a truth of principle than to reason upon it, a view that his reduction of the rules of syllogism to a mathematical rule (two quantities equal to a third are equal) partially explains.[30]

However, the gist of his argument is that all logical truths (or truths of consequence) are fundamentally hypothetical. Using an argument which was to become typical, Buffier argues that the high praise given to mathematical reasoning is misleading. Far from being the paradigm which metaphysics should emulate, mathematical reasoning is more aptly described as an example of logical reasoning and exemplifies the hypothetical status of such reasoning. Therefore, to say that there is no science but in geometry or in mathematics is to say that there is no science but that which can very well subsist without the reality of things. While mathematical reasonings may *seem* to solve factual problems, their demonstrative strength nonetheless arises solely from the hypothetical associations of ideas.[31]

Buffier offers many examples to support this view, one of which, the sphere on a needle, is like a *leitmotiv*. Geometricians, he says, talk of the properties of perfect spheres, and their statements are valid

29. *Raisonnement*, no. 136, pp. 174–75.

30. *Métaphysique*, nos. 71–72, pp. 298–300; see also *Raisonnement*, nos. 66–88, pp. 81–111; nos. 121–23, pp. 158–62; no. 129, p. 167; no. 132, p. 171; no. 288, pp. 350–52; no. 364, pp. 450–51. Buffier's rule implies a reference to the axiom "the whole is greater than the part." For negative reactions toward Buffier's logical reduction, see *Mémoires de Trévoux*, September 1714, p. 1573, and October 1732, p. 1694. A more positive reaction is that of Abbé Prévost, [164], pp. 213, 637–39. On the argument about mathematics during the eighteenth century, see E. Cassirer, [41].

31. *Métaphysique*, no. 87, p. 308; nos. 43–44, p. 281; no. 49, p. 284; *Traité*, nos. 85–90, pp. 39–41/pp. 59–63; Bouillier's ed., p. 240; *Raisonnement*, nos. 339–45, pp. 419–27, also in *Traité*, Bouillier's ed., p. 239.

with respect to their deductions. With regard to facts, however, what they say is "*if* there were a perfect sphere, it would have this or that property." Geometricians can logically hold that if the earth were a perfect sphere and were in perfect equilibrium, it could then be supported by a surface thousands of times smaller than the point of a needle. Such assertions do not appear very judicious, notes Buffier, insisting, however, that it is not the business of geometricians to verify whether the earth is such a perfect sphere, whether it could have the equilibrium required by the demonstration, whether there is a metal of the strength and thinness required by the inferences. In brief, given the logic of inferences, *if* there were such conditions, the earth *could* stand upon a needle. In associating ideas, we need not be concerned with the question whether or not the conditions on which hypothetical inferences are grounded are or could be met. This implies that when it is time to determine the real status of the object of thought itself, hypothetical reasoning cannot be used, either *pro* or *contra*. This is a point that Buffier will maintain throughout his justification of common sense.[32]

Indeed, this insistence on the hypothetical feature of logical reasoning is meant to show that reasoning must presuppose the truth of the premises on which it is grounded. In this context, logic itself must be complemented by first principles, for it is not sufficient to recall our ideas with precision and to relate them to each other: we also need to make sure that the ideas we connect in chain-syllogisms refer to a real object. In Buffier's terms, logical reasoning faces a "problem of facts": only if the facts about which we reason were guaranteed to apply to the actual world could he sanction geometrical (that is, logical) demonstrations in all sciences. It is precisely such a guarantee that "sentiment" and "plausibility" are meant to provide and which common sense—as a sentiment—conveys.[33]

32. *Métaphysique*, no. 50, p. 285; *Raisonnement*, no. 136, pp. 174–75, and nos. 340–42, pp. 420–26; *Traité*, Bouillier's ed., pp. 236–41; *Traité*, no. 199, pp. 81–82/pp. 131–32.

33. *Raisonnement*, no, 185, p. 229; no. 287, p. 350; no. 344, p. 427; nos. 309–12, pp. 371–72. Buffier's language is sometimes misleading inasmuch as it conveys a realistic type of epistemology (see *Raisonnement*, no. 309, pp. 370–71, and *Métaphysique*, nos. 63–64, pp. 293–94), but when he uses the term "objective" it usually refers to the fact that we deal with the object of thought as such and not with hypothetical inferences. Pascal had already used "coeur" to denote a rational disposition to judge by direct and

The most striking feature of Buffier's assessment of what his definition of common sense is not meant to convey lies in his original account of the nature of vulgar prejudices and in the methodological implications of this account when justifying principles of common sense. Buffier's persistent claim is that we must distinguish common sense from vulgar opinions and prejudices.[34] First of all, Buffier fully agrees with philosophical objections to common sense defined only as vulgar notions. Public opinion, in his mind, has nothing to do with common sense. Like Proteus, public opinion changes without reason. The public of public opinion is in fact many publics—multiform, full of contradictions and changing fashions.

Here the example of aesthetic appreciation is revealing. As Buffier says, if we define "good taste" as the approval of artistic masterpieces *only*, it would be naïve to rely on public opinion for a confirmation of this definition and for a discovery of what these masterpieces are.[35] To argue that the only legitimate public is the public who approve of masterpieces only is to confuse the issue: it would be as difficult to decide what is "good taste" on the basis of common sense as it would be to decide what is common sense on the basis of taste. In most questions, *vox populi* is so far from *vox Dei* that a contrary maxim is frequently confirmed: the truth is not made by the multitude.[36]

Just as he has found the use of words to be varied and relative, so Buffier's examination of vulgar prejudices reveals that he is aware, to the point of obsession, of the relativity of human opinions. He also recognizes the heavy influence of "civilisation," which he describes as

---

immediate grasping of the truth, and this in opposition to "reason" determining the truth by way of reasoning. Buffier's "common sentiment," as well as Pascal's "coeur," denotes a disposition to comprehend first principles inasmuch as these truths are principles of other truths. Pascal's "coeur" and Buffier's "common sentiment" connect the necessity to assent to certain judgment with their immediacy. See Pascal, [154], no. 282; see, e.g., no. 3, 260, 268, 275, 282, 384, 392, 395. On the question of sentiment, see D. Stewart, [193], 5: 415–17; J. P. Zimmerman, [204], pp. 42–64, 440–66; R. Mercier, [139], p. 431.

34. If Lanson is right in defining rationalism as an attempt to struggle against prejudices, Buffier must be called a champion of rationalism (see G. Lanson, [112], pp. 5–28, 409–30).

35. *Préjugés*, nos. 346–60, pp. 465–66.

36. "Dissertation sur le goût," in *Cours de sciences*, no. 26, pp. 1467 ff. *Traité*, nos. 81–82, pp. 37–38, 57–58.

a comedy or a set of historical habits. In this line, all norms are suspicious, for they result from partial views on most questions. Such, for example, is the idea that the French language is the clearest, or the view according to which jurisprudence exhibits man's universal reason: many languages are clear, and jurisprudence exhibits many rules of conduct and not *the* rules of justice.

For Buffier, the important point here is not that all men do not agree about the truth or falsity of many statements, but that, in most cases, such disagreements are legitimate. The postulate that one of two opposite opinions must be true is, according to Buffier, a vulgar prejudice. In a Baylian tone, he argues that this Yes-or-No rule is antiphilosophical: in most questions, including that of good and evil, there are many justifiable and legitimate viewpoints. Thus, for Buffier, what the prejudicial view takes as a falsehood is simply a countertruth, pregnant with truths.[37] In this context, there could not be a "legitimate" prejudice—an expression ascribed to Trembley de Genève—for full examination of a question will reveal many justifiable viewpoints on *most* questions.[38] What is a prejudice in the proper Buffierian

---

37. *Traité*, no. 63, p. 29/pp. 43–44. For a similar view, see M. G. C. Le Gendre, [115], pp. 7, 343; and *Préjugés*, no. 366, p. 469; no. 334, p. 457; no. 26, p. 329; nos. 304–6, pp. 444–46. Buffier also claims that it is a prejudice to complain about the multitude of "bad" books: taste and opinions being arbitrary, there might be good reasons to like or dislike any book. It is prejudicial to ascribe wit to only one sort of mind: there is no one entirely without wit, everyone has some talent, but none has all the talents of the human race. It is a prejudice to think that only a few persons reason well: all men reason according to the ideas they have in mind, so the man who thinks he is made of glass rightly reasons that he can be broken. The use of ridicule, in our discussions, is arbitrary as well: what we usually call "ridicule" or "extravagance" is often simply what does not fit our partial views and—the prejudice of the wise man—no one is in principle immune from ridicule, no opinion is entitled to be admitted on the basis of authority, even that of a "wise man." We cannot use universal agreement as a proof that an opinion is not a prejudice because, if a ridiculous opinion were believed by all men, Buffier ironically points out, we would ascribe it to "human nature" (see *Préjugés*, no. 90, p. 351; no. 99, p. 354; *Raisonnement*, nos. 329–36, pp. 398–416; *Préjugés*, nos. 287–325, pp. 438–55; *Raisonnement*, no. 177, p. 221). There were many books, in Buffier's time, concerned with the question of different sorts of mind. See, for example, de la Sarraz Franquesnay, [73].

38. See T. Jouffroy, [104], 1: 72; see also *Préjugés*, no. 119, p. 161; no. 112, pp. 358 ff.; nos. 202–16, pp. 381 ff.; no. 143, p. 373; no. 311, p. 448; *Traité*, nos. 513–20, pp. 212–14/pp. 363–71; *Métaphysique*, no. 2, p. 256; nos. 64–66, pp. 294–95; *Raisonnement*, nos. 162–66, pp. 208–13. Buffier's notion of prejudice as a phenomenon of intellectual life whose features are partiality and lack of sense of perspective is original. On this question, see F. Schalk, [180], and L. Marcil-Lacoste, [131].

sense of the word is the refusal or the failure to consider *several* standpoints in the points of view we discuss.

Thus, far from relying on public opinion in order to defend his notion of common sense, Buffier actually makes it a *methodological* principle to deny that all men agree or should agree on most questions. Indeed, the most important feature of what he calls a prejudice is a stubborn adherence to *one* point of view, out of ignorance, vanity, preconception, bias, and so forth. Furthermore, Buffier argues that his common sense is not meant as a magical cure for prejudices, because only a defense of paradoxes—the holding together of many viewpoints on a given question—will permit one to see how common sense itself can be distinguished from mere dogmatism.[39]

When two apparently reasonable maxims contradict each other, the only thing to do is to disentangle the varying aspects and standpoints from which they are being asserted. Buffier uses the question of the truth of sense data as an illustration of this kind of investigation. An interesting feature of this illustration is Buffier's usually overlooked claim that the common man, and not only the philosopher, does grant the legitimacy of doubts concerning sensory perceptions. According to one philosophical maxim, Buffier notices, we cannot trust our senses for we never know whether the conditions establishing their reliability are satisfied. According to the popular maxim, we are sure of what we see. In Buffier's mind, the latter is true inasmuch as we are sure of appearances, not of the things. He adds: " . . . the most stupid men . . . are convinced their eyes deceive them with regard to the true dimensions of objects; so that, while they judge, without reflection, that the sun is four feet in diameter, they are all ready, on the last reflection, to conclude that their first judgment is subject to error."[40]

In brief, the solution to vulgar prejudice is not an attempt to define

39. Notice that Buffier applies his analysis of prejudice to the unwarranted rejection by certain Scholastic philosophers of modern (Cartesian) principles (see *Traité*, no. 5, p. 4/p. 4; *Préjugés*, no. 161, p. 381). On this question, see K. S. Wilkins, [203], p. 85; V. Cousin, [51], pp. lxxxvi–lxxxviii; cxxxi; ccxxii–ccxxx; A. Sortais, [191], p. 40; A. R. Désautels, [60], pp. 15–16, 44; and the *Recueil*, [167].

40. *Traité*, no. 79, pp. 36–37/pp. 56–57; nos. 104–8, pp. 49–50/pp. 75–76. A similar analysis of the question of "taste" as a feeling or as a sensory perception is given in *Préjugés*, no. 157, p. 380; *Traité*, Bouillier's ed., p. 249; and *Cours de sciences*, "Eclaircissements," no. 61.

a "legitimate" public, but a suggestion that consideration of legitimate paradoxes be used as a cure for those who show stubbornness, partiality, and narrowness. In the previous example, what Buffier suggests is that the distinction between the appearances of objects as they are perceived without reflection (i.e., without some notion of natural sciences) and the appearances of objects as they are perceived with the aid of further knowledge will solve the contradiction between the two maxims; not by a firm Yes or No about the truth of either statement, but by a simultaneous Yes and No, which results from the acknowledgment of the different points of view from which these maxims were asserted.

As he says, Buffier is proud to be the apologist of subtle debaters, for their contests illustrate a fundamental relativity in most opinions. Buffier's philosophical defense of paradoxes is thus an epistemological plea for intellectual tolerance—the opposite opinion is not necessarily to be condemned—a point that did not please his colleagues of the Mémoires de Trévoux.[41]

What must be emphasized here is that when combined with his defense of paradoxes, Buffier's defense of common sense is a peculiar version of philosophical relativism. For him, indeed, the defense of paradoxes leads to a critical assessment of the nature of first principles. As he says, there is an important difference between prejudices and first principles, which a use of paradoxes renders explicit: far from being both true and false, given diverse perspectives, the truths of common sense have but one analysis, one light, one meaning, one perspective, *whichever point of view we have of them.* Therefore, not only should we encourage diverse perspectives, but we must also realize that this very exercise is salutary for the mind.[42] A lack of perspective

41. *Mémoires de Trévoux* May 1724, p. 955; September 1714, p. 1578; May 1730, pp. 833–34; August 1724, pp. 1483–84; March 1765, pp. 728–31. See *Préjugés,* nos. 19–20, pp. 324–25. On the limits of Buffier's logic of paradoxes when applied to practical issues, in particular the defense of Catholicism, see my [123].

42. *Préjugés,* no. 23, p. 327; *Métaphysique,* nos. 28–36, pp. 271–76; "Dissertation sur le goût," in *Cours de sciences,* pp. 1497 ff., nos. 2, 24–26, 32; *Traité,* no. 91, pp. 41–42/pp. 63–64; no. 82, pp. 37–38/pp. 57–58; *Traité,* Bouillier's ed., pp. 246–50. Buffier's view is quite different from that of Lelarge de Lignac: "Those prejudices which resist methodological doubts must be granted" (see Lelarge de Lignac, [116], pp. 72–73). Buffier's claim is original in the light of P. Hazard's statement: the champions of reason "never stopped to inquire whether in those very terms prejudice and superstition justly so called they were not including beliefs that were at once lawful and necessary" (see

would make the determination of first principles impossible, for, without this, propositions that are one-sided or prejudicial could be elevated to the status of first principles. But as vulgar prejudices are revealed by considering all points of view on the subject at one time, so this same consideration can help to discover the first principles of common sense, because they will be the same from all points of view. For certain questions, which Buffier declares to be essential, there is but one answer, no matter which point of view we take in considering them.[43]

We must acknowledge, however, that the sameness of first principles—by which Buffier means that all men would make the same judgment about the truth or falsity of a particular statement—*cannot* be perfect identity. Except in the case of a few logical truths, Buffier does not use the word "same" to refer to perfect identity.[44] At this point, Buffier not only espouses Bayle's criticisms of Spinoza's notion of identity, but also Locke's objections to "trifle propositions" given as first principles. For Buffier, to say that all men form the same judgment means that all men make similar judgments, which include points of difference but which, on the whole, present more resembling features than nonresembling ones. Part of the philosophical importance of common sense is that it forces an examination of the problem of relativity in the case of universal propositions that are not logical truths.

For example, Buffier argues that there is something which we call a "human face" and which is not identical between one man and another; there is something which we call "nature," although nature

Hazard, [90], p. 182; Hazard, [89], pp. 318–42; cf. *Préjugés*, no. 30, p. 331; *Métaphysique, no.* 74, pp. 299–300).

43. *Préjugés*, nos. 153–57, pp. 378–79; no. 23, p. 327; nos. 230–35, pp. 410–12; *Métaphysique*, no. 1, p. 255; no. 31, p. 273.

44. Buffier sees the philosophical system of Spinoza as the most obvious example of the reduction of all truths to logical (identical) truths. With Bayle, he argues that, in saying that all things are of the same substance, Spinoza confused the identity of abstraction (always perfect) and the identity of reality (never more than resemblance). We shall see the importance of this point in Buffier's justification of the appeal to common sense (see in *Cours de sciences*, "Dissertation 1: Qu'il ne sert à rien de faire de grands raisonnements contre Spinoza," pp. 1407–10, esp. nos. 400–403; also in *Métaphysique*, no. 37, pp. 276–77; no. 62, p. 293; *Traité*, no. 245, p. 105/p. 169; *Exposition*, no. 27).

is quite varied. In the same way, there are truths that are similar for all men, although they are admitted with varying clearness, easiness, and discernment by different men. After examination, we shall see that, on the whole, the impressions of truth we receive from certain propositions are more similar than our statements about them suggest. These are the impressions that Buffier will call "natural" in the sense that they constitute an element of similarity amid diversity.⁴⁵

This means, however, that there will be something paradoxical about common sense itself. To illustrate this point, let us use an example that Montesquieu greatly valued: if we were to state the principles of common sense as they apply to the notion of beauty, says Buffier, we would find that these principles create a paradox: for beauty is "that which is at the same time the *most common* and the *most rare* in things of the same species" or "that *particular* form the *most common* of all particular forms to be met with in the same species of things."⁴⁶ What is meant here is not, as it has been argued by Montgomery, to identify taste and common sense. It is to illustrate the *kind of sameness* Buffier has in mind when he says that we pass the *same* judgment. This view is reinforced in a full chapter, where the reasons why common sense is not common are clearly stated.⁴⁷

5. WHAT COMMON SENSE IS

In the *Traité* Buffier's main concern is to offer a positive account of his notion of common sense. He is thus a counterexample to the view that common-sense philosophers defend their doctrine by means of purely negative arguments.

To repeat his definition, common sense is "a disposition which Nature has placed in all men, or evidently in the far greater number of them, in order to enable them all, when they have arrived at the age

---

45. *Traité,* nos. 72–79, pp. 33–36/pp. 50–55; nos. 242–49, pp. 104–7/pp. 167–72; *Métaphysique,* nos. 32–39, pp. 274–77; *Préjugés,* nos. 246 ff., pp. 407 ff. In a word, human reason is similar in all men but not substantially the same (*Traités,* no. 217, p. 91/p. 146; nos. 72–74, p. 33/pp. 50–52; *Raisonnement,* no. 264, pp. 328–29; *Métaphysique,* no. 70, p. 297; *Préjugés,* nos. 9–11, pp. 319–21; *Métaphysique,* no. 33, p. 274). On the Buffierian logic of paradoxes, see my article, [123].

46. *Traité,* no. 94, p. 43/p. 66 (italics added). Montesquieu, [143], pp. 47, 94, 62.

47. *Traité,* nos. 72–79, pp. 33–36/pp. 50–55; see also Montgomery, [144], p. 125.

and use of reason, to form a common and uniform judgment with respect to objects different from the internal sentiment of their own perception, and which judgment is not the consequence of any anterior principle." When he says that common sense is a disposition, Buffier means that it is a stable tendency to judge that some propositions are self-evidently true. However, he insists, one must have reached the age and use of reason for common sense to be a disposition. As we shall see, as a disposition, common sense is a source of truth that should be distinguished from another source of truth, the internal sentiment. The latter is Buffier's version of the Cartesian *cogito*, to wit, the rational disposition by which we judge that certain propositions concerning our existence and our thought are self-evidently true.[48]

Immediately after his definition of common sense, Buffier offers us five examples of first principles of common sense:

(1) There are other beings and other men in the world besides me.

(2) There is in them something that is called truth, wisdom, prudence; and this something is not merely arbitrary.

(3) There is something that I call intelligence or mind and something which is not that intelligence or mind, and which is named body; so that each possesses properties different from the other.

(4) All men have not combined to deceive and impose on me.

(5) What is not intelligence, or mind, cannot produce all the effects of in-

---

48. It is in referring to common sense as a disposition that Buffier sometimes uses the argument from God's veracity in favor of his view. We cannot think that nature guides us in a wrong direction all the time, especially in essential questions, he says. God would have belied himself had he deceived us. However, Buffier's references to God at this point are also meant as indications of the limits of human understanding: what is *beyond* our faculties is as if it were not, and therefore the argument from God cannot be used uncritically. For example, we cannot invoke God's "intentions." We cannot judge of "miracles" except in considering the extent to which certain events are not "natural" given our knowledge of nature. (See *Traité*, no. 28, p. 13/p. 20; no. 37, p. 16/p. 24; nos. 75, p. 34/p. 52; no. 127, p. 57/p. 88; no. 141, p. 62/p. 96; no. 213, p. 88/p. 142; nos. 325–27, pp. 141–42/pp. 230–31; *Cours de sciences*, "Eclaircissements," no. 67; *Métaphysique*, no. 61, p. 292; no. 71, p. 298.)

telligence or mind, neither can a fortuitous jumble of particles of matter form a work of such order, and so regular motion as is found in a watch.[49]

Concerning his list of principles of common sense, Buffier laconically remarks that it is not definitive, although he insists that "at least" some of his principles should be retained. We shall see that the first example on his list—the existence of other beings and things—is central to his doctrine. For the moment, however, we must acknowledge that Buffier's discussion of the *positive* aspects of his notion of common sense is more largely concerned with the marks or qualities that permit us to discern first principles—and his examples are given as a way to test such marks—than it is with an exhaustive enumeration of first principles of common sense.

The most important aspect of Buffier's positive definition of common sense is the set of marks which, he argues, allows us to discern first principles. First principles must be:

49. Buffier has stated three lists of examples of first principles of common sense; the first list (here quoted) is taken from the *Traité*, no. 34, p. 15/p. 23. The anonymous translator of Buffier's *Traité* had added a sixth example (the translator's number 4): "What is generally said and thought by men in all ages and countries of the world is true." I think that the translator took this from Buffier's *Métaphysique*. As we can see from these two other lists, Buffier hesitated between universal consent and veracity in man as a first principle.

The second list in *Métaphysique*, no. 78, pp. 301–2, offers the following propositions (translation L.M.-L.):
"1. There is something existing outside myself and what thus exists is distinct from myself.
"2. There is something which I call soul, mind, thought in other beings and in myself, and what we call thought is not what we call body or matter, nor material thing or corporeal thing.
"3. What is known by the sentiment or the experience of all men must be taken as true and we cannot disagree with it without breaking with common sense."
The third list in *Métaphysique*, no. 82, p. 304, is the following (translation L.M.-L.):
"1. There exists something outside myself and I am not the sole being in the world.
"2. There is such a difference between what I call mind, or soul, and what I call body or matter, that I cannot seriously confuse one with the other, nor judge in good faith that the properties of the former, that is, figure and motion, can in any manner suit (*convenir*) the properties of the latter, that is, sentiment and thought.
"3. What is affirmed by the experience and testimony of all men is incontestably true."

(1) so clear, that if we attempt to defend them or attack them, this must be done with propositions which are less clear and less certain;

(2) so universally received among men, in all times and countries and by all degrees of capacity that those who attack them are, compared to the rest of mankind, manifestly less than one to a hundred or even a thousand;

(3) so strongly imprinted in our minds that we regulate our conduct by them, notwithstanding all the speculative refinements of those who imagine contrary opinions; and who even act according, not to their own imaginary notions; but to those very first principles which are universally received.[50]

Among these qualities of first principles, the first one—their superior clearness—is the most important. The other marks serve to emphasize its epistemological priority. In order to see this Cartesian ingredient of Buffier's philosophy, it is necessary to analyze the sense in which he connects the notion of self-evidence and the notion of universal consent. This question is puzzling. For example, in discussing universal consent, Buffier sometimes argues that a proposition which is "clear to most men" is certainly clearer than its opposite. At other times he is reluctant to appeal to "all men" and prefers to appeal to "reason." The ambiguity of his position appears in his conclusion: "Reason universally determined is the common sense of which I talk."[51]

My claim is that Buffier sees universal consent as a fringe benefit from the self-evidence of first principles.[52] His definition of the qual-

---

50. *Traité*, nos. 51–53, p. 22/pp. 32–33.

51. *Traité*, Bouillier's ed., pp. 244–51, *id.* in *Cours de sciences*, "Eclaircissements," nos. 45–70.

52. Part of the problem is to find out the "signs" that may be used in order to detect the rational sentiment of mankind. Buffier asks: " . . . what judge is to decide whether the character of a sensible man belongs to the philosopher or to me, when I think seriously that something is impossible which they think possible?"

His answer is the following: "I am persuaded that I shall be justified by the sentiments of all mankind, except a very few, who lose and perplex themselves in endeavouring to find a possibility where the rest of mankind can discern none. It is, therefore, the business of the philosopher to *prove to me*, that rational nature resides only in him and a few of the same stamp, whilst it is unknown to all the rest of mankind" (see *Traité*, no. 62, p. 28/p. 42 [italics added].

Buffier thinks that the evidence of first principles is perceived by "direct discernment," and in such matters he argues that philosophers must be aware of their tendency to prefer "clarification" to "light" (see *Préjugés*, no. 11, p. 321; no. 155, p. 379; *Traité*, no. 68, p. 32/p. 48; nos. 75–78, pp. 33–36/pp. 51–54).

ities of first principles is meant to reveal a simple fact: "the necessity [men] normally experience of judging clearly such a thing on such a subject."[53] For him the truth of first principles is provided by the primordial clearness of the proposition to which we assent. Such clearness appears to be a crucial element for determining that some propositions are first principles if our judgments about such propositions are made attentively, firmly, constantly, without prejudice, and in such a manner that our assent implies a propensity to act in a certain manner.[54]

For Buffier there is another way to verify the truth of first principles of common sense. A first principle is necessarily clear, evident, and self-justified, and thus a valid counterargument must present a demonstration that is clearer than the principle itself. If such a demonstration were provided, then we should conclude that the proposition was not a first principle. The latter possibility must not be ruled out. Buffier emphatically insists that it is crucial not only to enunciate the first principles of common sense but, more important, to compare the evidence and clearness of the proofs or disproofs given for them. In turn, this suggests that attempts to prove or disprove a first principle are not in themselves an argument against the philosophy of common sense. The appeal to one's own intellectual experience requires a correlative evaluation of the clearness of the counterclaims.

Buffier also argues that first principles are self-justified. His basic claim is that there is an implicit appeal to universal consent in the idea of self-evident propositions. Indeed, given the relativity of mankind's opinions, what is common in the thoughts of all men can be so only because of our natural sentiments of truth. In other words, because we acknowledge that the relativity of men's opinions results from cultural influence, we restrict the epithet "natural" to judgments whose similarity among men results from our most internal impressions of truth. We can say that a proposition is self-evident if it is in keeping with what nature has always dictated to us in our most internal impressions, sentiments, or perceptions.

---

53. *Traité*, no. 66, p. 31/p. 47 (translation L.M.-L.). The English translation says: "The business is only to be convinced of a simple matter of fact, that is, of the necessity they naturally experience of judging clearly such a thing on such a subject." See also *Préjugés*, no. 228, p. 409; no. 244, p. 415.

54. *Raisonnement*, no. 206, p. 252.

There are, Buffier argues, natural impressions which it is impossible to belie and which are, in fact, confirmed by our experience. We have never seen these opinions contradicted or, if so, we have been unable to take these denials seriously. Because all men have the same nature, first principles of common sense are democratic entities, so much so that if we had grounds to think a first principle was not admitted by most men, we should entertain serious doubts about its truth and status. Let us add that, contrary to Bouillier's claim, Buffier did distinguish two sorts of first principles, those which extend to all situations and dispositions of men and those which are particularly attached to certain situations and dispositions. It is only inasmuch as the latter *could* be admitted by all men that we call them first principles.[55]

Buffier's implicit appeal to universal consent can be further documented and explained by his view that we cannot guarantee the validity of such an appeal. We cannot consult each individual in order to confirm a first principle. Moreover, polling people (even if it were possible) would not satisfactorily establish the intrinsic validity of first principles.[56] Before Buffier, Elie Benoist had argued that in such matters we should not merely count the voices but also evaluate the truth of even unanimously accepted statements. Quite in this line, Buffier insists that we weigh the clearness of our first principles by comparing it with the clearness of counter or alternative views.[57]

For Buffier there is another reason that we cannot rely on universal consent in order to show the validity of first principles. Indeed, *his* first principles of common sense are those which make possible our empirical procedures, for they provide the evidence that an object of thought is based in reality. The rules for determining the extent of validity of human testimony would be useless if we had no assurance that there are other beings, or we were convinced that all men attempt to deceive us or that there is no difference between reasonable and extravagant utterances. Also, the rules of sense testimony would be invalid had we no assurance that there are external things and bodies.[58]

---

55. *Métaphysique*, no. 228, p. 409; no. 244, p. 415; no. 75, pp. 300–301. Bouillier, [33], p. xxviii, argues that Buffier failed to distinguish an empirical and an absolute "universal" consent.

56. *Traité*, no. 84, p. 38/pp. 58–59.

57. *Métaphysique*, no.s 83–85, pp. 304–5. See P. Rétat, [173], pp. 25–31.

58. *Métaphysique*, no. 87, pp. 307–8; *Traité*, nos. 136–53, pp. 60–66/pp. 94–103.

Just as with logical and mathematical procedures, empirical procedures are far from being self-justifying. In fact, they are doomed to stipulate principles for which they cannot provide grounds, except perhaps by illustrating the interest of their consequences. Buffier thinks that comparing the clearness of first principles with that of counter or opposite proposals is more revealing than appealing to universal consent, which actually derives its force from such clearness.

On the whole, Buffier thinks, this comparison will show that the arguments for and against first principles are not equally strong. When the denial of a first principle is obscure, when it leads to endless disputes or inquiries among men of most subtle capacities, and when, further, these denials are not demonstrated in the opponent's own behavior, we have signs that the plausibility of our first principle is much greater than that of the counterclaim.[59]

For instance, if one questions the certainty of the existence of bodies, is it clearer, asks Buffier, to prove it by saying that God has given us an idea of them and that if this idea were not true, God must deceive us? This proof, he continues, contains three or four propositions each of which is neither clearer nor more immediately obvious to the mind than "there are bodies." Shall we attempt to *disprove* it by saying, for example, that I might experience all I do without the existence of bodies? Again, argues Buffier, this possibility is far from being more obvious than our natural sentiment that bodies exist: if such a possibility were based on our natural sentiment, we would naturally judge and act as if experience did not suppose bodies. But then, what would we experience that gives us the idea that bodies exist?[60]

To take Buffier's central example, we cannot seriously think that we are the only being in the world. We feel a necessity to judge that there are other beings, although we do not have logical arguments that prove this more clearly than our self-justified assertion. There is, however, no clear argument that seems able to disprove it. Further, we cannot help thinking that a rejection of this truth would be unreasonable. Besides, the fact that most denials of this principle are merely verbal is a sign that they are not serious. As Buffier points out, in all these comparisons a counterdemonstration is proposed,

59. See Buffier's notion of probability in this line (*Traité*, nos. 157–95, pp. 67–79/pp. 105–25).

60. *Traité*, nos. 55–58, pp. 23–25/pp. 33–37.

and it is said that there are no answers to the objections raised. Perhaps there are none, but those who cannot answer the objections are not more convinced than those who proposed them. This is to say that neither the opponent nor the defender of the view that others exist seems to take the objections as crucial.[61]

Buffier holds that the same kind of defense can be given for the *existence* of reason in our fellow men, the *veracity* of their (uniform) judgment, and the *existence* of an intelligent cause of order. However, he focuses on the assertion that other beings and other things exist because he sees this principle as a necessary precondition for any valid talk about the properties and relationships of beings and things. The denial of the existence of other beings and things would make it impossible to assess the validity of all further statements about them. This argument suggests that the five examples of the principles of common sense that Buffier listed are related as follows: the assertion of the existence of other beings and things is supplemented by the assertion of their most striking properties. Even the assertion of the existence of an intelligent cause for the order of natural events cannot be understood without a reference to a "striking" property of an intelligent being, its capacity to be the cause of orderly manifestations.

Having thus analyzed the ways in which Buffier connects his notion of self-evidence to that of universal consent—the latter being a fringe benefit of the superior clarity of first principles[62]—let us further clarify

---

61. Buffier's other detailed examples are free will and hazard (*Traité*, nos. 58–70, pp. 25–33/pp. 37–50; *Préjugés*, no. 318, p. 451).

62. At this point one can see that Buffier's common sense is very different from the Lamennaisian notion of general authority against individual reason—even though his *Traité* has been presented as the first exposition of Lamennais's view (see [31]).

On this point Carlos Sommervogel notes, [188], no. 38: "Le disciple de la Mennais, éditeur de cet ouvrage, a eu soin de supprimer le passage où le Père Buffier déclare que le sens commun est une règle de certitude, non pour toute espèce de vérités mais uniquement dans les choses dont la connaissance est parfaitement à la portées des hommes qui en rendent témoignage." We can add that inasmuch as Lamennais's principle refers to human testimony (and Buffier sees all sorts of authority in this line) there is no proportion between the two doctrines: Buffier thinks that the internal sentiment and common sense are the fundamental rules of the truths we have, rules that make possible subsidiary rules for sense testimony and human testimony, including the subsidiary rule, for any testimony, not to contradict reason. On the question of authority, it is also interesting to notice that a reviewer of Buffier's views in the *Mémoires de Trévoux* (September 1724, p. 1552), had tried to explain that the Bufferian common sense refers and applies to the authority of the Church, at this point making a connection

the sense in which he argues that it would not be *reasonable* to reject first principles of common sense. This will give us an opportunity to see in what sense the argument from practice and ordinary life is introduced in Buffier's defense of common sense.

Sometimes, Buffier argues, our difficulties in speculation can be solved by reflection upon our actual practice in life. His example is the following: when we have to make a decision, we know that we have to start somewhere and to weigh the plausibility of alternatives. When we have to decide what ought to be the first steps in our reasoning, we can reasonably take this procedure as a model. To be reasonable is thus not only to reject the procedure of infinite regress, but more importantly to recognize that the necessity of starting somewhere calls for the necessity of weighing alternatives.[63]

An important consequence of this notion of reasonableness is that in weighing the plausibility of alternatives, one will be led to recognize the limits of human reason. For Buffier, indeed, to be reasonable requires that reason admit that the situation created by a mitigated form of skepticism must be accepted. In considering the objection that his defense of common sense does not provide solutions to many problems raised by philosophers, especially by metaphysicians, Buffier writes:

It may perhaps be asked, whether it is worthwhile to write a treatise on spiritual beings, when it ascertains nothing with regard to the most sublime and extensive subjects of common metaphysics? I say, in answer, that it is learning a great deal, to see distinctly we can acquire no knowledge of certain matters; and that all we might have learned of them may, or ought to be forgotten, as incapable of giving satisfaction to a rational mind.

It is perhaps the most solid fruit of metaphysical knowledge, to make us fully sensible of the limits of our understanding, and of the vanity of so many ancient and modern philosophers, who have thought it better to use a lan-

---

nowhere explicit or obvious in Buffier's philosophical writings (see *Exposition*, no. 11, pp. 153, 284; *Traité*, no. 521). The only passage where Buffier clearly relates the authority of the Church and common sense is in *Sentimens chrétiens, sur les principales véritez de la Religion; Exposez en Proses, en Vers, et en Estampes* (Paris: Joseph Mongé, 1718), p. 6. He says that common sense can be found in the teaching of such great and solid minds as the Fathers of the Church. This passage starts: *If one does not trust one's own light . . .*

63. *Préjugés*, no. 111, p. 358; no. 146, p. 375; nos. 34–60, pp. 332–39; no. 89, pp. 350–51; *Métaphysique*, nos. 72–73, pp. 298–99; *Traité*, no. 194, p. 79/p. 125.

guage that is incomprehensible than to repress the ridiculous ambition, and the dangerous vanity, of saying things that neither are, nor can be, understood by any person. For my own part, it has been my constant aim, throughout this whole treatise, to explain first truths, and the sources or principles of our opinions, in the clearest manner possible, in order to avoid, or lay open, the errors into which the inferior ranks of men and the ignorant are apt to fall for want of thinking; and many philosophers by giving into the contrary extreme and thinking too much. With this view I have been careful to admit, as notions, none but clear and precise ideas; and to acknowledge no principles, but the judgments adopted by common sense.[64]

Thus Buffier's insistence that first principles of common sense are true and his insistence that they must be admitted as first steps in any reasoning should not hide the fact that, up to a certain point, his defense of common sense does admit the truth of arguments for skepticism or, to use E. Labrousse's expression about Bayle, that it is a form of "metaphysical agnosticism."[65] We have seen that his defense of paradoxes against the vulgar prejudice that a statement must be true or false was crucial to his view of first principles. *Nolite judicare* is, for Buffier, a sound and rational position in many important cases. In particular, this seems to be the case, for him, with studies in natural philosophy, physics, jurisprudence, theology and medicine, and, to a large extent, history. To use a striking example, whose metaphysical importance cannot be missed, Buffier says:

. . . all the first truths that can be discovered in natural philosophy are comprised in its uncertainty and incomprehensibility. We have seen that the essence of things in general, and the nature of every substance, is impenetrable to our capacity. We have likewise observed that all we conceived of matter and form were no more than general and vague ideas, which can afford us but a very superficial knowledge of natural bodies.

And indeed, on the one hand, we know nothing but by experience, which extends no further in us than our sensations and the reach of our senses, which are confined within very narrow limits. On the other side, natural bodies, each in its form, are constituted only by certain modifications, cir-

---

64. *Traité*, no. 479, p. 199/p. 334; *Préjugés*, no. 307, p. 446; no. 365, p. 469.

65. E. Labrousse, [109], p. 56. If we do not recognize the limits of human reason, we open the door to mere imagination, says Buffier (see *Métaphysique*, no. 81, pp. 303–4; *Préjugés*, no. 299, pp. 441–42). For associations between Buffier and Huet on this point, see P. Mercier, [139], p. 183; P. Vernière, [198], pp. 436, 503; A. R. Désautels, [60], pp. 180–83; see also M. L. Wiley, [202]; E. Cassirer, [41], pp. 55, 84–85. In this sense Buffier objects to what Y. Belaval has called "le dogmatisme du sentiment" (see [14], p. 604).

cumstances, or qualities of rest or motion, of figure or arrangement, or of quantity or situation, in parts so imperceptible that our senses cannot reach them; so that, in order to discover what they are, we have no other resources but conjectures and systems, examples and comparisons, and probabilities or possibilities, which, at bottom, afford us no certainty of anything: they are limited, therefore, to opinions, that we consider as sufficiently supported when we can thence form a chain, or consequences, in which no contradiction appears . . . . a judicious person will not be prevented from looking upon it as a species of romance.[66]

Not only does Buffier admit that it is reasonable to suspend judgment on most questions discussed in many sciences, he also recognizes that reasonings on the basis of first principles will not lead to propositions that are as clear as first principles are. He has chapters on "what is clear about" many philosophical notions—such as being, essence, quality, unity, multiplicity, possibility, finiteness, action, freedom, immortality, and so forth—*given our first principles*. And, in general, what is clear is not very extensive.[67]

For example, common sense assures us that bodies exist, but we still have to apply subsidiary rules in order to judge the validity of sense testimonies. What is clear concerning these testimonies is summed up in the following (negative) manner: the senses do not give us the "truth" about the nature of the unknown object that produces a sensation in us, or about all the external characteristics of the object, or about the nature of the impression produced in other perceptive beings. Senses are reliable with regard to what *appears* to be the case and, more precisely, in what *appears* to be the case in important *needs* of ordinary life. Senses are not there for our (theoretical) curiosity,

66. *Traité,* English ed., pp. 353–54; *Raisonnement,* no. 44, pp. 58–59; *Traité,* nos. 187–89, pp. 77–78/pp. 121–22; no. 194, p. 79/p. 125; nos. 153–56, pp. 66–67/pp. 103–5; no. 444, pp. 183–84/p. 304; nos. 500–532, pp. 207–18/pp. 351–81.

67. Buffier's basic point is that one way to make sure that the first principles we use in our reasoning are not arbitrarily determined is to admit that the different levels of clearness and evidence include what seems less clear. According to an Aristotelian maxim, we should expect only as much evidence as the nature of the case permits. With common sense, the nature of the case requires only as much evidence as our natural sentiments of truth provide (see *Traité,* no. 6, pp. 3–5/pp. 2–5; no. 39, p. 17/p. 25; no. 82, pp. 37–38/p. 57; no. 465, p. 192/p. 321; *Raisonnement,* no. 72, p. 90; no. 184, p. 228; no. 283, p. 347; *Préjugés,* no. 151, p. 377; *Métaphysique,* no. 58, p. 291; no. 80, p. 303).

says Buffier, but in order to meet our (practical) needs.[68] Thus common-sense principles give us a limited level of certainty (body exists): but it is not the case that they guarantee the certainty of all data supplemented by sensory perceptions or the truth of all statements to be found in the natural sciences.

In other words, the appeal to common sense is not meant as an appeal to a set of propositions that would settle all the questions that "common metaphysics" attempts to answer, very often in a dogmatic fashion. To appeal to common sense is to appeal to a reason that is "between thinking too little and thinking too much." We must recognize the truth of self-evident propositions while admitting that all their implications are not clear or obvious, while acknowledging that to answer all questions or objections concerning them would sometimes require that we go beyond the limits of reason. In turn, to realize that many issues remain obscure even when one acknowledges self-evident propositions is not to say that nothing is done by such a recognition. A defense of common sense involves an awareness of the limits of human reason. We are so much filled with the dogmatic spirit, complains Buffier, that when we suggest a doubt, we appear to lack good sense.[69]

6.   BUFFIER'S JUSTIFICATION OF THE APPEAL TO COMMON SENSE

As we have said, Buffier's definition of common sense was meant as a first step in his justification of the validity of an appeal to it in philosophy. We have already mentioned some of his arguments in favor of common-sense principles: the qualities of first principles, in particular their superior clearness; the necessity of making a reasonable decision concerning the first steps of reasoning; the recognition of the limits of human reason.

These arguments are important but they do not include what Buffier sees as the *main* foundation of an appeal to common sense in

---

68. *Traité*, nos. 106–15, pp. 50–72/pp. 79–91.

69. On the contrary, Buffier holds that we must offer our "probabilities" as propositions, which should not be passed as truths (*Traité*, nos. 36–41, pp. 16–18/pp. 23–26; *Métaphysique*, no. 76, p. 301; *Raisonnement*, no. 264, pp. 328–29). For a similar approach, see Louis de Beausobre, [13]. For a different view, see J. P. de Crousaz, [53], [54], [55]; C. de Gorini, [78].

philosophy. Buffier argues that the most important support for his doctrine lies in a better understanding of the *cogito*, the internal sentiment of our thought and existence. Buffier wants to show that it is possible to *deduce* the validity of an appeal to common sense from certain marks of evidence characteristic of the internal sentiment and the mechanism of logical truths.

The importance of this argument in Buffier's doctrine has not yet been acknowledged. Known as a vigorous attacker of metaphysical solipsism, Buffier has been misrepresented as a philosopher who does not recognize the validity and importance of the *cogito*, that is, as an opponent to what he takes to be the origin of solipsism itself.[70] What has been overlooked, however, is the fact that at the basis of solipsism Buffier sees an *uncritical* use of the Cartesian *cogito*. Consequently Buffier's attempt to provide a version of the *cogito* that would overcome such problems has been missed.[71] The guarantee of his doctrine of common sense is derived from the similarities and relationships between common sense and the internal sentiment. Buffier indeed insists: "first principles of common sense and of the internal sentiment have *essential* relations between them."[72]

Buffier does not define the internal sentiment in the ways in which he has defined common sense. What we have, instead, is a discussion of its role and status as the model of all truths. From Buffier's discussion we can delineate his notion of the internal sentiment by saying that it is an enlarged *cogito*, to wit, a source of truth that refers specifically to human consciousness, to man's awareness of what passes within his mind. Accordingly the internal sentiment is summed up in the statement "I think, I feel, I exist." As we shall see, this expression

---

70. In the *Traité*, no. 15, p. 9/p. 12, Buffier says that an "English" philosopher is said to hold this view. In *Métaphysique* (one year after) he refers to a "Scottish" philosopher holding this view (no. 61, p. 292). Apparently Buffier refers to Berkeley. See Francisque Bouillier, [33], p. xxxvi; J. R. Armogathe, [8], pp. 131–35; Harry M. Bracken, [21], pp. 109–10, Appendices D, E, F. Armogathe says that in the eighteenth century the designation "solipsisme" was not known but that of "solipse" was, in France (see p. 47). The *Mémoires de Trévoux* (1713) says the Egoists are Malebranche's sectarians (p. 922). See also W. Hamilton in his *Works* of T. Reid, 1: 269–93.

71. Except J. Souilhé, [192], pp. 118–20, and A. Sicard, [184], p. 373, most commentators present Buffier as an anti-Cartesian philosopher or as a philosopher not very favorable to Descartes (see Armogathe, Ardley, Bernard, Bouillier, Chastaing, Cousin, Désautels, Gilson, Laforêt, Grave, Sortais, Strasser, Wilkins, etc.).

72. See *Traité*, Bouillier's ed., p. 7; English ed., p. 7.

is not to be confused either with a sensationalist interpretation or with a purely psychological interpretation of the *cogito*. For Buffier, the *cogito* has both an existential and a logical meaning. In saying, "I think, I feel, I exist," he wants to refer to the interior sense we have of our own existence and thought, of what passes within ourselves.

The superior status of the internal sentiment over common sense is clearly asserted by Buffier. He insists that the internal sentiment is the prior rule of all truths: "Nothing else can give us a more home [intimate] conviction that the object of our thought is as truly existent as our thought itself; for the object, the thought, and the inward sense we have of them are really nothing but ourselves, who think, exist, and have an interior sense of those things."[73] Thus "I think, I feel, I exist" is the origin and the principle of all truths, the most immediate, the clearest, the most evident of all truths for men.

In his assessment of the uncritical uses that philosophers make of the *cogito*, Buffier argues that they are inclined to interpret incorrectly the highest evidence by mistakenly *reducing* its epistemological meaning. Such reductions, rather than the *cogito* itself, are at the roots of solipsism, the denial of any existence but one's own. In discussing this issue, Buffier gives many examples of reduction.

His first example is the reduction of the *cogito* to an enthymeme. This gave rise to the question whether Descartes proposed his own existence as a consequence of his actual thought when he said, "I think, therefore, I am." Buffier comments:

If Des Cartes absolutely pretended to give us thereby a fresh conviction of our existence, as some people have supposed, his endeavours were useless and puerile: but those who defend him assert that his only view in urging such an argument was to give an example of the analysis of the most simple consequences that can be drawn from a principle; for, in fact, *I exist* is a consequence of the proposition *I think*, as we cannot think without existing. *I think*, however, is not a consequence of the proposition *I exist* since we may exist without thinking: but the consequence here is so intimately united with its principle that there can be no danger of mistake; and yet it requires some acuteness to perceive how far one is not the other. Thus, the famous consequence, *I think, therefore, I am*, is strictly true and just: it has but little merit, however, as a consequence, and still less as a discovery.[74]

---

73. *Traité*, nos. 9–13, pp. 7–9/pp. 9–11.
74. *Traité*, no. 12, p. 8/pp. 10–11 (Buffier's italics).

The *reduction* of the *cogito* to an enthymeme is not the only problem philosophers have created. Buffier feels that the philosophical interpretations of the internal sentiment lead to the following arguments and are restricted to them.

Suppose one maintains that the internal sentiment alone provides criteria for truth. It follows that, being immaterial, it cannot vouch for any perception of material objects, not even one's body. Our bodies or any bodies are very distinct from the immaterial impression we feel, and as we have no means to reach the cause of our impression if this cause is material, we have no evidence of the existence of a material object. Because we only feel immaterial impressions and because the latter can be felt by the soul without the existence of bodies, we can have no certainty in such matters. In fact, if it is true that the mind cannot, because it is spiritual, produce any impression upon the body, the more a mind is spiritual, the less it can move a body: an infinite mind is infinitely incapable of doing so. Besides, the internal sentiment cannot assure us that we are asleep or awake, for any statement implying a supposition of the existence of our body cannot be evident, given this interpretation of the evidence of the internal sentiment.[75]

Nor can the internal sentiment testify to one's own existence in the past or in the future. We have, say philosophers, no evidence but by an internal perception presently operating. We have, indeed, the perception of a remembrance of what happened to us. However, this remembrance is no more than the inward perception of what we are thinking at present, that is, a thought distinct from the thought we had yesterday, which no longer exists. Remembrance being no more than inward perception, it follows by parity of reason that lack of memory is no evidence against what may be supposed with regard to the previous states of our existence. We may have animated a crocodile or we may have existed eternally, even if we have no remembrance of these states. Our perception of what we judge and believe about our past existence is not the inward perception of the past itself, but a perception of the thought we presently have about the past in our beliefs. Thus the internal sentiment cannot vouch for our past or future existence.[76]

---

75. *Traité*, nos. 14–24, pp. 9–12/pp. 12–17; see also *Traité*, no. 55, p. 24/p. 36.

76. Buffier has no great confidence in memory as a source of truth either (see *Traité*, nos. 153–56, pp. 66–67/pp. 103–5).

The internal sentiment cannot assure us that we have the privilege of free will, for, again, we may conceive we are free without being free at all. If the internal sentiment was concerned only with one perception at a time, we could never perceive the alternative possibilities which a choice requires. Furthermore, if free will assumes a choice between present or future goods, between the senses or the reason, the internal sentiment cannot help, being incapable of bypassing the limits of present and immaterial perception.[77]

Being private, the internal sentiment cannot assure us that others exist. As the internal sensation carries no conviction but of itself and is altogether interior, it follows that we have no evident certainty of the existence of any being distinct from ourselves, whichever impressions we feel we receive. "Let the soul, in fact, reflect as long as it will on its own impressions, the occasion of which it ascribes to intelligences different from itself, it must reason, thereon as it does with regard to bodies."[78] Because the soul remains within itself, there is no evidence that its constitution is not such as to have all those ideas and impressions by itself. Even though we ascribe intelligence like our own to other beings, we are not sure that they exist distinct from us.

To be sure of the existence of beings other than ourselves, a difficult problem within the Cartesian tradition, one can argue that we have a metaphysical evidence of God's existence and therefore that such a proof holds for the demonstration of the existence of other beings. Sometimes, let us notice, Buffier is willing to argue that we cannot think that nature guides us in a wrong direction all the time: God would have belied himself had he deceived us. Yet Buffier's considered view is that the Cartesian argument from the veracity of God is not a legitimate way of showing the truth of first principles of common sense. This argument, he says, is groundless from the standpoint of the internal sentiment.

Some philosophers, Buffier argues, hold that if we consider the idea we have of God, we realize that it necessarily implies his existence and that, therefore, we can conclude that God exists, for we have this "ontological argument" as evidence. Anticipating Kant's criticisms of this argument, Buffier objects that given the epistemological features of the internal sentiment, this demonstration does not reach far. On

---

77. See also *Traité*, nos. 58–60, pp. 25–27/pp. 39–40; no. 428, p. 176/pp. 284–85.
78. *Traité*, no. 22, p. 12/p. 17.

the contrary, it begs the question, because in order to conclude that God (a being distinct from us) exists, we already have to admit that the existence of another being is more than a possibility. But it is this very supposition that the internal sentiment cannot guarantee. The ontological argument actually proves that God exists in our thought, but not that God exists. It proves perhaps that we cannot form an idea of God without including the idea of his existence, but all these notions are internal truths, which demonstrate nothing outside our ideas, our mind, and our perceptions. To prove something demonstratively is to remain within the strict limits of the internal sentiment itself. "Metaphysical evidence," Buffier argues, is the perception of what we immediately experience within ourselves, of our thoughts, ideas, or sentiments: the consequences there deduced are likewise a perception of our own thought.

Let us add that Buffier shows a certain interest in a demonstration which would parallel the ontological argument. To have an idea of oneself logically implies having an idea of what is distinct from oneself (the idea of myself implies that which is not myself) and, therefore, the other exists.[79] However, given the mechanism of the internal sentiment, this demonstration would prove only that we have an idea of others, not that others exist. Such a demonstration would be better than the ontological argument, at least inasmuch as, for Buffier, a demonstration that each being is not "the sole being in the world" is logically required before we could demonstrate the existence of such *another* being as God. However, Buffier concludes that both demonstrations are powerless to prove real existence outside thought.

... as the existence of a being really distinct from us is a thing different from the intimate perception of our own thoughts or ideas, it cannot be proved by a metaphysical evidence taken in this sense .... Some Geometricians are led into palpable error, imagining that things demonstrated by Geometry exist out of their thought, exactly similar to the demonstration formed of them in their mind ... whereof, unless we suppose God and ourselves to be the same being, it will be impossible ... to find a metaphysical demonstration of the existence of God .... no truth whatever with respect to an object

79. In fact, Buffier rejects this demonstration rather straightforwardly in his *Métaphysique* (see nos. 63–64, pp. 293–94).

different from our ideas and internal perception is susceptible of that kind of evidence.[80]

Thus the philosophical views on the *cogito* present many limitations. As Buffier points out: on the basis of such interpretations, it is impossible to make sure that a material, a past, or an external object exists (or did exist). Invoking the far-reaching absurdities of the foregoing consequences, Buffier notes that such arguments tend to exclude all certainty of everything distinct from ourselves, such as God, creatures, other beings, bodies, and even all that we have said, done, or thought a moment before the actual thought we form of those matters. "This would be to leave the world without any principle of truth as to what is distinct from ourselves, with regard to those things that affect and interest us the most, and which are the great incentive to action and the mainspring, as it were, of our whole life."[81]

In other words, the logical consequence of the philosophical understanding of the *cogito* is metaphysical solipsism, that is, the doctrine according to which one cannot be sure of the existence of anything but oneself or one's consciousness. Such a doctrine, Buffier says, would condemn all human beings—who believe in the existence of other beings—to be "dissident visionaries."[82]

However extravagant solipsism seems to be, Buffier's philosophical reaction—as Armogathe has shown—is unique.[83] While opponents to the Cartesian system had pushed polemics so far as to create a phantom-sect, the Egoists (a sect described in highly derogatory moral terms and, incidentally, sometimes identified with the Jesuits), Buffier does not treat solipsism as a mere absurdity. On the contrary, he argues that though solipsism would not *seem* to deserve attention because of its extremism, it nonetheless is a philosophical theory consistently derived from the *cogito*. Furthermore, there is no doubt in

---

80. *Traité*, nos. 48–59, pp. 20–21/pp. 30–32. On Buffier's references to God, see *supra*, n. 48. On other aspects of his anticipations of Kant, see [171], pp. 786–89 and my article, [130].

81. *Traité*, no. 28, pp. 13–14/p. 20; *Métaphysique*, no. 64, p. 294. In his discussion on the limitations of the internal sentiment, Buffier conveys both the positive use of contrariety in thought and the difference between contrariety and contradiction.

82. *Traité*, no. 7, p. 3/p. 5.

83. J. R. Armogathe, [8], pp. 131–35.

Buffier's mind about the logical validity of the skeptical inferences. If solipsism is erroneous as it stands, it is a *valid error*:

There is . . . *no contradiction in saying that we have no evident certainty of the existence of bodies.* What in fact constitutes in us that supreme light, the source of all other, which is universally acknowledged as such? Is it not the perception and knowledge we have of our own existence, which enables each of us to say with the fullest and clearest conviction, *I exist, I am, I think?* And this knowledge is in one sense the same with, or at least includes, the following: I am *one,* and not *two*; I am *myself* alone, and not another; for whoever says *myself,* says *one* to the exclusion of any other, and says *one* that is not two. To object to this would be to object to *anything being really what it is;* which would be a puerile objection, or rather downright nonsense. As therefore, no person can refuse the title of the first truth to the sense he has of his own existence, in like manner the idea of unity in himself is also a first truth. Such is evidently the source of our idea of unity. I have, therefore, the clearest and most immediate idea of unity, and of plurality or multiplicity, which is contrary to it.[84]

In other words, as the *cogito* permits one to assert one's own existence as unique, and as the evidence for this truth is the highest possible, it would seem to follow that the *cogito* cannot guarantee the existence of any other being. Indeed, the very perception of one's own existence, by the notion of unity that it carries, is the perception of oneself with "the exclusion of any other." The law of identity and the law of noncontradiction agree in favor of the solipsist conclusion. Surely, says Buffier, one cannot argue that there *is* a contradiction in the argument, nor can we adequately counter this view by saying that it is ridiculous:

From the extravagance of the propositions contained in the last chapter, many will perhaps imagine that they have been inserted rather with a humorous intent that in order to prove anything solid; but, should any of our readers entertain such an idea, it is our request that they may examine, with the

84. *Traité,* no. 89, p. 41/pp. 62–63; nos. 234–36, pp. 100–101/pp. 161–62 (italics added).

strictest severity whether they are not necessarily deduced from their principle, and that too as clearly as any geometrical demonstrations.[85]

Buffier also holds that we cannot adequately counter the solipsist conclusion by invoking a weak form of *reductio ad absurdum* based on the law of "contrariety" rather than the law of contradiction. One cannot rest on the argument that, because the solipsist conclusion is "manifestly" absurd, its opposite is by virtue of the law of contrariety "necessarily" judicious. As Buffier puts it:

A more important reflection to be made [about the *cogito*] is that every consequence which is clearly deduced from our actual thought partakes of the nature of its evident certainty in the supreme degree; and such are those demonstrations we term metaphysical, or geometrical, which are nothing but our actual thought applied to different circumstances.[86]

Thus, although the law of contrariety can be invoked *against* the absurdity of the solipsist conclusion, the highest evidence itself can be invoked *in its favor*. In trying to reject a conclusion that seems absurd, we then cannot deny that the deductions of solipsist conclusions have greater force in being clearly and logically derived from the internal sentiment and its utmost evidence.

The fact that Buffier believes solipsist conclusions to be "valid errors" can be further evidenced by his rejection of metaphysical attempts to prove true what the skeptics think we cannot prove. As we have seen with the ontological argument, Buffier thinks that the metaphysical demonstrations confuse the issue and fall into a peculiar kind of *petitio principii*. Starting with the model of evidence offered by the *cogito*, philosophers realize that certain objects of thought are distinct from that for which the internal sentiment vouches, and they conclude that these (distinct) objects must be demonstrated to exist. Then they deduce a series of internal truths of consequence in a

---

85. *Traité*, no. 24, pp. 12–13/p. 18; cf. *Traité*, no. 89, p. 41/pp. 62–63. It is important to notice this point, because Buffier talks of madness, insanity, fanaticism, subtleties, ridicule, originality, impertinence, conceit. He also talks of "degrees" of extremism. All these expressions refer to forms that denials of first principles take (see *Traité*, no. 76, pp. 34–35/p. 53; *Préjugés*, nos. 287–306, pp. 438–45, and no. 334, p. 457; *Traité*, Bouillier's ed., p. 248; *Cours de sciences*, "Eclaircissements," nos. 57–58).

86. *Métaphysique*, no. 50, p. 285; *Traité*, no. 13, p. 9/p. 11; no. 86, p. 40/p. 60; cf. *Traité*, no. 25, p. 13/p. 18 and no. 234, p. 100/p. 161.

geometrical order, failing to realize that logical truths can only testify to the agreement of our ideas with thought. Therefore, while admitting the gap between what our internal sentiment shows to be evident and what is not like our sentiment, philosophers forget, in their deductions, the very problem they were meant to face: what is external cannot be proved to be by internal truths. On the contrary, logical deductions simply develop the evident internality of our thoughts, illustrating how easy it is to be satisfied with internal operations.

To put it crudely: the skeptical denials are more accurate and logical than such "metaphysical proofs." They do not run into circularity and do defend, within a strict commitment to the characteristics of the internal sentiment, the fundamental distinctions that any logical reasoning must maintain.[87] Nonetheless, skeptical denials are difficult to accept. Apparently the utmost certainty (I exist) leads logically to the utmost skepticism (No one but me exists). This is odd, not only because solipsism is perceived as absurd by most men, but more importantly because the solipsistic consequences are of the same nature as their principle in being internal, immaterial, present, and evident.

At this point Buffier argues that we must (and that we can) discover the epistemological origin of what appears as a "valid error." Philosophers, he says, define "truth" as the "conformity of thought with its object"; they thereby assume that in order to prove any object of thought true, we must establish that the characteristics of any object are the same as the characteristics of the thought. If we add to this assumption the philosophers' view of the internal sentiment (the latter functions in recognizing itself only), we see what the origin of the problem is. Because philosophers assume that the internal sentiment provides us only with rules of identity and epistemological likeness, they conclude that there is no source of certainty concerning any object which does not have the (internal, immaterial, present) characteristics of the internal sentiment.[88]

Shall we deny that the internal sentiment is the source of all truths? Buffier certainly does not want to reject what he considers to be the prior rule, the basic model of truth. Shall we deny that the conse-

---

87. See *Traité*, Bouillier's ed., pp. 239–41; *Raisonnement*, no. 142, pp. 184–85; nos. 339–44, pp. 419–27.
88. *Traité*, nos. 85–88, pp. 39–42/pp. 59–63. For an enlightening analysis of the Cartesian rule of epistemological likeness, see R. A. Watson, [201].

quences are absurd? This cannot be done, for there is something obviously absurd in them. Shall we say that there is no distinction, no gap between internal and external objects? Buffier rejects this move, which he holds would confuse ideas and realities, abstractions and existences, systems and facts.[89] Shall we say that logical demonstration can bridge the gap between internal and external objects? This view, although it avoids skepticism, is no less extravagant than the absurd consequences that we were trying to avoid: in arguing that "what is true of our idea is true of the thing" one presupposes that something distinct from ourselves is, at the same time, not different from ourselves. This, says Buffier, is quite unintelligible and quite beside the point raised by the solipsist.[90]

Buffier does not question the epistemological value of the appeal to the internal sentiment, even if such appeal is limited to the notion of epistemological likeness. The gap between the internal and the noninternal is genuine, and skeptical philosophers are right in paying attention to it. It is so important that no one can claim that it is illogical to deny the idea that there is any tie whatsoever between the internal and the noninternal:

We may further observe how erroneous it is in those who pretend to prove that a certain object really and truly exists distinct from us, by saying that no *contradiction can be shown* in what they advance relative to the existence of that object. It is indeed enough to inform us that they have advanced nothing against an internal truth . . . for the existence of an object separate from us is not proved by mere conformity of ideas that are only within ourselves.[91]

In his commitment to the highest certainty of the *cogito* and to the distinctions for which the skeptics so strongly argue, Buffier is led to a solution which, in his view, will leave the validity of skeptical approaches untouched while providing us with a more complete account of our rules of truth. He charges that modern philosophers not only fail to make certain distinctions but, more precisely, he reproaches

---

89. *Métaphysique*, nos. 49–54, pp. 284–88; no. 37, pp. 276–77; *Traité*, Bouillier's ed., p. 241.

90. Buffier has many ironical examples of definitional strategies which amount to a series of literal connections (see *Raisonnement*, no. 140, pp. 181–82; nos. 341–42, pp. 423–26; *Traité*, Bouillier's ed., p. 239; *Traité*, no. 48, pp. 20–21/pp. 30–31).

91. *Traité*, no. 88, pp. 40–41/p. 62 (Buffier's italics).

them for failing to give the (Cartesian) criterion of the distinctness of ideas a complete and positive status in our judgments. For the moment it seems that in matters of truth the pattern of interpretation is the following: "to distinguish" (to see that X is not like the characteristics of the internal sentiment) *implies* "to deny" (to conclude that X does not exist).

For Buffier, if nonskeptical philosophers have failed to acknowledge the importance of the distinction between internal and external truths, and if skeptical philosophers have failed to acknowledge the importance of other distinctions such as between truths of principle and truths of consequence, truths of existence and truths of the intrinsic nature of things, it is because all philosophers have failed to follow out the implications that a perception of distinction has for our thought. By reducing the truth of all propositions to tautologies and to statements about objects that imply a likeness with the features of internal sentiment, skeptical philosophers overlook the important role that the perception of distinction has in the assertion of similarities (i.e., no strict likeness or identity) between objects of thought. At this point Buffier suggests that identity and likeness used as a rule for judging the truth of all statements does not do what philosophers think it does.[92] To save the internal sentiment from its perilous position, more careful analysis is necessary.

What Buffier has to show is that the rules of identity and epistemological likeness are not, regardless of the evidence for them, the *sole* rules that the highest evidence *itself* makes possible. He wants to show that the philosophical understanding of the *cogito* is natural and, given certain qualifications, valid, but that as it stands, it is an *unwarranted reduction* of the internal sentiment itself. Accordingly he devotes considerable attention to examples in which the pattern of interpretation ("to distinguish" implies "to deny") does not apply, even in the *cogito*.

Of course, the internal sentiment refers to oneself in a manner which shows that "the object, the thought, and the inward sense we have of them are really nothing but ourselves who think, exist and have an interior sense of those things."[93] Furthermore, as already

92. *Raisonnement*, nos. 253–54, pp. 313–14; no. 330: see in the edition of 1714, pp. 405–6; this passage has been corrected in the sense in which I use it.
93. *Traité*, no. 9, p. 7/p. 9.

noticed, the reference to oneself in the internal sentiment is the origin of the very idea of unity, which *excludes* multiplicity. But, observes Buffier:

. . . an important reflection occurs on this occasion; and philosophers might have made the same, instead of spending their time in vain researches after the nature of unity which is necessarily known to us; and it is, that this unity, so essential to us, is properly applicable only to beings such as me, of which I have the immediate sentiment by my own existence. I alone, I say, and other beings like me, can be truly, properly, and formally *one*; as unity, taken in that sense, excludes in the being in which it is found every possibility of division.[94]

But if, by the internal sentiment, one has the proper notion of unity, which excludes the possibility of division, this is not to say that the impossibility of division rests on strict identity, or in the total absence of distinction. As Buffier points out, the *cogito* itself is much better understood if we realize that it vouches for the evidence of truths related to both one's existence and one's thought. "I think, therefore, I exist" is an evident and important truth, which shows that by the same perception we have an internal sense of both our thought and our own existence: " . . . the consequence here is so intimately united with its principle, that there can be no danger of mistake; and yet it requires some acuteness to perceive how far one is not the other."[95] Relative to these two elements of the internal sentiment, Buffier notices that the copula has an existential function distinct from its predicative function, a distinction of which philosophers do not seem aware.[96] The *cogito* is thus a paradigm of the immediate conjunction of thought and existence and, far from granting only a logic of perfect identities, it demonstrates the possibility of conjunctive truth.

The internal sentiment itself shows that it is possible to overcome the gap between thought and existence, and its evidence applies to the conjunction of the two realms. That is to say, the *cogito* provides evidence not only for identity sentences but also for conjunctive propositions, which are self-evidently true. Actually, the conjunctive truth

94. *Traité*, nos. 234–36, pp. 100–101/pp. 161–62.
95. *Traité*, no. 12, p. 8/p. 10; *Raisonnement*, p. 320. This passage is not in the edition of the *Cours de sciences*.
96. *Métaphysique*, no. 46, p. 282; *Raisonnement*, nos. 245–67, pp. 303–33.

of the internal sentiment seems even more important than the rule of identity: at least, it requires "some acuteness" to see how far thought and existence are distinct, though intimately related in the *cogito*.

If the internal sentiment, the paradigm of all truths, already permits the enunciation of a conjunctive truth, we can expect that our logical deductions will exhibit similar true conjunctions. Indeed, in an argument that anticipates the Kantian distinction between the analytic and the synthetic *a priori*, Buffier argues that there are two kinds of logical truths: "intuitive" and "conjunctive" ones.⁹⁷ The former consists in seeing that a predicate is contained within the idea of the subject, as when we say "three is three and not two." "This idea is this idea and not another idea" is an important rule of mental activity, as it is apparent, tautological, and thus always very clear and evident. Conjunctive truths, however, are not tautological, for their predicates *add* something to the subject, however tenuously. Thus when we say that "three is equal to two and one" we add something to the subject, something that "three is three" does not contain. In such cases, says Buffier, we perceive with separation or distinction what was seen united in intuitive truths.

Conjunctive knowledge proves that human consciousness is not doomed to repeat endlessly the same tautologies, however clear. It permits us to detect the resemblance that remains between different ideas when modifications are added. As Buffier says, conjunctive knowledge is true insofar as it comes "close" to analytic intuitive truths, that is, if we complement the notion of strict identity by the notion of sameness. In conjunctive knowledge we try to see how two ideas can still be called similar although they differ in certain respects; we try to see how far the addition of modifications could be made compatible with the notion of similarity.⁹⁸

---

97. *Raisonnement*, nos. 245–67, pp. 303–33. Buffier also uses the example of "two and two make four" in the *Traité* where he wants to show that a logical truth is hypothetical (see *Traité*, no. 86, p. 60/p. 39; *Eclaircissements*, no. 50, p. 21). Hamilton sees Buffier's intuitive/conjunctive distinction as the first designation of the Kantian analytic/synthetic *a priori* distinction (see [171], pp. 786–89 and my article, [130], on the question).

98. Buffier, who presents his view as a defense of the "principle of variety" in thought, is quite consistent in his many examples. He compares first principles to numbers that are used in many mathematical operations; he refers to the Cartesian "common notions"—they permit the passage from truth of principle to truths of consequences in not being identity propositions (see *Raisonnement*, no. 240, p. 307; no. 255, pp. 316–17; nos. 260–61, pp. 323–24; no. 265, pp. 330–31; no. 316, p. 314 [slight

Buffier admits that obscurity in thought arises with the addition of modifications to certain (intuitive) truths. It is easy for us to deal with tautologies but difficult to make a clear judgment when we also have to discern all the minute differences among the ideas that some of our judgments imply. Nonetheless, the existence of two types of logical truths shows that a "reflexive discernment" (an application of analytic and synthetic methods) is a necessary part of reasoning. Indeed, the common business of intellectual activity is to reach true conclusions which, although evident by means of a process of inferences, are not evident in the same way tautologies are. To demonstrate is to perform an activity where distinctions, even the smallest, often play a crucial and fruitful role. In this context, to say, as some logicians do, that the secret art of syllogism is to have one admit in conclusion what is already granted in the premises is not very sound. This is true only as a pedagogical device, applied to those who do not pay attention to what they think, says Buffier.[99]

However strong Buffier's attacks on the limitations of the *cogito* as

---

modifications in the two editions]; *Métaphysique*, no. 51, p. 286; *Traité*, no. 50, p. 21/ p. 28; nos. 410–15, pp. 169–71/pp. 278–83; *Grammaire*, nos. 12, 70, 80; *Raisonnement*, nos. 245–67, pp. 303–33). On Buffier's grammatical model, see A. Bailly, [11], pp. 273–77, and J. C. Chevalier, [43], pp. 602–16. Notice that Buffier uses a new grammatical model. Instead of analyzing propositions in terms of one subject, one predicate, i.e., one grammatical subject, one verb, one complement or attribute, he analyzes them in terms of one subject (noun-verb) and many modifications. In order to analyze the latter, Buffier refers to "conjunctions" (or "modificatifs"). In his *Grammaire*, Buffier lists ten sorts of "conjunctions" (copulatives ou comparatives, disjonctives, adverbatives, conditionnelles, continuatives, causales, dubitatives, exceptives, concluantes, de temps; see nos. 145–46, p. 656). This view is interesting when compared to his notion of probability (see *Traité*, no. 162, p. 69/pp. 108–9).

99. *Traité*, no. 554, p. 226/p. 398; *Raisonnement*, no. 126, p. 165; nos. 162–64, pp. 208–11. For example, Buffier holds that it is more difficult to assent to the maxim "It is impossible for a thing to be and not to be" than to say, "This is this" (see *Raisonnement*, no. 249, p. 307, and no. 17, pp. 19–20). Commenting on Locke's saying that "Whatever is, is" is not universally received, Buffier says: "We do not always reflect upon this idea; but it takes place in all our judgments, without our reflecting upon it. The author, therefore, on this occasion, seems to have confounded the reflective with the immediate thought: it is however certain, that even children themselves, more or less expressly, give their assent to this proposition, *Such a thing is that thing*: and we never can make one of them deny, or doubt inwardly, his foot to be his foot, or his hand to be his hand" (*Traité*, English ed., p. 401, Buffier's italics; see also *Raisonnement*, nos. 309–13, pp. 370–73; no. 31, pp. 44–55).

a rule of *all* truths, it is therefore clear that the elements which he finds in the internal sentiment are fundamental to his justification of the appeal to common sense.[100] Because he sees two main elements in the *cogito*, an existential element and a logical element, and because he feels these elements are related to two kinds of logical truths, intuitive and conjunctive, Buffier thinks that his new analysis will enable us both to acknowledge the truth of the distinction between the internal and the noninternal objects of thought and to establish their relationship.

At this point we face the most difficult moment in the justification of the appeal to common sense, a difficulty related to the puzzle of the "valid error." On the one hand, Buffier does not want to say that crucial distinctions like internal and noninternal are not important, or that they can be overcome by means of internal demonstrations. On the other hand, he does not want to say that we have no evidence

---

100. I cannot say that Buffier was the first to see the psychological and the metaphysical sides of Descarte's *cogito*, for Buffier insists on "immediacy" rather than on the actuality of the *cogito* as a rule of truth (see *Encyclopaedia Britannica*, 11th ed., vol. 4, art. "Buffier"). On the other hand, Buffier does not want to use the *cogito* as the basis for an ontology that would give a substantive and positive account of the intrinsic nature of things (see F. Bouillier, [18], p. 588). Nonetheless, Buffier certainly sees two main elements in the *cogito* to which I would refer as the existential element and the logical element. This view evokes the long-standing problem of the Cartesian *cogito*, both an intuition and a movement of thought (see H. Gouhier, [79], pp. 269–76, and G. Dreyfus, [64], pp. 117 ff.). In this sense, Buffier's views on the *cogito* are different from that of the Sensationalist School. On this, see J. McCosh, [137], and F. Picavet, [161].

Because Buffier attacks the *cogito* as a rule of *all* truths, many commentators have missed the extent and the importance of the support he finds in the internal sentiment in order to validate the appeal to common sense. G. Sortais, [191], p. 81, thinks that the Cartesian influence on Buffier has been overemphasized. E. Gilson, [77], pp. 16–17, claims that Buffier's method is directly opposed to that of the internal sentiment. P. Bernard, [16], pp. 1169–72, says that for Buffier the criterion for evidence is not the internal sentiment but common sense. J. R. Armogathe, [8], pp. 152, 316, says that Buffier rejects the *cogito* "because" Buffier does not mention the evidence of the internal sentiment in the *list* of first principles of common sense. In appealing to the internal sentiment, Buffier was much in the mood of the century. From Fontenelle to Destutt de Tracy, Maine de Biran to Rousseau, Condillac to Frayssinous, so many thinkers appealed to the internal sentiment as the origin of the highest of all truths that it is simply impossible to mention them—except, perhaps, another defender of common sense: the Marquis d'Argens, [7], pp. 143–86, who thinks, e.g., that "on peut aussi bien prouver l'existence en disant 'Je sens donc je suis' qu'en disant 'Je pense donc je suis.' "

of the existence of any being outside ourselves. The proposed solution is twofold: (1) there are fundamental distinctions between internal and noninternal objects, therefore we must accept the conclusions of the internal sentiment, and (2) there are also important similarities between internal and external objects, and therefore we need another source of truth to complement the internal sentiment. Common sense as a disposition is this other source of truth.

To understand Buffier's position, we have to show in what sense the two sources of evidence are both related and distinct. As we shall see, by virtue of common sense we admit the existence of something that we believe to exist outside our thought. However, the principles of common sense are propositions that include references to the internal sentiment, to which they *add* modifications. I think, I feel, I exist, says the internal sentiment. I am not alone in existing, says common sense. I am aware of something I call my intelligence or my thought, says the internal sentiment. I am not only aware of that but also of something distinct from it, that is, my body, says common sense. I have clear and distinct ideas that are intuitively true, says the internal sentiment. I cannot say that other intelligent beings do not have clear and distinct ideas and that what they say is merely "extravagant," says common sense.

Clearly, common sense functions through an awareness of distinctions such as those between me and other beings, the mind and the body, reason and mere extravagant opinions, prudence and imprudence, freedom and necessity, order and chaos, *strict* evidence and *arbitrary* assent. Of these distinctions, the first (myself and beings distinct from myself) is the most important, and it hints at a difference in kind between the two sentiments. If this first distinction is accepted, then similarities arise, as the fact that our bodies resemble other bodies and our mind, other minds. While asserting these similarities, Buffier defends certain differences (e.g., what we call a mind is distinct from what we call a body), suggesting that common sense is employed not only in the assertion of distinctions, but more importantly, in the defense of these distinctions as having been made correctly.

Thus Buffier wants to defend the internality of the internal sentiment while opposing the dogmatism of such internality—only myself exists. In his view, an object of common sense is not "external" because it has *no* internal features but, instead, because it cannot be reduced to the dogmatism of internality, which insists on saying "only internal."

Buffier maintains that we can say both "I exist" (on the basis of the internal sentiment) and "Not only myself exists" (on the basis of common sense). Given the positive role that the making of distinctions plays in our judgments, it is possible to add something (however vague) to a solipsist perception of oneself.

To be sure, when Buffier refers to what is outside the internal sentiment he uses very vague expressions such as "there is something which we call, say, a body." In fact, the only truth of which common sense can assure us is that something distinct from us exists. It cannot tell us what this thing is in itself. Most of our thoughts are concerned with internal issues only: internal sentiment and logical reasoning. But there is one moment where it seems that we reach beyond this, in the judgment common sense allows us to make concerning the existence of other beings and things. This judgment does not reach very far outside ourselves, for our reasoning on such objects will use truths of consequence, which can only unpack the internal features contained in our assents to external objects. But, at least, there is one moment where we are sure of something more than ourselves and our thoughts.

Buffier makes clear that the distinction between ourselves and other beings is most difficult where it concerns the existence of external objects. From the fact that Buffier defines common sense as a disposition by which we judge objects that are different from the internal sentiment, we should not infer that he holds that common sense guarantees the truth of judgments about the intrinsic nature of external objects. On the contrary, Buffier notes that, in philosophical theories, the distinction between ourselves and other beings implies much more than a passage from intuitive to conjunctive knowledge in the logical domain. For example, it implies a passage from a knowledge of ourselves to a knowledge of what exists distinct from us. But, Buffier objects, it is one thing to judge of the agreement of two ideas actually present to our mind (internal truth) and quite another thing to judge an idea to be in accordance with an object outside thought (external truth). Commenting upon Locke's ambiguous saying that "Existence is not required for real knowledge," Buffier distinguishes real and ideal knowledge in the following manner: "For my own part, I call *real* or *external* knowledge the congruity of our ideas with the existence of things subsisting distinct from us; and *ideal* or *internal* knowledge, the congruity between one idea and another, independently of the existence of things."[101] But this is not to say that there is no relationship between the two kinds of truth: Buffier maintains that all external truths are *at the same time* internal truths; the assertion of existence *outside* thought is made by a mind, an intelligence through its thought. We have to see how this difficult transition from internality to externality is possible.[102]

As we recall, the transition from knowledge of internal truths to knowledge of external truths cannot be made by means of logical demonstrations. The transition, now argues Buffier, cannot be made by means of clear and distinct ideas either. Apparently, therefore, the solipsist would be right in asserting the absence of certainty concerning the existence of any other being if the criteria for certainty in this case were the same as that required for certainty in ideas. But to know that a thing exists is not the same thing as knowing what this thing is in itself. To admit that we cannot assert of an external object what is true of internal ideas is not, however, to assume that our knowledge of existence must be logically dependent upon our knowledge of the intrinsic nature of the thing said to exist.

Inasmuch as the solipsist makes this assumption, Buffier holds that he is mistaken: man knows that a thing is, without knowing the intrinsic nature of this thing or how it came into existence. This, Buffier argues, is another (direct) consequence of the impossibility of knowing the intrinsic nature of things.

This last reflection is a full solution of a number of ridiculous difficulties with which the human mind perplexes itself; its nature is to know the existence of certain things, without being acquainted with their properties; and would it renounce the knowledge of the existence, because it is incapable of knowing its properties? This is the same thing as if a person should refuse to be convinced that he remembers and thinks, because he cannot explain to his satisfaction in what manner he remembers and thinks. The *manner* eludes our researches; let us give it up: we suffer ourselves to be perplexed with this, because we have no idea of it; and yet this very circumstance should free our minds from all perplexity; for any particular matter, of which we have

---

101. *Traité*, English ed., p. 415; see also *Métaphysique*, nos. 39–68, pp. 279–96.

102. *Raisonnement*, no. 360, p. 446 ff; no. 403, pp. 505–6; *Métaphysique*, nos. 39–40, p. 279; nos. 51–52, pp. 286–87; no. 54, pp. 288–89; *Traité*, nos. 216–23, pp. 88–9/pp. 142–45.

no idea, is, and ought to be, with respect to our reason and arguments, as if it did not really exist: now, what does not exist, we have no right to judge of, nor to form thence any conclusions contrary to those things we know to exist. A deficiency of knowledge, or a thing unknown, never destroys nor makes any alteration in real knowledge, or a thing known.[103]

Notice that the internal sentiment remains again at the heart of Buffier's argument. We are completely certain that we exist, even though we do not know how we came into existence. To say that we are a thinking substance does not explain everything about our thinking nature; it leaves unsettled questions related to the role of the will, the memory, and the imagination, not to mention the problem of innate ideas and all assertions that imply the existence of our body. Of course, we do know more about our thought than we know about things. Nonetheless, the evidence of the *cogito* and the way we assent to it indicate that we do not need to know either the cause of the impression of truth we feel or the intrinsic nature of our consciousness, in order to be sure of our existence. In the *cogito* no metaphysical development of the features of our intrinsic nature seems required to produce our immediate assent to it.

To know . . . in what the internal nature of the mind consists, what constitutes their real essence and their essential and physical differences from the body . . . This knowledge neither ought, nor can be, of a different nature from what human knowledge essentially is; and this is, it can never reach the internal nature of beings but it is not, therefore, the less evident or convincing.

We know not the internal nature of our mind as far as it may be known, or as God knows it; but we know it as far as we are capable of knowing it, or as is consistent with human understanding.[104]

---

103. *Traité*, no. 472, p. 195/p. 327. See also *Exposition*, esp. nos. 25–26; *Traité*, nos. 492–94, pp. 204–5/pp. 344–46; no. 227, pp. 96–97/pp. 153–56; *Traité*, Bouillier's ed., p. 148. Sometimes Buffier's language suggests that to know the intrinsic nature of a thing would imply to know fully its cause as well as its most fundamental properties, and this is impossible. Buffier's straightforward conclusion on his section on "cause" (related to action) is: we should cleanse philosophy of all that is incomprehensible (*Traité*, no. 323, p. 140/p. 228).

104. *Traité*, no. 403, p. 166/p. 274; no. 405, p. 167/p. 275. See *Traité*, Bouillier's ed., p. 244; *Raisonnement*, nos. 145–48, pp. 187–92; *Métaphysique*, no. 48, p. 283. See also *Raisonnement*, nos. 154–55, pp. 200–201, and *Traité*, no. 64, p. 30/p. 45. Buffier's point is that we do not need to know the intrinsic nature or the causes of our impressions of truth in order to be certain of the most evident and the clearest impressions we feel.

Our knowledge of existing things is limited, but in certain determined ways. A lack of knowledge in one area (the inner constitution of things) does not shake the knowledge we have in another area (the existence of things). Our notion of existence is very clear, very distinct, because it is the *only* simple notion we have that is clear by itself: we cannot divide the idea of existence into several parts. Thus we cannot *explain* a truth of existence, because to explain is to develop an idea by an analysis of more simple ideas comprehended under the idea to be explained. What philosophers have failed to recognize is that truths of existence are inexplicable because they are self-evidently true, that is, they are clearer than any explanation of them could be.

The conformity of our thought with the existing object cannot be claimed to result from a comparison between the features of our ideas and the features of the thing. It is the simplicity of the notion of existence that makes our impression of truth very clear. In the absence of knowledge of the intrinsic nature of things, the accordance of our judgment with the external object does not reach very far: it only reaches the sentiment we have of its being more than mere thought. But, argues Buffier, it clearly reaches that far.[105]

Thus when the solipsist argues that the passage from the truth of our existence to a truth of the existence of a being distinct from us is much more difficult than a passage from, say, intuitive to conjunctive truths, he reasons correctly. When he says, further, that it is impossible to deduce, from the knowledge of our nature, some knowledge of the nature of the thing distinct from us, he again reasons correctly. But when he concludes that we have no evidence of the existence of any being but ourselves, he reaches a false conclusion: our knowledge of existence is not epistemologically dependent upon the (impossible) knowledge of the inner constitution of things.

All truths, concludes Buffier, are internal, for all truths refer to a particularity of our thought. But the impressions of truth we feel by way of sentiment reveal that our immediate assent to the existence of other beings is as necessary as our immediate assent to our own existence.

---

105. *Métaphysique*, no. 52, p. 287; *Raisonnement*, no. 15, p. 15; *Traité*, no. 196, p. 80/ p. 129. Like Kant, Buffier uses the example of money: the idea of forty francs and its existence.

In fact, as the first rule of truth universally acknowledged by all, that is, the internal sentiment of our own perception, derives all its force from Nature, whenever the sentiment of Nature is found, there also will be found a true evidence and a necessary rule of truth.

In the nature of man, there is a principle which we feel, in spite of all vain subtleties, a principle which answers all reasonings, or rather a principle which is above all reasonings: that each of us exists in such a manner that other men and other beings exist with him.

. . . the existence of an object separate from us, is not proved by mere conformity of ideas that are only within ourselves: it can be proved only by the sentiment which Nature has placed in all men, or at least in the greater part of them, to enable them to judge of the existence of objects that are equally comprehensible by them all; so that when we are to judge of an object existing separate from us, we cannot be determined but by that *sentiment* or by some consequence thence deduced.[106]

Of course, the first principles of common sense and those of the internal sentiment do not touch the mind in quite the same manner, although they produce a similar immediate impression of truth. "I always apprehend the ambiguity," confesses Buffier. Internal objects make a more lively, striking impression upon the mind: they impress our mind from within, and it is always easy to assure their conformity with our actual thought. For example, the properties of the soul, as far as we can know them, are clearer than those of the bodies.[107] However, this is no reason to deny that we have similar impressions of truth concerning the existence of external objects. This would be to confuse the degrees of clearness and the reality of clearness by a failure to distinguish kinds. The vulgar dichotomy "either Yes or No" is once more misleading. Both common sense and the internal sentiment, because they are natural dispositions of the mind, provide

---

106. *Traité*, no. 13, p. 9/p. 11; no. 40, p. 17/p. 26; nos. 480 ff., pp. 220 ff./pp. 337 ff.; *Raisonnement*, no. 309, pp. 370–71; *Métaphysique*, nos. 64–65, pp. 294–95.

107. Buffier's language should not be misleading at this point: the only thing that we know about an external truth is the "effective nature" or the existence of a thing and not its intrinsic nature. But a knowledge of a thing which does not include a knowledge of its qualities (e.g., Buffier holds that to know a substance without knowing its accident is a mere abstraction) cannot reach very far. On the other hand, and consistent with his conviction that the internal sentiment is the clearest source of evidence, Buffier holds that the properties of the soul or of the mind are clearer than the properties of the bodies (see *Traité*, no. 334, p. 145/p. 237; *Métaphysique*, no. 49, p. 284; *Raisonnement*, no. 351, p. 435; no. 361, p. 447).

kinds and areas of evidence, of clearness, of distinctness, and of certainty.

It might be consistent to deny the truths of any existence except our own, but the consistency of such a conclusion is not guaranteed by the internal sentiment, or by the logical truths, or, and more importantly, by a better look at the nature of our judgment of existence, immediate judgments obtained by way of sentiment. And if, at this point, a skeptic asks: How do you know that your sentiments are true? Buffier would answer: In the same manner that I know that I exist and if this is no standard of truth, we have no standard at all, not even the *cogito*.

7. CONCLUSION

As we have seen, Buffier provides a precise definition of common sense . Common sense is a natural disposition to judge certain principles to be self-evidently true. These principles are primarily concerned with the existence of other beings and things; they also concern the most striking properties of these beings and things.

In defining common sense both as a disposition and as a set of first principles, Buffier distinguishes two kinds of arguments in favor of his theory. Common sense as a disposition is, by far, the most important element in his justification, but the justification of common sense as a set of first principles is also necessary for Buffier's doctrine. In the last case, Buffier argues that the superior clearness of principles of common sense —when we compare them to the clearness of alternative or of counterviews—is a guarantee of the truth of these principles.

However, because the internal sentiment seems to guarantee only the most clear and distinct principle of knowledge (I think, I feel, I exist) and because the assertion that only this principle is self-evidently true would contradict the principles of common sense (other beings and other things exist), the central issue of a justification of the appeal to common sense becomes the nature of the relationship between these different kinds of principles. At this point Buffier thinks that we can show that common-sense principles and the principles whose truth is guaranteed by the internal sentiment have "essential" relations if we consider them as resulting from distinct dispositions, which both provide genuine sources of certainty. The analysis of these "essential" relations explains how the solipsist conclusion, while logically deduced from the *cogito*, is the result of an unwarranted reduction of its role in guaranteeing the validity of first principles.

Buffier's main argument is that the *cogito*—when accurately analyzed—can be interpreted existentially to provide a guarantee for the possibility of a knowledge of the existence of other beings and things. This is possible because the *cogito* itself is a paradigm of conjunctive truth, of truths that do not result from the clearness of merely tautological statements. Thus it is in showing that common sense as a disposition has characteristics which resemble another disposition (the internal sentiment) that Buffier concludes that both these dispositions are equally natural and valuable sources of truth and certainty. For him the gist of the matter lies in a better account of the many rules of truth that philosophers (like the solipsist) are inclined to reduce to the rule of identity and the rule of noncontradiction.

Both internal sentiment and common sense are sources of certainty and of truths of principle. Both afford us truths that we ought to distinguish and recognize. In both cases, evidence for the truth of such principles is provided by the necessity of assent, which makes doubt academic because of the superior clearness of these principles to any counterargument. Both are rational sentiments, immediate impressions of truth whose content cannot be deduced from other propositions. In both cases there are judgments of existence that are accompanied by obscurities about the nature of the thing said to exist. The highest evidence itself, that of the internal sentiment, can thus be rescued from the dangerous position of solipsism by an appeal to the complex model of truth, which characterizes human reason and which grounds its unity.

If we now consider Buffier's doctrine of common sense , his definition and his justification of common sense as a disposition and as a set of first principles, we can formulate a general interpretation of his theory. By means of this general account, we should be able to mention briefly some weaknesses of Buffier's doctrine, as well as provide a clearer assessment of the sense in which his doctrine is grounded on a complex model of truth.

In arguing for common sense, we have see that Buffier does make numerous distinctions between his notion and many other notions, such as the Aristotelian *sensorium comune,* a new (Scholastic) faculty, an innate idea, a set of vulgar prejudices, or a set of strictly identical judgments. In fact, there seems to be no limit to the number of distinctions one should make while discussing common sense as a notion and as a source of first principles. In the last case, we know, for instance, that if we consider the way we pass judgement, we must distinguish truths of principles and truths of consequence. When we consider an object of thought with regard to whether or not it exists, we should distinguish real knowledge and ideal knowledge or external and internal truths. If we consider the real content of a judgment, we should distinguish objective and hypothetical truths. If we acknowledge the modifications that some predicates add to a subject, we must distinguish intuitive and conjunctive truths. If we consider the limitation of our knowledge, we should distinguish the (unattainable) truths of the intrinsic nature of a thing and the (attainable) truths of their existence, and so on. In making so many distinctions, Buffier's point is to avoid confusion. Yet, at the same time, this procedure exhibits his tendency to substitute distinctions for explanations.

Another weakness of Buffier's philosophy appears in his treatment of "truth of consequences," once the truth of common-sense principles is recognized. The point is, of course, to show that an appeal to common sense is not to be confused with an appeal to a naïve form of metaphysical realism. Yet Buffier's treatment of philosophical notions such as being, quality, possibility, freedom, and so forth tends to substitute a vague appeal to the limits of reason for the analysis of specific arguments. This would seem to involve a confusion of the issues of skepticism with vagueness for all matters that are not within the metaphysical domain.

Finally, another weakness of Buffier's philosophy appears in his somewhat psychological version of some of Descartes's theses. Beyond his argument for the *cogito* and for the clearness and distinctness of ideas as criteria for truth, Buffier's rather Lockean rejection of the possibility of metaphysical knowledge leads him to misrepresent Descartes's arguments, especially on the appeal to God, methodical doubt, or mathematics as a model of philosophical inquiry. In the last case, we have seen that Buffier is inclined to reduce the rules of logical reasoning to the mathematical rule that two quantities equal to a third are equal. Buffier's weaknesses in his defense of common sense must, however, be related to his view on "truth," a view which is not what many would expect from a common-sense philosopher.

"Truth," Buffier says, is an ambiguous word. Ordinary language refers to it mainly to focus on the good faith of a person saying what he or she thinks. In philosophy, truth has been defined as the conformity of thought with its object, the conformity of judgment with the nature of the things judged. However, Buffier argues, all these notions of truth need qualification. In fact, truth implies a reference to the particularity of thought, and it is vain to talk of truth without referring to a mind that says that so-and-so is true. Furthermore, as there is no limit to what the human mind may think, we should restrict the notion of truth to what is most immediately and clearly perceived and to which the mind cannot but assent.

By using so many distinctions, Buffier actually suggests that recognition of the complexity of issues involved in providing a justification of human beliefs is his most important point. Indeed, this recognition is directly opposed to the dogmatism of internality, which has placed human reason in the tautological position of solipsism from which it must be rescued. We must acknowledge that the human mind functions according to many rules and many criteria, and thus it is important, in our analysis, to offer the most precise notion possible of the many aspects of our thoughts. If, on the one hand, we can see the logical consistency of a solipsist conclusion derived from the *cogito* and if, on the other hand, we also see the absurdity of these consequences, this suggests that human reason actually uses more than the rules of identity and of noncontradiction in order to assent to self-evident judgments. The internal sentiment makes possible a logic of identity based on the idea of strict likeness between certain features of our thoughts; but common sense makes possible a logic of differences and similarities based on the idea of distinctness, which makes it possible to recognize the validity of conjunctive truths. These two possibilities are guaranteed by the *cogito*, which a better understanding shows to be a paradigm of conjunctive truths even though it is also the source of intuitive truths.

Buffier's justification of common sense as a disposition by which we perceive the truth of principles concerning other beings and things (their existence and their most striking properties) is thus an attempt to show that even though human reason judges according to different kinds of self-evident principles, it is nonetheless consistent in all its self-evident principles. His model of truth is more complex than that authorized by the rule of identity, the rule of noncontradiction, or the notion of logical consistency restricted to that of strict likeness. Common sense can be defended as a standard of truth in philosophy because, ultimately, it permits one to see the compatibility of the different first principles that are natural to human reason, and thereby to reject as invalid the claim that, in admitting the principles of common sense, we are bound to contradict the highest evidence of the *cogito*. In showing the principles of common sense and of the internal sentiment to be compatible—though different—Buffier shows that the unity of human (natural) reason is possible if we recognize that it is more complex than the solipsist model of truth would grant.

Notice that Buffier's rejection of prejudice is part of this awareness of the paradoxical nature of human rationality; human reason may say, at the same time, both Yes and No, because the human mind reasons according to many rules and many criteria. A genuine philosopher will look for explanations that render this complexity of issues intelligible. These explanations are found when he tries to discover the most natural impressions of truths, those on which the impressions of all men converge, self-evident propositions. In thus discovering that in self-evident matters the impressions of truth of one's *own* reason are not all of a kind but are compatible with one another, a philosopher discovers the philosophical ground for intellectual openness; if we acknowledge that, even in the case of self-evident propositions, there are complexities, we should not expect that it will be easy either to accept or to reject any other kinds of proposition. In turn, to realize that there are only a few self-evident propositions is to realize that there is a ground for a mitigated and smiling form of skepticism.

Indeed, an important consequence of Buffier's views of the complexity of the model of truth that is natural to human reason is his acknowledgment of the limits that characterize his doctrine of common sense. Common sense is restricted to providing certainty for only a few propositions. Furthermore, the general principles of common sense will be supplemented by data whose certainty is not guaranteed by these principles. Common sense is restricted in the knowledge that first principles convey: these principles permit one to assert the existence of things but not the intrinsic nature of the things said to exist. Common sense is restricted in its extension; it is not uniform or identical in all men. Common sense, finally, is restricted in its justification. In order to show that the evidence of the principles of common sense must be admitted in philosophy, one has to rely on arguments derived from the *cogito*. One also has to acknowledge that even though the evidence for the principles of common sense resembles the evidence we have in favor of the principle of the internal sentiment, it would be false to hold that this evidence has the same value.

The limitations of Buffier's notion of common sense result from his view of a complex model of truth because, while requiring the recognition of the *common* impressions of truth produced by self-evident propositions, this model also requires the recognition of the legitimate ambivalence concerning the truth of most propositions.

Buffier's acknowledgement of the limitations of the appeal to common sense derives from his awareness of the many issues involved in the recognition of self-evident principles and from his attempt to avoid confusing the certainty of these principles with nonobvious implications. Furthermore, Buffier insists that the very attempt to defend common-sense principles is possible only if one does not pretend to settle all the philosophical questions that are raised by admitting common sense. In thus defining common sense as a disposition to judge that a *few* principles are self-evidently true, Buffier emphasizes his conviction that there are crucial limitations to any appeal to natural evidence.

This distinction between first principles and other kinds of propositions, and the resulting limitation of the notion of truth to a few propositions, is not the only consequence of Buffier's complex model of truth. As we have seen, Buffier insists that the difference between the evidence for the principles of common sense and the evidence for the principles of the internal sentiment should not be used as a ground for rejecting common sense. We have also seen that he argues that this difference is less important than the similarities one can detect in analyzing both sources of truth. In this sense, Buffier has argued that we should not treat our common-sense principles as we must treat most propositions: with common-sense propositions we must see the ways in which the internal impressions of truth of all men converge, while with most propositions we must recognize that we shall feel a legitimate ambivalence about their truth.

However, this is not to say that we must suspend our reservations against the Yes-or-No prejudice when we deal with common-sense principles. On the contrary, it is to say that we should attack philosophical versions of this prejudice. According to Buffier, the reduction of all rules of truth to the law of identity and the law of noncontradiction is the epistemological version of this vulgar prejudice. His reason for insisting that the difference between the evidence for the principles of common sense and the evidence for the principles of the internal sentiment is not a valid ground for rejecting common-sense principles may be summarized as follows: unlike the prejudicial tendency to judge any statement by the rule of Yes or No, the tendency to judge that common-sense principles are self-evidently true is grounded on a model of truth that says Yes (I exist) and No (I am not alone in existence). In other words, it is in the most internal impressions of truth of all men that a philosopher can find the ground of the legitimate ambivalence that most judgments produce in our minds. At the very base of human reason, we find a tendency to judge that a few propositions are self-evidently true, and we also realize that in admitting their evidence, we have to say both Yes and No on the question of existence. Because of this, there should be no surprise in concluding that Buffier's philosophy of common sense—with its insistence on both the consistency and the limitation of human reason—is the ground of his mitigated and smiling skepticism.

III

Thomas Reid

1. DIFFICULTIES IN ASSESSING THE CORE OF REID'S DOCTRINE

BECAUSE MY PURPOSE is to show that Reid's justification of common sense is original, it is important to begin by acknowledging that, as other commentators have pointed out, he uses the term "common sense" in a variety of ways. In the context of our study, we must notice that, unlike Buffier, Reid did not start his philosophical undertaking by defining common sense. In fact, although his first book (1764) was titled *An Inquiry into the Human Mind on the Principles of Common Sense,* it is only in his second work, *Essays on the Intellectual Powers of Man* (1785), particularly in his "Essay on Judgment," that he deals systematically with the question of defining and justifying the appeal to common sense in philosophy.[1] Especially when he deals with perception, natural signs, and our ability to interpret nature, Reid seems willing to rely on common sense, even before he has systematically justified his use of this term.

As we shall see, Reid has good reasons for presenting his doctrine as he did. But before I enunciate my claim, let me discuss the problems other commentators have raised concerning his notion of common sense. First, his delayed elucidation of the meaning of common sense has been taken as a proof that, in his later work, Reid plagiarized Buffier's definition of the term. It must be recalled that in his "Essay on Judgment" Reid mentions Buffier's defense of common sense and

---

1. *Works,* pp. 413–75; esp., pp. 421b–426a.

that he quotes with praise the Buffierian view of the marks of first principles.

There are also other problems. Because Reid uses the term "common sense" in a variety of ways, the version of common sense derived from these different references has been held to be confusing. Indeed, although a few commentators on Reid's philosophy insist that his notion of common sense has one central meaning, most commentators have found from two to five different meanings in his uses of the term.[2] These meanings include (1) common sense as a faculty (itself confusingly identified as practical sagacity, intuitive reason, power of the mind, average intelligence, well-balanced intellect); (2) common sense as a set of principles (again, these principles are confusingly identified as ordinary beliefs, self-evident truths, data of consciousness, popular conclusions, intuitive judgments, laws of the mind); and (3) common sense as a doctrine or as a set of assumptions concerning the source of certainty, of evidence, of truth (and these assumptions are confusingly identified as philosophical or popular, as principles of deduction, or as necessary conditions in the exercise of rational powers).[3]

2. A few thinkers insist that the Reidian notion has one central meaning: a metaphysical theory of judgment (V. Cousin, [52], pp 364–72, 390; a noetic faculty of first principles (W. Hamilton) in Reid, *Works*, pp. 791, 743, n. A); a reference to common persuasion and to palpable suppositions (A. Lyall, [119], pp. 40–51); the source of evidence of judgments of existence and of necessary relations (S. Rome, [177], p. 228); the underlying assumptions and principles of beliefs (J. H. Jacques, [96], p. 710); a limited number of truths evident to all men (J. H. Faurot, [67], p. 182); the illuminative certitude provided by the testimony of our faculties in revealing extramental reality (A. Boutwood, [20], p. 166). Besides these analyses focusing on a central meaning of the Reidian notion, all other studies stress Reid's vague and ambiguous use of the phrase. Other studies include T. Brown, F. Bouillier, G. Ardley, F. Copleston, L. Dauriac, S. A. Grave, J. Ferrier, J. Fearn, T. Jouffroy, H. Laurie, P. H. Mabire, J. McCosh, D. F. Norton, J. Priestley, R. J. Petersen, and H. Sidgwick.

3. A. D. Woozley, ed., [168], p. xxxii, identifies (1) a body of propositions generally accepted as true although not demonstrably true; (2) the principle of matter-of-fact evidence underlying those propositions; (3) the power of the mind by which we detect the truth of those propositions.

J. F. Latimer, [113], p. 1, holds that Reid mixes two meanings of common sense: (1) popular conclusions reached by men of sound and well-balanced intellect; (2) intuitive original datum. Latimer further notices a "tone of Revelation" in Reid's defense of common sense.

S. D. Schwarz, [181], p. 166, thinks that Reid uses the term "common sense" to designate: (1) general propositions of everyday life which philosophy is wont to criticize

Reid's different uses of the term "common sense" have also led commentators to hold that inasmuch as there is a general argument, this argument is circular. Suppose, for example, that common sense is primarily meant to refer to human reason. Then it seems that Reid argues in the following manner: in the *Inquiry* he holds that common sense allows us to describe our intellectual powers, while in the *Intellectual Powers* he argues that only such a description would allow us to enunciate the principles which guarantee that common sense is a genuine part of reason.

Reid's apparently confused use of the term "common sense" is made even more puzzling by the fact that he often presents common sense as a valid tool for refuting skeptical theories.[4] This suggests that common sense is already a clear notion, at least inasmuch as it may be used against skeptical arguments. Some commentators on Reid have concluded that we cannot expect to find a positive notion of common sense in his writings because Reid uses the term in a defensive manner

----

and evaluate; (2) assumptions which philosophy makes as it criticizes the latter and which are not self-evident; (3) similar assumptions which are self-evident.

Stewart, [194], vol. 3 (*Elements of the Philosophy of the Human Mind*, vol. 2), pp. 36–37, refers to the ambiguity of Reid's use of the term "principle" as (1) datum, i.e. an assumption taken as a datum upon which reasoning proceeds; (2) elemental truth, i.e., a truth virtually taken for granted or assumed in every step of reasoning and without which, although no consequence can be directly inferred, a train of reasoning would be impossible. Stewart holds that the necessary conditions involved in the exercise of rational powers are not identical with first principles of deduction.

Olin McKendree Jones, [103], p. 46, lists the following meanings for common sense: (1) common experience; (2) principles, or natural principles of the mind (sensations and beliefs) or, natural laws of the mind; (3) evidence of general propositions, which brings us immediate truths of knowledge (apparently, for Jones, mathematical and moral knowledge); (4) opinion generally agreed upon though not self-evident.

Bernard Peach, [156], p. 69, sees three Reidian meanings for common sense: (1) a body of principles (contingent and necessary) commonly accepted as true but not known to be true either by demonstration or by induction; (2) self-evidence underlying the body of principles above and which is primarily revealed in common language and conduct; (3) a faculty (and its degree of effectiveness) by which we recognize the truth, the necessity, or the acceptability of these principles.

Grave, [80], pp. 84, 114, says that Reid muddles the meaning of common sense disastrously. The term refers to (1) mental powers; (2) set of beliefs and principles; (3) average intelligence; (4) practical sagacity; (5) intuitive function of reason.

4. The explicit aim of the *Inquiry* is to justify the common sense of mankind against skeptical subtleties, and in his later elucidation Reid says that common sense is more extensive in refutation than in confirmation (*Works*, pp. 209b, 425b).

and the ambiguities mentioned above simply result from the variety of skeptical claims he wishes to refute.[5]

I feel, however, that the foregoing problems occur mainly because Reid is aware of the difficulties involved in appealing to common sense in philosophy.[6] He claims, both in the *Inquiry* and in the *Intellectual Powers*, that principles of common sense must be taken for granted. But he also holds that certain preliminary steps are necessary before one can show the principles of common sense in "their proper point of view."[7] This suggests that Reid has *methodological* reasons for his refusal to start his philosophical defense of common sense with a definition of the term. And because Reid argues that the experimental method is the only valid method to be used in philosophy, we can expect his reasons for delaying his elucidation of the term "common sense" to be derived from his commitment to the experimental method. My claim is that Reid's understanding and use of the inductive method is central, systematic, and precise enough to explain fully his delayed clarification of the term "common sense."

Most commentators agree that Reid wants to use an inductive-introspective procedure in his philosophical works. There are disagreements about his success in applying such a method and about the extent to which he was aware of its epistemological limitations. There are also, more generally, disagreements about the possibility of using such a method to validate philosophical theories of the human mind. But almost all commentators agree that Reid's basic methodological credo is an attempt to substitute an accurate description of our intellectual powers arrived at through inductive analysis for deductive conjectures and hypotheses.

We have, therefore, something like unanimity on *one* aspect of Reid's thought: his professed methodology. My plan is to follow this meth-

---

5. See J. F. Ferrier, on the "positively anti-speculative turn of mind" of Thomas Reid, "a mixture of shrewdness and naivety altogether incomparable," in J. Passmore, [155], p. 43. On this question, see also Norton, [147], pp. 20–21.

6. For Reid common sense is a part of human nature that has never been explained (*Works*, p. 122b), and he insists that we find a standard in order to judge of the use and abuse of a term "frequently mentioned and rarely canvassed" (*Works*, p. 423b). In both the *Inquiry* and the *Intellectual Powers*, Reid argues that an enumeration of the principles of common sense is the chief desideratum in logic and that a clear explication of these principles is still to be done (*Works*, pp. 209b, 425b).

7. *Works*, p. 231b. See also pp. 122b, 423b, 209b, 422b.

odological thread to show that Reid's commitment to the experimental method explains why he arrives at his particular idea and doctrine of common sense. Interestingly enough, this has never been done before, because previous studies have emphasized Reid's doctrine rather than his method.[8] While certain authors have praised his intentions and method in general terms, sometimes as a means of mitigating certain of his doctrinal weaknesses,[9] the majority of commentators have failed to see the importance of the link between the Reidian method and doctrine, while some have denied this link altogether.[10]

8. There are two exceptions to this claim and we shall refer to them later: W. P. Krolikowski, [108], pp. 139–53, and L. L. Laudan, [40], pp. 103–32. In his discussion of "critical commonsensism," R. M. Chisholm characterizes Reid's method as "particularist" in opposition to Descartes's strategy, called "methodist" (see [45] and esp. [44]). For objections to Chisholm's characterization, see my article [122]. In more recent studies (see [12] and [74]), Reid's method is not a subject of analysis, except in D. F. Norton's presentation of the "Abstract" of Reid's *Inquiry*, [12], pp. 125–33. This explains why so many commentators mistakenly interpret Reid's claim that self-evident truths need no proof as implying that Reid does not provide a justification for the appeal to common sense in philosophy.

9. A few commentators have general comments on the relation between Reid's method and his doctrine of common sense. J. A. Laird, [111], p. 106: "Reid's common sense principles are similar to Baconian *axiomata media*, or instances of more fundamental principles." Grave, [80], p. 160: common sense presents vincula for coherent links permitting a coherence of experience and its presupposition. S. Rome, [177], p. 225: Reid attempts to supplement particular common sense judgments (fragmentary observations) with systematic conceptual knowledge. Gladys Bryson, [24], p. 23: the Scottish School tries to systematize, to order, to present in methodical form the diverse phenomena, to fit the particular in the general principles they called "laws of nature." A. Lyall, [119], pp. 42–48, 122: first principles to ground all knowledge cannot be ultimate generalizations of particular intuitions, for these generalizations have a probable evidence that implies that "truth" changes, a contradiction. M. R. Cohen, [46], p. 48: Reid's method proved utterly barren: his followers simply elevated every challenged traditional belief into a fundamental intuition of the mind. Most French commentators of Reid's philosophy praise his commitment to the inductive method: Royer-Collard, Jouffroy, Cousin, etc. For Cousin ([52], pp. 3, 303–15, and [50], Lesson 19), Reid's method is more aptly said to be Cartesian than Newtonian.

10. The link between Reid's method and doctrine has been denied by O. McKendree Jones and S. A. Grave, especially the latter. Jones, [103], pp. 68–84, alluding to the claim according to which Reid changed the meaning of common sense, from the *Inquiry* to his later works, wants to "assert strongly" that the very definition of Reid's principles did change from the empirical to the dogmatic: Reid starts out to explain a fact, finds himself in an impasse, and concludes that he had run into a first principle (p. 74). Thus, argues Jones, Reid changed "from one earlier form of empiricism to another closely akin to rationalism." Apparently, therefore, Reid's doctrinal tenets are the very

My claim is that only by focusing on Reid's methodology can one demonstrate the consistency and originality of his doctrine of common sense. The methodological consistency of his argument gives Reid's appeal to common sense a continuity sufficient to answer the charge that his introduction of a definition of common sense (supposedly plagiarized from Buffier) into his *Intellectual Powers* constitutes a discontinuity between his idea of common sense in the *Inquiry* and his idea of common sense in his later work. I want to show that there is no discontinuity between these works and that they must be considered as a consistent and original unit.

Recognizing the consistency of Reid's method also helps us to understand an important dimension of his epistemology: the extent to which his views on common sense are founded on his attempt to formulate the conditions for a truly experimental science of the mind. In particular, by considering Reid's method we can understand the sense in which there is no confusion in his many uses of the term "common sense." Rather, we shall see how Reid relates ordinary judgments and principles of knowledge; how he relates self-evident truths and the undemonstrability of first principles; and how he can claim that first principles of common sense are assumptions which must be admitted in all theories of knowledge.

In what follows, I propose to discuss Reid's views on common sense in two distinct parts, one specific and one more general. First, I shall focus on Reid's "Essay on Judgment," where in eight successive chapters he discusses judgment in general, common sense, opinions of philosophers concerning judgment, first principles in general, first principles of contingent truths, first principles of necessary truths, opinions about first principles, and prejudices. In following the order

---

roots of his ambivalent method. Grave argues ([80], pp. 130–46) that there is no positive connection between Reid's method and Reid's doctrines (pp. 140–42) and therefore that Reid's "inductive" inferences do not add very much to common-sense philosophy, i.e., to the argument between Hume and Reid. Hume and Reid differ in looking at empirical facts, claims Grave (p. 91). Grave admits that the (only) positive side of Reid's common-sense philosophy is a reformation in the method of philosophy (p. 132), but this "positive side" is a destructive one: the truths of common sense are inductive rediscoveries lost under the rubbish of hypothesis (p. 143; cf. p. 84). Grave has interesting suggestions for a genealogy of Reid's method: from Aristotle, Reid learns the necessity of first principles; from Descartes, the uniqueness of mental facts; and from Bacon, the method of induction (pp. 130–31). From Bacon, Reid would have learned that the prescriptive spirit of philosophers is the origin of many errors, a spirit Bacon refers to as a "second Fall" (p. 135).

Reid uses, my aim is to assess the method by which he proceeds to the elucidation and justification of the appeal to common sense. Reid's method, at this point, will be related to the methodological rules he has stated in his first essay of the *Intellectual Powers*. When necessary, I shall supplement my discussion of Reid's justification of common sense by summarizing the background material found in previous analyses of perception or conception. I shall also give special attention to the nature of Reid's objections to other philosophical views on common sense.

After this, I shall offer a more general account of the connections between Reid's method and his doctrine. My aim will then be to show that there are systematic connections between his treatment of common sense and his more general views on the conditions for a truly experimental science of the mind. Special attention will be given to Reid's understanding of the rules concerning the experimental method stated by Newton and Bacon and to his own suggestions for an accurate application of such rules in the specific field of a science of the mind.

This way of accounting for Reid's doctrine of common sense is made necessary by an important but, I believe, neglected fact: rather than offering a general treatise on the experimental method, Reid has *used* this method in his reflections on the intellectual powers of man. There is no way to analyze accurately his views on the inductive method without first understanding the ways in which he applies it. As we shall see, this understanding provides important clues for analyzing the systematic and critical views Reid held about the inductive method itself. This analysis shows that Reid's justification of common sense is grounded on the argument that common sense satisfies many of the necessary conditions for a truly experimental science of the mind.

2. REID'S METHODOLOGICAL RULES CONCERNING THE INTELLECTUAL POWERS OF MAN

Reid announces the general guidelines of his methodology in his first (preliminary) essay in the *Intellectual Powers*.[11] There he states the following four principles.

11. *Works*, pp. 219–45.

1. We should not pretend to give a logical definition when the nature of the things defined does not allow it. A logical or strict definition, Reid explains, is a definition that expresses the genus and species of the things defined by means of specific differences. However, he says, "there is no subject which offers more occasions to use words which *cannot* be logically defined than the subject of the powers and operations of the mind." There are many reasons for this, but the most important is that for a logical definition to be valid, we have to make sure that nothing which belongs to the subject when divided into genus and species is omitted. However, our reflections on the intellectual operations of men must proceed step by step and we cannot pretend to encompass every subject of inquiry under definitive and exhaustive headings.

In the absence of a logical definition of our intellectual operations, we must use common words in their commonly accepted sense, pointing out their various meanings when they are ambiguous and explaining their uncommon meanings when we are obliged to use less common words. As Reid says, every man who understands language has *some* notion of what it is to think, to apprehend, to believe, to will, to desire. Our aim is to start with the notion we have of the words we use when we talk of our intellectual operations and then, by attentive reflection, to form a clear and distinct notion of them. The best use of a definition, Reid says, is to prompt attentive reflection upon mental facts. Thus we may expect that, in analyzing "common sense" as the term should be used in philosophy, the technical meaning of the term will have to be continuous with the common meaning of the term, although our reflections should help us to form a clearer and more distinct notion of common sense itself.

2. Reid asserts that his entire inquiry does take certain principles for granted. He asks that we "deal with them as an upright judge does with a witness who has a fair character." The truly philosophical analysis of the principles of common sense starts at the moment of "hearing what may be pleaded against their admittance as first principles." Before we can do this, we must make sure that we see them in their "proper point of view." The evidence of first principles, Reid says, is not demonstrative but intuitive.

3. Reid asserts that, as in natural philosophy, discoveries about common sense will be made by patient observations, accurate experiments, and conclusions drawn by strict reasoning from observations

and experiments. More specifically, "no regard is due to the conjectures or hypotheses of philosophers, however generally received." He holds that nothing can be assigned as a cause of the operations of the mind which does not satisfy the Newtonian requirements for the ascription of cause as stated in the *Regulae Philosophandi*. As we shall see, this rule will be central to Reid's alternative method of discovering first principles.

4. Finally, Reid argues that analogical reasoning is of limited use and concludes that "we ought never to trust reasoning drawn from supposed similitude of mind and body." We shall see how this requirement is crucial for Reid's treatment of self-evidence, because he will try to delineate a model of causality different from the model used in a science of physical objects.

To this list of methodological principles, Reid adds a discussion of what he calls "proper means" to be used in applying these four principles. In our inquiry upon the mind, the chief source of knowledge should be an "accurate reflection upon the operations of our own minds." Reid distinguishes reflection from consciousness, for reflection is an attentive and voluntary examination of the operations of the mind through which the understanding can make its own operations its objects. Consciousness, in *this* respect, is a superficial view of the operations of the mind, an awareness of present mental operation while the mind is engaged with something other than its own operation, usually external objects.

Reid lists other things that provide information about the mind: (1) the structure of language, which is the expression of human thought; (2) the course of human actions and conduct, which shows the effects of human sentiments, passions, and affections; and (3) the opinions of man, including prejudices and errors, which can be seen as the effects of the "constitution" of the human mind. The reference to the "constitution of the mind" is important because Reid uses this expression to designate, in general terms, that which his philosophy is supposed to provide: a better (scientific) knowledge of the way in which the human mind is framed, through an inductive assessment of the natural laws that govern men's intellectual powers and operations.

The chief proof Reid will offer for his doctrine is that the reader who reflects upon the operations of his own mind and upon the "signs" we use concerning the mental operations of others will agree that the Reidian description is accurate. Hence inductive-introspection is used both to develop a doctrine about the way minds work and to provide proof for such a doctrine.[12]

3. THE IMPORTANCE OF REID'S DECISION TO ELUCIDATE THE MEANING
    OF COMMON SENSE IN HIS "ESSAY ON JUDGMENT"

Having described Reid's statement of his methodological rules in general terms, we turn to his elucidation of the meaning of common sense in his "Essay on Judgment." The notion of common sense as discussed here is central to Reid's philosophy.[13] This location in the "Essay on Judgment" indicates that, in order to understand Reid's idea of common sense, we must begin with careful reflection on the activity of judging. As Reid says:

There are notions or ideas that ought to be referred to the faculty of judgment as their source; because if we had not that faculty they could not enter into our minds and to those that have that faculty and are capable of reflecting upon its operations they are obvious and familiar. Among these we may reckon the notion of judgment itself; the notions of a proposition, of its subject, predicate and copula; of affirmation and negation, of true and false, or knowledge, belief, disbelief, opinion, assent, evidence.[14]

In thus referring such notions as belief or evidence to the faculty of judgment, while arguing that these notions are crucial for a clear understanding of the meaning of common sense, Reid shows his awareness that *defining* common sense is a complex undertaking. We are trying to provide means to discover the natural laws by which the human mind performs the activity of judging. The act of defining is itself a judgment about the proper use of the term and therefore offers a chance to analyze (definitional) judgments. On the other hand, the attempt to define common sense is part of the attempt to discover, through inductive methods, the nature, the origin, the extent, and

---

12. *Works*, pp. 443a–3b, 142b.

13. For Reid, his new analysis of judgment will be the test of the "way of ideas," the greatest obstacle to a true system of the mind: "The common theory concerning ideas naturally leads to a theory concerning judgment, . . . as they are necessarily connected, they must stand or fall together" (*Works*, p. 427a; cf. pp. 210a–211b. On this question, see *infra*, pp. 139 ff.).

14. *Works*, p. 414a.

the status of judgments. Reid's elucidation of the meaning of common sense through an analysis of judgment will reveal an inductive account of knowledge, which he hopes will provide continuity between common understanding and science.[15]

According to Reid, we cannot offer a logical definition of common sense. What we can do is explore the many operations of the mind where judgment plays a role and try to discover resemblances and differences among them. As we shall see, in his justification of common sense, Reid will focus on the connections he sees between such activities as sensing, conceiving, judging, and reasoning. The elucidation of the connections we can discover between these mental activities. This is important because it suggests that we cannot understand Reid's chapters on common sense without considering his *Inquiry* and his *Intellectual Powers* as a consistent whole.

According to Reid, the philosophical notion of common sense cannot be established before reflection upon the sensing activities that provide the materials for an analysis of judgment. Indeed, he devoted his first book, the *Inquiry*, to the problem of perception, and particularly to the ways in which judgment occurs in seeing, hearing, smelling, touching, tasting. In the *Intellectual Powers*, Reid begins with an essay on perception ("Of the powers we have by means of our external senses"), which is a summary of his discussion of this in the *Inquiry*. In brief, the justification of common sense gains an essential part of

15. Reid wants to make sure that our definitions are not directed by untested analogies (*Works*, pp. 220b, 364b, 414a, 392a, 392b; cf. p. 689b). For him, to use "common words" in their common acceptance is "to make a virtue of necessity" (*Works*, pp. 218a–220b; see also pp. 319b ff.); although crucial to reach people's notions, language is not a final test: language reaches no further than people's notions and speculations, which are sometimes "ill-defined and vague" (*Works*, p. 474a). In our attempt to "start with clear definitions and self-evident axioms" in a science of the mind, as in mathematics, we must realize that such definitions and axioms are to be arrived at by inductive methods (*Works*, pp. 77b, 217a, 230a). On this question, see *Works*, pp. 472a, 434a, 702a; pp. 458a–459b; 424–425a; pp. 76a, 364a–365a, 393a, 413b, 220b, 77b, 364a. On defining as an attempt to discover the grammar of nature, see Adolphe Garnier, [75], pp. 68–69, who disapproves Reid's attempts to define terms. M. F. Sciacca, [182], pp. 67–71, thinks that the Reidian definitions and assumptions prevent Reid from genuinely applying the Baconian-Newtonian method. On Reid's definition as a technique to generate better induction, see L. L. Laudan, [40], esp. p. 120. On Reid's attempt to offer a new inductive logic, see Lusignan, [118].

its significance and strength from its grounding in an inductive-introspective reflection on the sensing activities. As Reid puts it:

I thought it most decent and proper to write not in the Synthetical but in the Analytical method; that is, not to lay down my conclusions first and then seek for facts to confirm them; but to take the facts in the order the senses present them & consider what may be inferred from them. I rather chuse the character of an enquirer than of a doctor and therefore as becomes a fair enquirer take a precognition of facts before I draw my conclusions . . .[16]

However, the philosophical status of common sense cannot be established within the limited scope of the *Inquiry.* The data that have been collected concerning perception must now become the basic materials for further reflection. Reid holds that in order to explain the philosophical status of some of the judgments that he had shown occurred in perception, it is necessary to reflect upon conception, abstraction, judgment, and reasoning. The justification of common sense gains its full significance and strength from its grounding in inductive-introspective reflection on judgments.[17]

Thus in his elucidations of the meaning and justification of common sense, Reid has many issues in mind, and in analyzing his chapters on the question, we have to consider the conclusions he has drawn from his inductive account of the sensing activities. In point of fact, Reid's arguments for the true meaning of common sense cannot be understood if we do not consider these conclusions as the materials from which he proceeds to further reflections.

The main conclusion of Reid's reflections on the judgments we make by means of the senses is that "Nature presents no object to the senses or consciousness that is not complex."[18] For him perception is a complex operation in four important ways: It is (1) the result of a train of operations; (2) an act of the mind composed of three ingredients;

16. Birkwood Collection, T. Reid, MSS 2131.6 (II), (2); see also *Works,* pp. 91b, 163b, 104a, 217b, 201b, 472b. On this, see Stewart, [194], pp. 265 ff.

17. For example, one needs to reflect on reasoning in order to see the difference between intuitive and discursive judgments (see *Works,* pp. 210b, 223b, 489a, 489b, 157a–59b). On this question, see J. H. Faurot's article in [74], pp. 229–44; D. A. Tebaldi's article in [12], p. 28; and J. Immerwahr's article in [74], pp. 245–56.

18. *Works,* see pp. 216–17b; 103a, 206a. On this, see also K. Lehrer, [12], p. 2; D. N. Robinson, [12], p. 44, N. Daniels, [12], p. 38.

(3) an act of the mind in which two types of judgment arise, necessary and contingent; (4) the root of the tree of knowledge.[19]

Perception is the result of a train of operations. We perceive no external object except by means of certain bodily organs and we perceive no object unless some impression is made upon a sense organ, an impression that is communicated to the brain (probably) by the nerves. The impression made upon the organ, and communicated to the brain, is followed by a sensation and, last of all, this sensation is followed by the perception of the object. In referring to perception as the result of a train of operations, Reid mentions "connections" between different elements, such as bodily impression, sensation, and perception proper. Such connections must not be mistaken for logical connections. As he says in his "Abstract of the *Inquiry*":

> For aught we know Nature might have given us Sensations of Mind such as we have without connecting them invariably with certain material Impressions made upon the bodily organs. In like manner for aught we know, Nature might have given us both the conception and the belief of external things, without connecting them invariably with certain Sensations. For no man can give a shadow of reason why the latter should always precede the former.

Besides, as will become clear later, Reid's references to "invariable" connections between the different elements of perception as a train of operations must not be taken out of context, that is, without reference to the generalizing process of induction, together with Reid's obvious concern with exceptions.

Concerning perception as the result of a train of operations, Reid insists on two points. First, for a perception to occur, it is necessary that some impression be made upon the organs, but it is not necessary that we know the nature of this impression. Perception is familiar to us and indeed the *main* link of the "mysterious chain" that connects

---

19. For what follows, see *Works*, pp. 114a–115b; 130a–132b; 182a–188b; 245a–260a. See also the important "Abstract of the *Inquiry*," presented by D. F. Norton, [12], pp. 125–33. Reid's theory of sensation and perception is certainly central to his account of common sense. Conversely, an assessment of Reid's method as it relates to common sense is indispensable in order to interpret accurately Reid's theory of sensation and perception. For example, many alleged inconsistencies or equivocations in Reid's theory of sensation and perception (e.g., in T. Duggan's [74], pp. 205–20) would seen to derive from a failure to interpret it on the basis of his method.

the material and the intellectual world, because "we cannot be un-conscious" of the step that follows the impression, the sensation. The second point on which Reid insists is that we must distinguish a sensation and a perception. A sensation (such as "I feel a pain," "I smell a rose") has no existence except when it is felt: its *essence* is to be felt. Sensations, however, are complex acts of the mind even though they are feelings. As Reid says, "When I feel a pain from the gout in my toe, I have not only a notion of pain but a belief of its existence and a belief of some disorder in my toe which occasions it." Notice that the mind is active in sensations; it is active to the extent that, for example, we give enough attention to our sensations to remember them.

A perception, on the other hand, is the complex act of the mind by which we perceive external objects and their qualities. Perception has three ingredients: (1) some conception or notion of the object and of its qualities; (2) a strong and irresistible conviction and belief in the present existence of this object; and (3) the "immediacy" of such belief, that is, the fact that, in perception, our convictions are not produced by reasoning but, rather, by an immediate assent to the judgment we make.[20]

We must realize not only that the sensing activities involve a train of operations which are, like our sensations and perceptions, of a complex nature, but we must also notice that the judgments which arise in perception are of two types, if we consider the fact that they may be related mostly to contingent, but also to necessary truths. As Reid writes in his manuscript:

A Necessary truth must allways be immutably true the contradictory proposition is impossible. Whereas a Truth that is contingent must be mutable & the contradictory proposition is not impossible   Necessary Truths stand upon their own Bottom. (& no reason can be given why they should be true) No

---

20. *Works*, pp. 464b, 282a. For example, Reid says: "When I grasp a ball in my hand, I perceive it at once hard, figured and extended. Feeling is very simple, and hath not the least resemblance to any quality of body. Yet it suggests to us three primary qualities perfectly distinct from one another as well as from the sensation which indicates them. When I move my hand along the table, the feeling is so simple that I find it difficult to distinguish it into things of different natures; yet, it immediately suggests hardness, smoothness, extension and motion—things of very different natures, and all of them as distinctly understood as the feeling which suggests them" (*Works*, pp. 123b–24a).

cause can be assigned of their truth . . . . But every contingent truth must have a foundation & a Cause distinct from itself. And this foundation must rest upon Will & Power.

From the perspective developed about perception as the result of a train of operations, we may say that all judgments of sense are contingent, because we can give no reason why we perceive as we do. Yet, while perceiving, we are led to make judgments that refer to contingent truths and to necessary truths. As Reid puts in in his manuscript:

there are natural suggestions, particularly, that sensation suggests the notion of present existence, and the belief that what we perceive and feel does now exist; that memory suggests the notion of past existence, and the belief that what we remember did exist in time past; . . . certain sensations of touch, by the constitution of our nature, suggest to us extension, solidity, and motion, which are no wise like to sensations, although they have been hitherto confounded with them.[21] . . . when I attend to colour, figure, weight, I cannot help judging these to be qualities which cannot exist without a subject; that is, something which is coloured figured, heavy. If I had not perceived such things to be qualities, I should never had any notion of their subject, or of their relation to it. By attending to the operations of thinking, memory, reasoning, we perceive or judge that there must be something which thinks, remembers, and reasons, which we call the mind. When we attend to any change that happens in nature, judgment informs us that there must be a cause of this change, which had power to produce it; and thus we get the notions of cause and effect, and of the relation between them. When we attend to body, we perceive that it cannot exist without space; hence we get the notion of space, (which is neither an object of sense nor of consciousness,) and of the relation which bodies have to a certain portion of unlimited space, as their place.[22]

21. *Works*, pp. 111a–b; see also pp. 108a–13a, 123b–24a, 183a, 198a–99a, 460a.

22. *Works*, p. 421a. On this ground Reid will later include contingent and necessary truths among the dictates of common sense, a view that has puzzled many commentators. Interestingly, there is a tendency to interpret this inclusion as representing a confusion in Reid's works either between his doctrine and his method or among several methods. Thus we are told that Reid passes from sensualism to spiritualism (M. C. Hippeau, [93], pp. 425–31); that Reid's system is dualistic, containing realism (empiricism) and intuition (idealism) (R. Petersen, [160], p. 22); that Reid is metaphysically a realist and epistemologically an intuitionist (S. Rome, [177], p. 110, n. 1); that Reid, apparently passing from empiricism to rationalism is, in fact, passing from empiricism to dogmatism (O. McK. Jones, [103], pp. 68, 73–74); from a scientific (or causal) explanation to a philosophical analysis of perception (D. A. Tebaldi, [12], p. 28); from indirect realism to direct realism (J. Immerwahr, [74], p. 245).

Finally, we must realize that the analysis of perception is complex because, in the tree of knowledge, perception is the root, common understanding is the trunk, and the sciences are the branches. As Reid says, in ordinary life, we draw the most obvious conclusions from these perceptions in so natural a manner that it is difficult to trace the line which divides the one from the other: "a farmer *perceiving* that his stable-door is broken open and some of his horses gone *concludes* that a thief has carried them off" (italics added). In a like manner, the science of nature dwells so near to common understanding that we cannot discern where the latter ends and the former begins; "I perceive that bodies lighter than water swim in water and that those which are heavier sink. Hence . . . every man, by common understanding has a rule by which he judges of the specific gravity of bodies which swim in water; and a step or two more leads him into the science of hydrostatics."[23]

Thus, on the basis of his analysis of the sensing activities, Reid concludes that while it is difficult to describe perfectly all the elements and the links that are naturally suggested to the mind because of these complexities, nonetheless it is apparent that our natural functioning is not passive in sensing; that it is not restricted to impressions (physical) or to sensations (feelings) but includes also perceptions of external objects. It is also apparent that our natural judgments are not restricted to the class of necessary judgments. Besides imaginary and abstract conceptions, we have conceptions of existing things; besides necessary relations of ideas, we make contingent judgments concerning relations. These are the important data on which Reid grounds his hope for a better (scientific) system of judgment, a system that should make us see the proper meaning of common sense, if we further reflect on such facts and draw (inductive) conclusions from an analysis of conception and judgments.[24]

4. REID'S ELUCIDATION OF THE PROPER MEANING OF COMMON SENSE

In his elucidation of the meaning of common sense,[25] Reid wants to argue (1) that sense, in its most common and proper meaning, signifies

---

23. This is one reason why the first exercises of our faculties are hidden like the sources of the Nile in an unknown region (see *Works*, pp. 417b, 11a, 80b, 326a).

24. In this sense Reid says that he is not offering a "new theory" (see *Works*, pp. 185a–86b, 309b).

25. For what follows, see *Works*, pp. 421b–426a.

judgment, though philosophers often use the term in another way; (2) that common sense, as a sense, signifies judgment; it signifies common judgments; (3) that these common judgments make up what we call common understanding; and (4) that "the same degree of understanding" that makes a man capable of common judgments concerning the conduct of life also makes "him capable of discovering what is true or false in matters that are self-evident and which he distinctly apprehended."[26]

Reid argues that we must use "common sense" as understood from its "unambiguous" meaning in common language. In common language, he says, common sense is as unambiguous and as well understood as the "county of York." It means a degree of understanding common to all men. It means that men are rational beings in that they all possess understanding, which is "the inward light given by Heaven to different persons in different degree." In common language, Reid argues, we call "seeing" a sense because we judge of colors by it. In a similar manner, we call "common understanding" common sense because we make common judgments, by means of the senses.

As Reid's former analysis of perception has shown, it is quite proper to say, with the common man, that sensing involves judging. By means of the senses, we have perceptions of external objects and of their qualities, and these perceptions involve conceptions and beliefs. It is also quite proper to say, with the common man, that common sense refers to common judgments. Again, Reid's former analysis of perception shows that those common judgments we make in the direction of our life are "the most obvious conclusions drawn from our perceptions." For example, "when I look at the moon, I perceive her to be sometimes circular, sometimes, horned, and sometimes, gibbous. This is simple perception and is the same in the philosopher and in the clown: but from these various appearances of her enlightened part, I *infer* that she is really of a spherical figure. This *conclusion* is not obtained by simple perception, but by reasoning."[27]

---

26. *Works*, p. 422b; see also p. 476a.

27. *Works*, p. 145b (italics added). According to Reid, reasoning and common sense are "gifts of nature" (see also pp. 463a–b, 421b, 415a–b). In his manuscripts Reid has listed many operations where common sense plays a role. By that faculty which we call common sense, we compare objects that are presented to us and discern various affections and relations belonging to them, such as identity or diversity, number, similitude, contrariety, proportion, sum, difference, quantity, matter, form, action, passion,

Hence the common meaning of common sense is correct in referring to common understanding, because it is natural to think that we have the *power* to make the judgments we actually make in perceiving and in drawing obvious conclusions from our perceptions.

If we raise the objection that the reference to common sense in common language does not explicitly mention the fact that all men have understanding, Reid's answer is that the reference to understanding is too obvious to need explicit mention: "Men rarely ask what common sense is; because every man believes himself possessed of it, and would take it for an imputation upon his understanding to be thought unacquainted with it."[28] If we object that the degree of understanding varies from one man to another, Reid answers that there is a basic level of understanding common to all men with whom we can converse. Tasks such as managing business affairs, behaving responsibly toward others, following the rules of law or following the political rules of our societies require understanding. Surely the degree of understanding required by such tasks must be possessed by

---

subject and accident, whole and parts, quality, time, place, genus and species, and innumerable other relations.

Elsewhere Reid lists the following operations as falling under the province of common sense: perceiving the obvious relations of things; distinguishing in the same object things that are different; observing in different objects things that are common; our natural and intuitive judgments about things that are not grounded upon reasoning but must be the foundation of all reasoning; reflection upon what has past in our minds; distinguishing; generalizing; discovering; reflection; judging; reasoning; comparing (numbering); classing (dividing, defining, compounding); Judging. [Birkwood Collection, T. Reid, MSS 2131.6 (II) (5)]. For another version of the meaning of common sense, see Appendix, *infra*.

28. *Works,* p. 423a. The importance of the reference to a tribunal will be analyzed later (pp. 134 ff.). In Reid's manuscript we also find a passage on common sense as "an object of attention to Men of Business in all Ages, & particularly to Lawgivers Magistrates and Civilians; As it is Common Sense that makes man capable of acting his part in human Society, & that makes him accountable for his conduct; the Laws of all Nations, and the practice of all Tribunals, distinguish with more or less Accuracy, those of the human Species who have this talent from them who [(want it)] whether through unripe Age, or Dotage, whether from Insanity or Idiocy or Lunacy. Such are not the proper Subjects of Law and Civil Government, they cannot transact business validly for themselves nor be accountable for their conduct towards them . . . . It were to be wished that a Power of the Understanding that has so Many Effects in Society & which has always been so much an object of attention to the Busy part of Mankind, had been attended to & Delineated by those Philosophers who have treated of human Understanding" [Birkwood Collection, T. Reid, 2131.6 (II) (6)].

those who perform them. Furthermore, this "common" level of understanding is clear enough to permit us to discern easily those who lack it: men's actions and speeches allow us to determine, for example, whether a man may or may not be a witness at the bar.

Reid argues that, in assuming that men are capable of certain tasks in ordinary life, we are presupposing that they possess understanding which allows them to make rational judgments about both practical and theoretical problems. Having argued—in referring to his former analysis of perception—that sensing involves judging and that judging involves understanding, Reid still has to show that the degree of understanding required by the performance of practical tasks in common life is the same as that which makes a man capable of judging of self-evident truths. Notice that for him the role of common understanding in practical affairs is more apparent that its role in theoretical matters. In this Reid fully agrees with Hume, who allows common sense a decisive role in conduct. However, Reid further argues that common sense also has an important role in theoretical questions, and this leads us to his elucidation of another aspect of the common use of "common sense."[29]

This aspect, Reid acknowledges, is only *implicit* in ordinary life. Usually, he says in quoting Shaftesbury's *Sensus Communis*, we appeal to common sense in a context of disagreement. When we are unable to reach an agreement in a discussion about morality, politics, religion,

---

29. *Works*, pp. 422b, 458a. Reid does not mention explicitly that common sense has a decisive role in conduct or in morals for Hume, but his quotation from Hume's *Essays* or *Enquiry* suggests that he is aware of the area in which Hume admits that common sense has an important role. To be clear, Reid admits that there are sciences concerned with action and others with speculation, as his own distinction between active and intellectual powers already indicates. Moreover Reid admits that in matters of deep speculation, the multitude is and must be driven by the few (*Works*, p. 520a; see also p. 469b). However, for Reid, the distinction between action and speculation is methodological, and in certain basic issues he holds that they are both determined by "Nature." Notice also that the "action" to which Reid will refer while elucidating the "appeal" to common sense will be the "action" of discussing. As we shall see, for Hume's impressions as a guarantee of the truth of *ideas*, Reid will substitute man's action, language, and opinions as vouchers for man's assent to certain proposition. For other indications on this development, see Norton, [148]. On the usually overlooked fact that Hume does give common sense an important role in morals, see Norton's article and D. C. Stove's article in [150] and my articles [128], [123]. On Reid's own view on morals, see M. S. Pritchard, [74], pp. 283–98, and H. Jensen, [74], pp. 299–310.

and the like, our final appeal is to the common sense of the speakers.
When such an appeal is made, everyone accepts that there is a solution:
in saying as a final answer, "Use our common sense," we imply that
common sense will show the speaker which solution is correct. This
situation is not satisfying, says Reid, because all disputants are left
with an (apparently) empty reference and it is not clear that the opinions implied would not be contradictory. As Shaftesbury says, common
sense is as hard to determine as "catholic or orthodoxy" in religion.[30]

However, Reid asks us to reflect on our use of the term "common
sense" in this context, because it indicates that when we appeal to
common sense in such cases, we are referring the question to a final
court of appeal. The crucial fact that needs examination here is that
we do not refer to any authority beyond common sense to provide a
decision in such disagreements, but instead (Reid suggests) to propositions that we hold to be self-evidently true. However, it is hard to
discover what these propositions are: as Shaftesbury said: "that which
was according to the sense of one part of mankind was against the
sense of another." In other words, one cannot merely *affirm* that
common sense is a final court of appeal because we judge of self-
evident propositions by it.

At this point Reid makes an important *methodological* claim. As Priestley said in comparing common sense to a judge (or, in Reid's terms,
to a tribunal of final appeal), "What can a judge do without evidence
and proper materials from which to form judgment?"[31] In other words,

---

30. *Works,* p. 423b.
31. *Works,* pp. 422b, 425a, 452b. As Reid writes in his manuscript: "I shall now
attempt to reduce to certain general Heads of Classes the Principles of Common Sense
upon which the various Branches of Human Knowledge are built.

"This, perhaps, may appear to some, to be a very humble task, & unfit for such an
Audience.—The A.B.C. may be explained to Babes; but men expect other entertain-
ment . . . . Men are apt to think their Understands are disparaged when they are put
in Mind of the Principles of Common Sense. I conceive the present State of Philosophy
not onely justifies an attempt of this kind but requires it . . . . The first Principles in
the various Branches of Science, if we except Mathematiks and Nat Philosophy, have
never been properly distinguished from the Truths deduced from them . . . . As this
is the State of Philosophy it seems not onely to be justifiable but necessary to turn back
to the Alphabet of Science, and to consider what are its first Principles. For untill men
agree in these there can be no hopes of their agreeing in any thing else. No Man can
Reason without Principles nor can two Men Reason together, without common Principles" [Birkwood Collection, T. Reid, 2131.6 (II) (8)].

if it is the case that referring to common sense actually means a reference to self-evident propositions, there is a good (philosophical) reason for common sense being seen as a tribunal of final appeal. But the way to check this is, for Reid, to codify the list of self-evident propositions that are at the basis of human understanding. It is to show that there are propositions which are self-evident to all men, and that when we use common sense to designate these propositions, we have indeed discovered the highest tribunal of reason and the proper meaning of common sense.

Let me add that because in this chapter on common sense Reid offers a "cloud of testimonies" in order to show that his use of the term "common sense" is not new, some commentators have missed in fact that the focus of his argument is *methodological*. Before arguing that it is proper to say, with the common man, that we call seeing, touching, smelling, hearing, and tasting senses because we *judge* by them, Reid had argued that we must reflect on the sensing activities—and he did quite carefully in his *Inquiry*. Now, before arguing that it is proper to say that we call common sense a tribunal of truth because we *judge* of self-evident propositions by it (as is implicit in the use the common man makes of the term "common sense"), Reid argues that we must reflect on the ways in which we perform the activities of judging. Notice also that the extent to which we can refer to common sense as "common understanding" or as "a power of reason" is the extent to which we can provide a list of common judgments, in the first case, and a list of self-evident judgments in the latter. In proposing a codification of self-evident propositions as the way to solve the difficulties raised by the true meaning of common sense, Reid suggests that the inductive-introspective procedure requires that we reflect on our *operations* and delineate their *contents* before we can draw conclusions about the existence of a power or a faculty in the mind.

The reason that Reid does not try to delineate the differences between ordinary beliefs and first principles of knowledge in his chapters on common sense is not because he confuses these but because his aim is to *discover* what kind of continuity exists between common judgments and first principles of knowledge by undertaking a new experiment about judgments: the codification of self-evident propositions. The extent to which common sense can be used as a philosophical standard will be the extent to which we can provide a list of self-evident propositions, which guarantees that common sense truly is the highest tribunal of reason: the part of reason that enables men to judge of self-evident propositions.

5. REID'S ANALYSIS OF PHILOSOPHICAL OBJECTIONS TO THE COMMON MEANING OF COMMON SENSE

Reid recognizes that there is a conflict over the true meaning of common sense with ordinary men on one side, and most philosophers on the other side. Indeed, with the exception of Buffier and Berkeley, who both mention common sense as a power of the understanding, most philosophers neglect or reject common sense in their theories. There are many reasons given for this, and Reid argues that the most important of these reasons are ill-grounded.[32]

Philosophers, he says, have defined the senses, both internal and external, as faculties (or in Reid's terms, "powers") by which men *passively* receive ideas or impressions from objects. They hold that the mind becomes active only in judgment, when it compares ideas (passively received) and perceives their necessary agreement or disagreement. The role of the senses is to provide us with ideas, and the role of judgment is to compare them. Given this definition of the senses, the common meaning of common sense cannot be philosophically valid. We cannot say that common sense "means" common judgment in the same way that sensing means judging because, properly speaking, we do not judge when we sense: we receive ideas.[33]

For Reid this view is not accurate. His previous analyses have shown that the mind is already active (i.e., judicative) *while* perceiving. Judgments take place in seeing, hearing, smelling, tasting, and touching: it is a concomitant of these activities. The dichotomy between sensing and judging in terms of the passivity/activity of the mind is artificial. Moreover, creating such a dichotomy precludes the possibility of our reflecting upon actual judgments by refusing to allow an active func-

32. Notice Reid's awareness of the fact that the relativity of human opinions is one of the main philosophical objections to common sense (*Works*, p. 423b). Though approving the use of wit and humor against philosophical objections to common sense (*Works*, pp. 458b–459b), Reid does not think—with Fénelon—that "it is sufficient to laugh instead of answering" (*Works*, p. 424b) or—with Hume—that it is sufficient "to leave an opponent to himself" (p. 425a).

33. *Works*, pp. 421b–422a; see also pp. 463a–b.

tion of the mind where the philosophical definition has stated there could not be one.[34]

Philosophers not only define the senses as passive and ideas as passively received, they also define "ideas" as representative substitutes, in the mind, of the things existing outside the mind. The philosophical accounts of such representatives vary throughout the history of philosophy, and Reid discusses such variation at great length. However, he holds that it is a standard view in philosophy to define ideas as "representatives," as "images," as "copies," as "pictures." This standard view gives rise to many epistemological problems such as the problem of the conformity of thought with its objects (whether, e.g., the "copy" is an exact picture of the thing, whether we can know the thing while we only perceive its representative, etc.).

For Reid, such problems are, to a large extent, pseudo-problems. Indeed, his entire *Inquiry* is an attempt to show that there is no such "representative" or "picture" in the mind, although there are some conceptions that may be called fancies, pictures, or copies.[35] Inasmuch as philosophical accounts of the senses and of judgment rest on this general hypothesis of "representative ideas," their theories must be rejected as invalid: they cannot apply to the manner in which all reasonable beings usually judge. In rejecting, as a mistaken hypothesis, the notion of "representative ideas," we also reject the view that judgment necessarily implies that we "compare" ideas in order to find their "similitude." As Reid says, the notion we have of the relationships between our notions is not always got by comparing them. For example, a certain kind of sound suggests to us that a coach is passing in the street. Yet in this belief there is no comparing of ideas, nor is there the least similitude between the sound we hear and the coach we imagine and believe to be passing.

There is also a third problem in the philosophical definition of judgment: the reduction of judgment to the perception of *necessary* connections between ideas. This problem is related to the reduction of ideas to "abstract conceptions," that is, to conceptions of objects

34. *Works*, pp. 246a–247a. For Reid the objects of the senses are "chaos," "rudis indigestaque moles," when judgment does not occur (see *Works*, pp. 418a).

35. *Works*, p. 111a. Reid says: "I think there is hardly anything that can be called *mine* in the philosophy of the mind, which does not follow with ease from the detection of this prejudice" (*Works*, p. 88b; see also pp. 431b, 209b, 421b–422b, 443a, 463a, 463b).

that have no spatial, temporal, existential—in a word, contingent—properties. But this is to argue that a very large section of judgment—indeed, the greatest part of human knowledge—must be ignored. These philosophical definitions of judgment cannot make room for the fact that we have conceptions of existing things and that we make judgments concerning their contingent relations. Even less can philosophical theories serve as an adequate basis for discovering the laws that are applied in contingent judgments.[36]

For Reid it is because they fail to ascribe a wider epistemological role to the senses that philosophers not only overlook the contingent and necessary judgments that arise in perception but are also led to significant inconsistencies. They admit as genuine knowledge certain judgments which occur in perception but which do not fit their narrow models. For instance, they admit that we have a sure knowledge of our existence, which could not result from a comparison of ideas;[37] they ascribe fallacies to the senses—but these could not occur if no judgment took place in sensing.[38] Finally, there is a gap between their definition of the raw materials of judgment (ideas) and their definition of the *mechanism* of judgment, which proceeds from simple apprehension, to judgment, and then to reasoning. But, says Reid, all the qualifications that philosophers make about the different kinds of ideas (general, abstract, particular, strong, lively, faint, languid, distinct, indistinct, clear, obscure, wavering, steady, eternal, vanishing, etc.) are not part of their definition of the first step of judgment, that is, "simple apprehension" as a bare conception of a simple notion. That is to say, the philosophical models fail to acknowledge the kinds of judgment that arise in perception while introducing qualifications on the kinds of ideas that are explicable only if such judgments do take place.[39]

On the basis of his own analysis of the sensing activities, Reid con-

---

36. *Works*, see pp. 454b–455a; pp. 185b–186a; p. 365a; pp. 484b, 442a–b, 468a–b; pp. 427b–429a, 441b–442a, pp. 433a, 430b. In his "Essay on Conception," Reid divides the classes of conception under three headings, and subdivides the second class here referred to in order to distinguish imaginary conceptions from abstract ones (*Works*, p. 365a). Interestingly enough, Reid's discussion refers importantly to the analogy of painting and of "copies."
37. *Works*, pp. 432b, 443a, 463b.
38. *Works*, pp. 208a–210a, 339b, 416a.
39. *Works*, pp. 360a–368b.

cludes that other philosophers' accounts of the sense, ideas, and judgments must be rejected and, accordingly, their objections to the common meaning of common sense. Reid's main argument is that the philosophical accounts of judgment are not scientific because they neglect important facts concerning perception and because their models cannot account for the complexity of such acts.[40] The conflict over the true meaning of common sense must be resolved on the side of the ordinary men in the following sense: while the philosophers' views on the senses, ideas, and judgments are not grounded on facts and are embedded in several difficulties, the common use of the term "common sense" is shown to be pregnant with philosophically important ideas; the idea of the mind as active (i.e., judicative) in the acts of sensing; the idea that judgment is a notion covering both contingent and necessary propositions; the idea of immediacy, that is, the absence of an intermediary (e.g., an image) between the mind and its object when we judge and the absence of a process of inferences that would produce men's assent to certain propositions.

6.   REID'S ANALYSIS OF THE PROBLEM OF FIRST PRINCIPLES

However important it is to recognize the difficulties involved in other philosophers' views of sensing and judging, it is even more important to analyze the difficulties they have created in their analyses of first principles.[41] Recall that the common appeal to common sense indicates that this is an appeal to a final court of decision in case of disagreements. In philosophy, says Reid, we find a similar situation: when, in a discussion, reasoning is at an end, it is often the case that we are quarreling about first principles. However, if the common appeal to common sense is apparently empty (we still do not know what common

40. This is the point of Reid's objection to Locke's division of ideas in terms of ideas of sensation and ideas of reflection: Reid thinks that Locke should have added a third category of "such ideas as *accompany* ideas of sensation and of reflection" [see Birkwood Collection, T. Reid, MSS 2131.6 (II), (5)]. On Reid's criticisms of philosopher's views, see Grave, [80], pp. 86–98: Grave argues that Reid is wrong in reading a *factual* denial in philosopher's *language*. A more accurate approach is proposed by D. N. Robinson's article in [12], pp. 44–55.

41. *Works*, pp. 434a–468b.

sense says is self-evident), we should not imagine that the appeal to first principles in philosophy is in a better position.[42]

Ordinary men, says Reid, differ greatly about first principles. But philosophers have not reached any more agreement in their discussions about first principles, either about their identification and number, or about their use in reasoning. What one philosopher takes to be a first principle, another labors to prove, while another altogether denies it. For example, "the sun exists, whether we think of it or not" was held as a first principle in ancient philosophy. Descartes, Malebranche, Arnauld, and Locke have tried to prove it by weak arguments, while Berkeley and Hume altogether deny it. The number of first principles presents a problem too. The Ancients were rather redundant and adopted many vulgar prejudices along with first principles: "this system was founded upon a wide bottom but in many parts unsound." The Moderns are extremely parsimonious: they have narrowed the foundation so much that "every superstructure raised upon it appears top-heavy." Finally, certain philosophers (Reid mentions Locke) think that first principles, because they are either tautological or fabricated at will, are not very useful in reasoning or in philosophy.[43]

The situation is puzzling because, as Reid puts it, everyone agrees that there *are* self-evident principles, and even Hume admits as self-evident the existence of the operations of our minds. It looks as if

42. Reid's suggestion to check whether the unsatisfactory results of both an appeal to common sense and an appeal to first principles would proceed from the same cause, namely, that we are discussing self-evident truths, could have been suggested by Fénelon's strategy concerning the *cogito*. See L. Marcil-Lacoste [125].

43. *Works*, pp. 462a–464b; see also pp. 205b–206a, 282a, 428a. On the number of first principles, Reid also wrote: "I do not insist upon it that the first Principles which a Man builds upon, should always stand by themselves in rank and file as they do in the Elements of Euclid or the third Book of Newtons Principia; . . . Yet methinks it is not unreasonable to ask that they should in one way or another be distinguished so as that their pretensions may be known, & they may not be confounded with things which belong to another Category . . . . That there may be innumerable selfevident Propositions I acknowledge; but the greater part of these will be found to be trifling propositions as Mr. Locke very justly calls them . . . . if we confine ourselves to those first principles that are really usefull and make them as general as the Nature of things will admit I see no reason to apprehend that in any branch of Science their Number will be any just objection to their Being particularly Pointed out" [Birkwood Collection, T. Reid, 2131.6 (II) (6)].

the factual existence of self-evidence was overwhelmed by philosophical problems of identification, number, or use of first principles. When we consider the question of first principles in philosophy, we must admit that we are in "a field of battle where every inch of ground is disputed." Because we still do not know what the *A*, *B*, *C*, of human reasoning is, our reasoning spends its force in the air and produces only sects, disputes, animosity, revolution, conjectures, and hypotheses. The codification of self-evident propositions is necessary not only for common-sense philosophers, but such codification is a desideratum in logic. If, according to Hume, nothing could correct bad reasoning but good reasoning, Reid's point is that good reasoning proceeds from first principles that are *not* the result of reasoning. In this domain our choice is between fictions (principles *presumed* to be self-evident) and facts (principles that *are* self-evident to the human mind).[44]

For Reid, if we say that a principle is self-evident, we must be able to show that all men actually agree on it. What would the expression "self-evident" mean if only a few philosophers actually assent to self-evident principles? It must be possible in principle for all men to agree about principles that are self-evident and distinctly apprehended. To suppose, says Reid, "a general deviation from truth among mankind in things self-evident for which no cause can be assigned is highly unreasonable."[45] And, he asks, "Why should it be thought impossible that reasonable men should agree in things that are self-evident?"[46]

Reid explains the paradoxical situation concerning first principles—

44. *Works*, pp. 442b, 443a; pp. 435b–436b; see also pp. 62b, 416a, 425a, 482a, 95b. See also Hume's letter, 18-2-1751, in J. Y. T. Greig, [82], 1: 150–51, and Hamilton's n. A, *Works*, pp. 743 ff. In the context of first principles, discussions upon "truth conditions" become fruitless: for Reid no criterion for truth can be "real" unless it is in keeping with the fundamental and "real" laws of human beliefs (*Works*, p. 376b). But in establishing first principles, we need "marks," which Reid does not hesitate to call "criteria": "Supposing Axioms to have some Utility in Philosophy, it may still be a Question that seems to have been too little considered how or by what criterion they are to be distinguished from prejudices of Education and other false Principles which it must be acknowledged have often passed for first principles" [Birkwood Collection, T. Reid, MSS 2131.6 (II), (6); cf. *Works*, p. 416a].

45. *Works*, p. 440b. See also pp. 485a, 424a, 122b, 188a, 477b–478a. For other interpretations, see L. L. Laudan, [40], pp. 111, 120, and W. P. Krolikowski, [108], pp. 142–43.

46. *Works*, p. 422b; cf. p. 440b.

if they are self-evident, why is there so much disagreement over them?—
as due to the fact that philosophers have not actually tried to discover
these principles by scientific (i.e., experimental) methods. Instead,
they have misguidedly attempted to formulate *a priori* theories about
what must be held as self-evident.[47] Behind such endeavors is the
mistaken assumption that only a few men are entitled to state what it
is to know. Ultimately this assumption is a denial of the fact that all
men are rational beings endowed with understanding. For Reid we
cannot admit that all men have a common degree of understanding
and yet refuse to admit that all rational beings have the capacity to
recognize self-evident principles. Again he concludes that only an
experimental codification of self-evident propositions will provide the
proper materials from which we can judge in what sense the common
appeal to common sense as a final tribunal in matters of truth can be
coextensive with the philosophical appeal to first principles of knowledge. But in attempting to discuss propositions whose truth is guaranteed by their self-evidence, we still have to discover the means to
distinguish what is solid and well supported by facts from vain fictions
of human fancy.[48]

7. REID'S ALTERNATIVE MODEL IN THE TREATMENT OF SELF-EVIDENT
PROPOSITIONS

In basing his approach on the assumption that all men can agree
about self-evident principles distinctly apprehended, Reid still has to
show that the agreement of human reason about self-evident principles is not only an epistemological rule but also a fact, which philosophers have been prevented from explicitly acknowledging because
of their mistaken theories.

One difficulty in developing this alternative approach to self-evident
principles is that the "evidence" that can be presented for them is not
definable and that its force is better felt than described. Besides, there
are many kinds of evidence. Reid's problem is to find a method that
allows him to determine which principles are self-evident.[49]

47. *Works,* pp. 456b, 442b–443a, 435a.
48. Birkwood Collection, T. Reid, MSS 2131.6 (II), (9); see also *Works,* pp.
422b–425a, 441a–441b.
49. *Works,* p. 328a. On this question, see *Works,* pp. 326b–330a. This point is overlooked, e.g., by P. Vernier, [12], p. 20; N. Daniels, [12], p. 37; L. Turco, see my review
[126].

At this point Reid introduced a crucial device: we must distinguish between intuitive judgments and judgments grounded on arguments:

It is not in our power to judge as we will. The judgment is carried along necessarily by the evidence, real or seeming, which appears to us at the time. But in propositions which are submitted to our judgment there is great difference—some are of such a nature that a man of ripe understanding may apprehend them distinctly and perfectly understand their meaning, without finding himself under any necessity of believing them to be true or false, probable or improbable. The judgment remains in suspense, until it is inclined to one side or another by reasons or arguments.

But there are other propositions which are no sooner understood than they are believed. The judgment follows the apprehension of them necessarily, and both are equally the work of nature, and the result of our original powers. There is no searching for evidence, no weighing of arguments; the proposition is not deduced or inferred from another; it has the light of truth in itself, and has no occasion to borrow it from another.[50]

Earlier Reid had argued that the common nature of all kinds of evidence is that they are all fitted by nature to *produce* belief. When we see evidence, it is impossible not to judge. Correlatively—and methodologically this is crucial—Reid thinks that when it is shown impossible not to judge, then we can assert safely that there was evidence sufficient to support our judgment.[51] When, further, no source of evidence could be shown to play a role in our judgment other than our understanding of the proposition, then we can safely assert that there was self-evidence. In the case of intuitive judgment, the apprehension of the proposition is necessarily accompanied by a belief: both the apprehension and the belief are the work of nature. What is characteristic of propositions that are not self-evident is that in such cases a distinct apprehension is not sufficient to influence man's judgment or belief: "something farther" is then needed.[52]

Perhaps evidence, as in many other respects it resembles light, so in this also— that, as light, which is the discoverer of all visible objects, discovers itself at the same time, so evidence which is the voucher for all truth, vouches for itself at the same time.

50. *Works*, p. 434a; see also pp. 413a–b.
51. *Works*, pp. 328a, 328b, 434b, 416a, 74b, 485a, 461b.
52. Birkwood Collection, T. Reid, MSS 2131.6 (II), (6).

This, however, is certain, that such is the constitution of the mind that evidence discerned by us, forces a *corresponding degree* of assent. And a man who perfectly understood a just syllogism without believing that the conclusion follows from the premises, would be a greater monster than a man born without hands or feet.[53]

We are now in a position to understand the gist of Reid's alternative argument. It is difficult to agree on self-evident propositions because we cannot understand what self-evidence is *a priori.* Furthermore, it is difficult to describe what self-evidence is because we seem able to discern only the effects that self-evident propositions produce in our mind; that is, a certain intensity and an immediacy of assent to certain propositions. However, these difficulties are resolved when we understand that if we say that a proposition is self-evident, we surely mean to say that it is self-sufficient to produce our assent. Thus when we need something more than the apprehension of a proposition in order to decide whether or not we should assent to it, we can surely say that this proposition is not self-evident. When, conversely, we cannot see that another source of assent besides our understanding of a proposition plays a role in our judgment, we can assert safely that the proposition is self-evident to us.[54]

In other words, Reid treats the notion of self-evidence on the model of an unknown efficient cause whose effects are discernible in the ways we assent to certain propositions. As he says, "a man comes to know his own mental abilities just as he knows another man's, by the effects they produce when there is occasion to put them to exercise."[55] Such effects may be seen in men's language, actions, and opinions. We need to reflect upon the signs of men's beliefs and, in order to do so, we should increase the signs we use. For example, we cannot restrict our introspective reflection to the Humean "impressions" that are meant as guarantee for the truth of men's ideas. In the case of

---

53. *Works,* p. 448a (italics added), p. 482b.

54. *Works,* pp. 328b, 434b, 438a–440b, 416a, 74b.

55. *Works,* p. 458a; see also pp. 438a–440b. On this question, see Sydney Rome, [177], pp. 225, 313; Reid's point is that Hume's philosophical relations presuppose natural relations. Antonio Rosmini-Serbati, [178], 1:86–91, argues that Reid's basic mistake is to envelop "original judgments" in a cloud of mystery: a judgment not preceded by some universal idea (notably that of existence) is an impossibility. For an enlightening analysis of Reid's view of judgment as a first operation of the mind, see Victor Cousin, [50], 4:371 ff., and T. Jouffroy, [104], 1:xxx, ff.

self-evident principles, the crucial test concerns not only the ways in which we conceive of, but also the ways we assent to, certain propositions.

We must treat the notion of self-evidence in a scientific manner, as the (self-sufficient) cause of our assent to certain propositions. We know—as one of Newton's greatest discoveries shows—that the *utmost* that natural philosophy can reach is the ascertainment of a law of nature according to the effects it produces. As Reid says:

> . . . we have no reason to ascribe Active power to any Being that is not endowed with some Degree of intelligence and will. The consequence of this is that we know not the real Efficient Cause of any Natural Phenomenon whatsoever. When natural philosophers pretend to show the Causes of Phenomena they either pretend to what is beyond the Sphere of Human Knowledge or by *Causes* they mean only Laws, according to which the unknown Cause Acts.[56]

In the case of self-evidence, the utmost that we can reach is the discovery of the laws of assent to certain propositions, namely, the discovery of propositions where the apprehension is immediately followed by an assent to the proposition we consider.[57]

But if we realize that our knowledge is limited to that of the effects which self-evident propositions produce in our mind, we also realize that what is truly self-evident to all men can be distinguished from those principles which unjustly assume that title. This determination is made by the use of what Reid calls "rational means," that is, means that help us to distinguish what is supported by facts from that which is hypothetical.

> . . . in such controversies, every man is a competent judge; and therefore it

---

56. I. Ross, [179], p. 20; see also *Works*, pp. 527a–b, 57a–58b, 458a, 65a, 73b, 76a, 76b.

57. Our knowledge is limited, being restricted to the operations of the mind or, that is, to the effects and operations revealed when exercised. In a crucial example, that of the necessary existence of a thinking being, Reid overtly acknowledges that even though we are conscious of the operations of a thinking being (such as deliberation, affirmation, negation, conversation, the use of personal pronouns), we cannot say *"what* this Being *is* which thinks, reasons or wills." On the other hand, we are conscious of the operations of the mind; we further know that "that which operates must exist." Thus the limits of our knowledge directly point to that which can and must be asserted: in this case, the existence of a thinking being. On this question, see P. Vernier, [12], p. 15.

is difficult to impose upon mankind . . . . opinions which contradict first principles, are distinguished from other errors by this: That they are not only false but absurd; and, to discountenance absurdity Nature hath given us a particular emotion—to wit, that of ridicule—which seems intended for this very purpose of putting out of countenance what is absurd, either in opinion or practice . . . . although it is contrary to the nature of first principles to admit of direct or apodictical proof; yet there are certain ways of reasoning even about them [*ad hominem, ad absurdum,* universal consent] by which those that are just and solid may be confirmed, and those that are false may be detected. Opinions that appear so early in the minds of men that they cannot be the effect of education or of false reasoning, have a good claim to be considered as first principles. . . . when an opinion is so necessary in the conduct of life that without the belief of it a man must be led into a thousand absurdities in practice, such an opinion, when we can give no other reason for it may safely be taken for a first principle.[58]

Thus we can make sure that the beliefs we see as self-evident are generally acknowledged as such: these beliefs are admitted by the learned and the unlearned; their denial is usually perceived as ridiculous; their denial may also be shown to lead to absurdities both in deductive reasoning and in conduct. Of course, Reid's "rational means" do not prove that self-evident propositions are true. They are meant to show that we have instances of belief shared by the learned and the unlearned and that such instances have many signs of being irresistible beliefs.[59]

Every man of common sense who is not a philosopher is *irresistibly* determined to believe the reality of the objects which he sees and handles and of those qualities of extension, figure, motion, colour, and smell which are attested by senses to belong to them . . . . The belief that men have of the objects of their senses could neither be so early nor so universal as we find it to be if it were a prejudice of education or of false philosophy. The universality of it, its growing up with us from infancy, and the necessity of it to our conduct in

---

58. *Works,* pp. 435a–441a. A. Garnier argues that Reid is wrong in making the appeal to universal consent an axiom (see [75], p. 8;); and A. Boutwood ([20], pp. 154–71) argues that Reid makes such an appeal a "fringe benefit" of first principles. On this, see *infra,* Section 12, where I show that Reid uses the appeal to universal consent in a Baconian manner.

59. *Works,* pp. 239a, 233a. For another view, see P. Vernier, [12], p. 18.

the common occurrences of life give it all the characteristics of a first principle.[60]

In treating his "rational means" as indications of the *generality* of men's assent to certain *irresistible* beliefs, Reid suggests that they do not constitute the final proof that certain propositions are self-evident. This introduces another dimension to his method of codification, which is central to his understanding of the kind of induction required in a science of first principles. This is the attempt to demonstrate the ultimate status of his first principles by means of an eliminative procedure that is, perhaps, the main feature of his codification.

As we have seen, Reid treats certain immediate assents to particular propositions as the effect of self-evidence (cause). But he also has to show that men's assent to such propositions is not borrowed from sources other than the apprehension of the proposition. At this point he asks whether reasoning, experience, custom, or education can have produced the assent which seems immediate.[61] Reid does not attempt to eliminate systematically all other *possible* causes of assent to principles he claims to be self-evident. Instead, his concern is to show that the *specific* other causes invoked by certain philosophers in order to account for men's assent to a *given* (first) principle do not cope with the examples of assent he considers. His main contention is that standard alternative explanations invoked by philosophers—such as experience and reasoning—do not accurately explain the *particular* assent

---

60. Birkwood Collection, T. Reid, MSS 2131.6 (II), (9).

61. *Works*, pp. 122a, 188a, 477b–478a, 329a–b, 443a, 452a. It is on Reid's eliminative procedure that Krolikowski, [108], pp. 142–43, has focused. He sees in it an adaptation of the Newtonian method. The latter includes: (1) observation, to wit, experiment and rigidly selected factors in complex phenomena; (2) breakdown into simple factors amenable to mathematical description; (3) explanation and prediction of other phenomena in which (2) operates as a cause. According to Krolikowski, Reid's adaptation of Newton's method includes: (1) observation, but little importance of the facts selected; (2) ascesis of prejudices, as education, fashion, philosophy; (3) analysis into simple and original principles of the human mind; (4) reconstruction of (1); (5) further use of (4) as basis to demonstrate various phenomena. The Baconian influence is left open as a question on the third phase of the Reidian process, as if there would be some resemblance between Bacon's simples and Reid's judgments. It seems to me that the Baconian methodological influence is more plausible in phase (2). On this question, see the next two sections.

to self-evident propositions, nor do they fit the general law from which such particular cases proceed.[62]

Concerning experience, Reid argues that when our immediate assent to certain propositions cannot be referred to preceding and similar examples, then our assent can hardly be said to be produced by experience, a conclusion drawn from a repetition of similar examples. Further, learning something by experience implies that we collect and compare data; but when we cannot recollect when we have learned that this or that principle is true, again we can hardly claim that we have learned it by experience. Finally, our assent to necessary propositions cannot be produced by experience, which informs us of what is and not of what must be.[63]

The same kind of argument is used by Reid when he deals with deductive reasoning as one of the sources invoked by philosophers in order to account for our assent to certain self-evident propositions. In such cases, reasoning proves nothing at all or it begs the question, and therefore it is difficult to maintain that reasoning can produce our assent to self-evident propositions. When, further, assent is given as soon as we are conscious of the proposition, then reasoning can hardly be invoked as a cause of our assent: in such cases, reasoning simply did not occur.[64]

The point of the eliminative procedure is, then, to show that we have a series of propositions that are no sooner understood than they are believed, without further operations such as deductive or inductive reasoning. On the one hand, therefore, we have judgments where the assent naturally follows the apprehension of propositions and, on the other hand, we have philosophical accounts incompatible with such assent. In a scientific manner, we must conclude that the connection between the apprehension and the assent in the case of self-evident propositions is a *law of nature* in the sense in which natural philosophy concludes the existence of such laws: by considering the effect, here the immediate assent. This immediate connection between the apprehension and the assent to self-evident propositions is what we call the law of assent to first principles.

62. *Works*, pp. 448a–449b, 455a–461b.
63. *Works*, pp. 449b, 455a–461a.
64. *Works*, pp. 448a, 455a, 461a.

8. THE BACKGROUND OF REID'S ALTERNATIVE

In order to understand the full meaning of the alternative Reid is presenting concerning an inductive treatment of self-evidence, we must understand it in relation to his final goal: an answer to skepticism. In so doing we see again that Reid's theory of perception—when connected with his analysis of conception—lies at the base of his method concerning first principles.

In the *Inquiry*, Reid had said that there would be no answer to skepticism if perception did not include beliefs, for example, about the existence of the thing perceived, that is, if only ideas occurred in perception. Ideas are transitory: they exist only when we are conscious of them. It follows that no object of thought can have a permanent existence. If we reduce the activity of judging to the activity of conceiving or to the ideas existing when we conceive them, it will follow that no judgment can be made concerning, for instance, the continued existence of the self.[65]

However, in analyzing perception we have noticed that it contains two elements, a conception and a belief about the truth of this perception, which are immediately connected together. The immediacy of this connection is what Reid called "a third element," by which he meant not only that there is no intermediary substitute (a representative idea) between the mind and the object, but also that there is no intermediary process of inference (by inductive or deductive reasoning) that could produce our irresistible assent to the judgment we make in perception. Reid now insists that in our analysis of the activity of judging we must account for two elements (conception and belief) and that we must discover their connection. This claim about judgment in general—that it always contains two ingredients, a conception and a belief—is inferred from our analysis of perception and thus will permit us to discover the continuity between common understanding and science in matters of judgment, especially in our judgments concerning self-evident propositions.[66]

Reid's basic claim is that the belief or conviction involved in judgment has not been sufficiently recognized and analyzed as being distinct from the conception that is also included in every judgment. He

65. *Works*, pp. 106b–107a; see also pp. 327b ff.
66. *Works*, *pp.* 91b, 103b, 104a, 217b, 366a, 466a, 422b, 438a, 414a.

argues that judging is different from conceiving or from having a bare apprehension of something. "If it could be said that in love there is something more than an idea, to wit, an affection of the mind, may it not be said with equal reason, that in belief, there is something more than an idea, to wit, an assent or persuasion of the mind?"[67] If so fundamental an ingredient of judgment has been forgotten by philosophers, there is hope that a better system, one including this ingredient, would lead to agreement on self-evident propositions.

We must use a model in which the conception of a proposition and the belief or conviction about the truth of the proposition—the latter being distinguished from the former—are seen in causal connection. If we analyze any judgment, it must involve an apprehension of the proposition and an assent (or a denial) of the truth value of that proposition. This model is sound because, Reid says, "a man cannot be convinced of what he does not understand." He continues: a sound judgment and a clear and steady apprehension are so connected that we do not know which comes first. There is, in this sense, what he calls a "bird-and-egg" problem about judgment, but this problem itself shows that the model of causal connection between the two ingredients of judgment is adequate. Propositions must be conceived before they can be judged, but something different from a mere conception must occur before we can say that we have judged this or that proposition to be true or false.[68]

For Reid, in using the model of a causal connection between the conception and the belief or conviction, we have a methodological means to discover what is supported by facts and what is hypothetical when we reflect on judgment. Reid will argue that we can make sure

---

67. *Works*, pp. 107a–b; 414a, 360a–362b, 376b–379b, 397a, 183a–b, 258a. See also Letter IX, 1-12-1778, in I. Ross, [179], for a clear statement on perception, conception, and belief. On this precise point Reid rejects Descartes's model; see my article [124] and similar views in P. Heath, [74], pp. 220–28, and P. Vernier, [12], p. 14, Reid is misread in M. Hooker, [12], p. 89, and in P. D. Cummins, [12], p. 62.

68. On the relationship between conception and assent, two interesting examples can be used. According to Reid, Hume denied that we have an idea of power and that we could have clear ideas of mathematical figures. In answer, Reid argues that we have a *conviction* concerning those ideas, as our actions (such as deliberation in the first case or mathematical derivation in the last) show. The argument is: we cannot be convinced of what we do not understand (see *Works*, pp. 446a, 452b, 409a, 412b, 415b, 419b, 430b, 521b, 409b, 414b, 260a). For related issues see also *Works*, pp. 87a, 482b, 240a, 466a, 475a, 210b–223b, 417b, 414a, 366a, 308b.

that men do conceive a self-evident proposition if we can show that they are convinced of its truth.[69]

In arguing that our model for self-evident propositions should recognize the actual features of men's beliefs or convictions (immediate, strong, impulsive, compulsory, self-sufficient), Reid also wants to reject the idea that men's conceptions can be made the *exclusive* test for the truth of all judgments. His favorite example is the *reductio ad absurdum*. This procedure, Reid argues, would be impossible if we assented to everything that we conceive and if we were unable to conceive propositions without assenting to them. We cannot argue that our conceptions are the exclusive test of truth, for we do not assent to all that we conceive; for example, we can clearly conceive but we do not assent to a self-contradictory proposition. The argument here is the following: conception is not always accompanied by an assent (conception is not always judgment), while in judgments assent (or dissent) always accompanies a conception. In our reflection on judgment, we must make sure that more than mere conception is present.

There are other limitations to the use of conceptions as the exclusive test for truth. Our conceptions do not always refer to existing things: there are fancies. Consequently, our conceptions cannot be the test for existence: it is a prejudice to think that whatever we conceive must have existence. Besides, in our attempts to discover the most *general* phenomena we can reach in an inductive approach to judgments, we must notice a significant difference between our conceptions and our convictions.[70]

---

69. Assent is no more voluntary than to see when the eye is open (*Works*, p. 74b). The notion of will is restricted to an "exertion intended to effect something which I believe to be in my powers" (Letter XIV, 6-10-1780, in [179], pp. 48–51). An action is said to be involuntary when one cannot hinder it by one's own will (p. 50). The springs of action differ in operating in a way that resembles impulse or persuasion (Letter VII, 27-2-1778, [179], p. 32). Attention, deliberation, fixed purpose, and determination are voluntary actions, i.e., they imply a large share of will. Thus the assent to self-evident propositions is not a voluntary act in the Reidian-restricted sense of the word.

70. *Works*, pp. 414a, 360a–363b, 376b–379b, 397a, 431a. In his manuscripts Reid writes: "So far is it from being true that our bare conceptions are the measure of possibility, that in many instances even when Judgment and reasoning is taken in to the aid of conception we are at a loss to determine what is possible and what is not. Mathematicks and even Arithmetick afford many instances of Impossibilities which are not obvious, but have been discovered by long trains of the most abstract Reasoning

The characteristics of our conceptions are subjected to a great variation among men, while the use of philosophical standards renders this variation even greater; our conceptions may be clear, distinct, steady, lively, strong, abstract, general, transitory, obscure, indistinct, feeble, weak, and so forth.[71] This variety, itself a genuine subject of inquiry, already suggests that it would be difficult to use any of such characteristics as a leading thread toward a *general* account of judgment. On the other hand, we must notice that the assent (apart from the apprehension of the proposition) puts all men on the same level: as Descartes and Cicero have seen, for all men all assent follows *some* evidence.[72] Furthermore, as Reid argues, natural evidence forces a corresponding degree of assent. In thus using the features of men's assent as the effects of men's conceptions, we can reach a general account of men's judgments: the variations between men's beliefs will be seen as the result of their different conceptions. In any case, such variations will not show that men lack the capacity to assent to what they understand.[73]

Let me add that Reid thinks that the distinction between conceiving and assenting to a proposition is particularly apt in the case of self-evidence: the main difference between intuitive judgments and judgments grounded on arguments lies in the way we assent to them. Immediate assent can follow the conception of propositions about both contingent and necessary things or relations, because the act of thinking (or for this purpose, the acts of conceiving, of assenting or rejecting) must be distinguished from the object of thought about which we conceive a proposition and to whose existence and properties we assent. Thus this twofold model of conception and assent allows

----

. . . . to distinguish in all cases between what is possible & what is impossible is not so easy matter as has been imagined by Philosophers. It is not the clear conception of a thing that will warrant us to affirm it to be possible. An no Man ever affirmed that an obscure conception is an Evidence of Impossibility . . . . Take away all Arguments drawn from Fact or from the real Existence of things; and I conceive there are very few things if any that we could pronounce to be possible. We know from Experience that certain things are possible because they are in our own Power, we know that others are possible because they actually exist, or because they have existed or shall exist. But beyond this our knowledge of Possibility is extreamly limited" [Birkwood Collection, T. Reid, 2131.6 (II) (9)].

71. *Works*, pp. 414a, 360a–362b, 376b–379b, 397a, 431a.
72. *Works*, pp. 366b, 353a–361a, 376b–379b, 397a, 411a, 378a–b, 363b.
73. *Works*, see pp. 435a, 438b, 416a.

us to discover which propositions are self-evident among our judgments about contingent things.[74] In the case of self-evident propositions we must also make sure that what Reid calls "a third element" (the *immediate* conjunction of the apprehension and the assent) is present. Thus if we reflect on conceiving and judging, our methodological principle for the codification of self-evident principles is twofold: (1) a proposition to which we do not assent immediately cannot be held as self-evident, however sophisticated our accounts of the conceptions it involves are; and (2) a proposition to which we assent strongly as soon as we understand it can be taken as self-evident, if we can show that nothing but our conception of it has produced our assent.

9. REID'S CODIFICATION OF SELF-EVIDENT PROPOSITIONS

Let us now consider the ways in which Reid uses his methodological model of self-evidence in his codification of first principles. Usually, Reid says, first principles "force assent in particular instances more powerfully than when turned into a general proposition . . . . The sceptic may perhaps persuade himself, in general, that he has no ground to believe his senses or his memory; but in particular cases that are interesting his disbelief vanishes and he finds himself under a necessity of believing both."[75] For example, Hume—the skeptic par

---

74. *Works*, see pp. 447b, 154a, 224a, 277b, 292a, 298a ff., 368a, 373a ff., 430b. Notice also that the exclusion of contingent truths would jeopardize Reid's claim for the continuity between common understanding and science (see *Works*, pp. 185b–186a).

75. *Works*, pp. 416a, 448a. According to S. A. Grave, [80], p. 104, there is no inconsistency between theory and practice if only empirical: what the philosophers question does not concern empirical facts but metaphysical assumptions. The basic mistake of Reid's appeal to common sense is a confusion between linguistic oppositions and factual oppositions at the ground of Reid's confusion of the empirical and metaphysical levels of common-sense beliefs. In fact, Reid would have to show that language has a double reference (empirical and metaphysical) in order to show that philosophical claims *really* go against common sense (pp. 98–102). For Grave it is illusory to confine people to what they *can* mean even though common-sense beliefs can have metaphysical implications (pp. 98, 96). However, in Reid's view of the importance of induction and, in such a method, of the importance of particular cases to be generalized, the inconsistency between a theory (denying a first principle) and a practice (admitting it in particular cases) gains a theoretical or at least a methodological status. In a sense one can say that Reid tries to show that it is not the case that "The great triumph of scepticism is to show that speculation and practice are irreconcilable." See Hamilton's note, *Works*, p. 457a. On this question, see *Works*, pp. 454b–455a, 438a–b, 462b, 83b, 297a; see also B. Brody, [12], p. 11.

excellence—persistently admits that in ordinary life he believes his senses, his consciousness, his memory. Reid asks us to reflect on the "ingenuity" of Hume's confession."

As may be recalled, Hume argues that we must follow Newton's "chief" rule of philosophizing: "where any principle [e.g., an explanation] has been found to have great force and energy in one instance, we must ascribe to it a like energy in all similar instances."[76] For Reid it is inductively inconsistent to admit the truth of one particular instance of belief and to deny the truth of the general rule derived from such similar instances. On the contrary, the experimental method, when we apply it to the question of judgments, demands that our general conclusions be drawn from particular instances of beliefs.

The second thing to notice in Reid's codification is what I shall call the "plainness" of his propositions. We can illustrate this by considering some of his particular examples of beliefs as well as the general statement of first principles of contingent truths (F.P.C.T.) or of first principles of necessary truths (F.P.N.T.), which he sees as the premises on which these particular beliefs are grounded. Before turning to Reid's distinction between contingent and necessary truths, we must focus on the nature of the connection between (particular) cases of belief and (general) first principles, because this connection is central to Reid's view of necessity.

Thus, Reid says, we can see by observation of those around us that we talk to each other; we impute certain actions or omissions to our fellow men; we expect the sun to rise tomorrow; we believe the world to arise from something (from an egg, from a struggle between love and strife, from chance, from a concourse of atoms, from God). We could not, he continues, talk to each other unless "we believed in the existence of other beings" (F.P.C.T.); we could not impute to man his actions unless "we believed that he has a degree of power of them"

---

76. D. Hume, [95], p. 204. For Reid, the second of Newton's most important discoveries is "to acquiesce in a law of nature according to which the effect is produced as the utmost that natural philosophy can reach" (*Works*, pp. 76a–b, 57a, 236a–b, 250a, 271b). Notice that Reid admits that if the skeptics were not "half sceptic" (i.e., if they denied *all* self-evident principles in speculation and in practice), the problem of a codification would radically be without remedy. See *Works*, pp. 434b, 102a, 110a, 130a, 208a, 234a, 266a, 299b, 489b; see also Birkwood Collection, T. Reid, MSS 2131.6 (II), (9). On this and its influence on G. E. Moore, see K. Lehrer, [12], p. 4.

(F.P.C.T.): we could not believe the world to arise from something unless "we believed that what exists must have a cause" (F.P.N.T.). Suppose we did not believe in the existence of other people, in their intelligence, in the existence of some power over our action, in some regularity in natural phenomena or in the existence of a cause for a change in nature; then it would be impossible to account for the facts of our particular beliefs. Even more, if we did not believe the foregoing, it would be impossible not only to give sense to our conduct but merely to perform the actions involving such beliefs: "If it were in our power to throw off our belief upon our practice and conduct, we would neither speak nor act like reasonable men."[77]

Reid does not discuss the appropriate ways to translate particular assent in particular cases into general propositions. This is surprising, especially if one considers his admissions that it is *when* turned into general propositions that self-evident principles present the most difficulties and that to retrace the path from particulars to universals is very difficult.[78] We can, however, interpret Reid's silence as a result of his conviction that it is in particular instances that self-evident principles are most universally—although implicitly—acknowledged, by both skeptics and dogmatists, by both the learned and the unlearned. Reid does attempt to show that the transition from particular instances of beliefs to general principles can and does occur.[79] His

---

77. *Works*, pp. 455a, 393a, 402a, 443a–b. Reid says that the agreement lies, "as it were, on the surface"; only two terms used in the codification will be defined by Reid: "consciousness" as distinct from reflection, and the "I" as distinct from the Humean succession of impressions (*Works*, pp. 443a–b). On this question, see also *Works*, pp. 435a–b, 475a, 233a. It would be interesting to compare this claim with G. E. Moore's claim that common-sense propositions are indubitable, although we can be very skeptical as to what the correct analysis of such propositions is. See, e.g., "A Defence of Common Sense" in [145]. Charles Sanders Peirce has interesting comments on the "surface" agreement. See [158], pp. 481–99, and his letter to Lady Welby (May 30, 1911), in [157], p. 426.

78. See Reid, [170], pp. 23, 16.

79. S. A. Grave, [80], p. 116. The function of common sense seems to be the authorization of a transition from empirical facts to metaphysical facts, which we find inevitable. Notice, however, that metaphysical first principles are but one subclass in Reid's codification. In his manuscript Reid wrote: "That whatsoever is, is, And That it is impossible for the same thing to be and not to be, may if I mistake not be put in the same Category as trifling Propositions. I know of No conclusion of any Consequence that was ever drawn from them. When then Should Science be encumbered with such

translation is "simplicity itself": when we feel a pain and believe it to exist (particular case) we cannot say that "we do not believe in the existence of internal operations" (F.P.C.T.). If a man performs those operations that are the effects of his consciousness (such as deliberation, affirmation, negation, conversation, the use of personal pronouns) and at the same time affirms a disbelief in his existence as "myself, my mind, my person" (F.P.C.T.), "I must" says Reid, "consider him in the same light with the man who swears he has tasted nothing but water for two days, while the very breath he utters carries copious steams of gin."[80]

The Reidian translation is causal: the individual cases of belief are the effects of a general law of assent to self-evident propositions, which characterizes our intellectual powers. We should state as simply as possible the general laws of belief that our particular beliefs express in order to make sure that our theories account for the actual judgments we make. It is this connection between particular effects (assent) and the law of thought (cause) expressed in a propositional (general) form that guarantees the validity of our general conclusion. And as the eliminative procedure shows that we cannot account for such judgments except by the immediate connection of the assent to the apprehension of the proposition, we can conclude that we have a self-evident principle.

The agreement of all reasonable men lies, as it were, "on the surface." What Reid means by this is that the reflexive sophistication concerning self-evident propositions need not be great, at least not in the act of immediate assent to such propositions. However, the "plainness" of Reid's examples should not be misrepresented. Far from being, as Grave puts it, a destructive method, philosophically

---

useless impediments? . . . That First principle in Natural Philosophy that Effects which are similar in their Nature ought to be ascribed to the same or to similar Causes, comprehend in its womb thousands nay millions of particular Propositions which must be admitted if the general proposition is admitted. To . . . enumerate all the particular self-evident Propositions which this general one contains would indeed be impossible & if possible would be meer trifling. But the general Proposition is easily marked and easily referred to when any conclusion drawn from it is disputed" [Birkwood Collection, T. Reid. 2131.6 (II) (6)].

80. *Works*, pp. 393a, 402a, and Birkwood Collection, T. Reid, MSS 2131.6 (II), (9); see also Reid, [170], pp. 23, 16. On this question, see V. Cousin, [52], pp. 3, 303–15; V. Cousin, [50], pp. 369–75, 407; M. F. Sciacca, [182], pp. 21–25, 67–74.

speaking, Reid holds that if we look at the agreement of reasonable men, we shall have the basis of a new science. In this new science, the most important facts (however plain) will not be denied, and sophisticated thought will now be useful because it will be sufficiently grounded. This procedure is meant to show in what sense there is a continuity between common understanding and science.[81]

We can illustrate the last point by a few examples. As Reid says, "When I perceive a tree, my faculty of seeing gives me not only a notion . . . of the tree but also a belief in its existence, and in its figure, distance, magnitude." Such instances of perceptual judgments imply that we believe, as a self-evident principle of *contingent* truths, that "those things do really exist which we distinctly perceive by the senses and are what we perceive them to be." Again, we do not only perceive figure or motion: we perceive them to be qualities. Such beliefs imply that we believe as a self-evident principle of *necessary* (metaphysical) truth, that "the qualities which we perceive by our senses must have a subject which we call body." In a similar manner, our ordinary judgments concerning, say, the gravity of bodies that swim in water imply that we believe as a self-evident principle of *contingent* truths that "in the phenomena of nature what is to be will probably be like to what has been in similar circumstances." As Reid says, take away this principle, and the experience of a hundred years makes us no wiser with regard to what is to come, and the whole fabric of natural philosophy falls on the ground.[82]

Thus Reid offers his examples of common-sense principles as "plain" examples because he wants to make sure that his list truly shows the continuity between common understanding and science. However, the plainness of Reid's list of first principles should not be misrepresented as the result of merely descriptive generalizations of instances of particular beliefs. First principles are *implicitly* recognized because they function as premises of particular judgments. Because we can discover such premises only by a knowledge of their effects (particular beliefs), the more we stick to particular instances the greater probability we have to state correctly what is self-evident for all men. On the other hand, the general statements at which we arrive, through Reid's method, do not constitute a mere enumeration of particular

81. *Works*, pp. 435a–b, 475a, 233a, 455a.
82. *Works*, pp. 441a–462b; see also pp. 44a–b, 795a–b, 521a–b.

beliefs: they are explicit enumerations of the self-evident propositions (cause) from which the particular beliefs proceed.[83]

Given Reid's treatment of self-evidence, we can now understand the sense in which he claims that his first principles of both contingent and necessary truths are necessary. Reid distinguishes contingent and necessary truths in the following manner:

The truths that fall within the compass of human knowledge whether they be self-evident, or deduced from those that are self-evident, may be reduced to two classes. They are either necessary and immutable truths, whose contrary is impossible; or they are contingent and mutable, depending upon some effect of will and power, which had a beginning, and may have an end. That a cone is the third part of a cylinder of the same base and the same altitude, is a necessary truth. It depends not upon the will and power of any being. It is immutably true, and the contrary impossible. That the sun is the centre about which the earth, and the other planets of our system, perform their revolutions, is a truth; but it is not a necessary truth. It depends upon the power and will of that Being who made the sun and all the planets, and who gave them those notions that seemed best to him . . . .
. . . The distinction commonly made between abstract truths and those that express matters of fact, or real existences, coincides in great measure, but not altogether, with that between necessary and contingent truths. The necessary truths that fall within our knowledge are, for the most part, abstract truths. We must except the existence and nature of the Supreme Being, which is necessary. Other existences are the effects of will and power.[84]

In dealing with first principles, it is important to acknowledge that Reid treats the notion of necessity without an exclusive reference to logical necessity, but in such a way that his list of first principles also includes such logical necessity. In the case of necessary truths, which are nothing more than what they are conceived to be, predicability

---

83. We can illustrate this by considering Reid's decreasing use of the term "power." In the *Inquiry*, when discussing natural judgment, he often says that "by an original power of our mind, we are under a necessity to believe this or that." But in his chapters on common sense, Reid is trying to determine the specific laws of belief that permit us to make the judgments we make in perception. He is trying, in other words, to give a more precise meaning to the notion of "power" that he was using in his *Inquiry*. This is plausible given the fact that he treats evidence on the model of an efficient cause (power) and this cause as the premise of judgments. On abstract ideas being "deontologized," see P. D. Cummins, [12], p. 72.

84. *Works*, pp. 441b ff. On this, see R. C. Sleigh, [12], p. 83.

and the impossibility for such propositions not to be true are the main source of our assent. It is impossible to conceive *and* assent to "two and two equal not four," "good breeding is worse than ill breeding," "thought can be without mind," or "something can exist without a cause."[85]

But Reid has a more extensive view of necessity than mere logical necessity. Indeed, even in the case of necessary truths, their necessity pertains also to what can be called their imperative indispensability in life, conduct, thought, and science. Taking advantage of two meanings of necessity—that of unavoidable constraint and that of indispensable requirement—Reid argues both that his first principles are unavoidable (they are necessarily assented to immediately) and that his first principles are indispensable (we could not act, think, or reason without assuming them). In other words, first principles are necessary to life and conduct, but also to thought and science, and it is when we have occasion to use these principles *in science* that we call them axioms.[86]

This range of necessity is at the root of the apparent confusion in Reid's codification of first principles to which we alluded earlier. Reid seems to alternate between an appeal to descriptive general laws and a more transcendental procedure, stating what beliefs should be invoked to make possible the (particular) assent to some propositions. In point of fact, Reid's first principles are both descriptive laws and beliefs without which no mental activity would be possible. This bipolarity is a direct result of his claim that common-sense principles pertain both to common understanding and to first principles of knowledge. The descriptive side of this endeavor is related to common understanding, while the transcendental side is related to first principles of knowledge.

85. *Works*, pp. 414b, 429a, 407a, 111a, 323a, 73–77b. On this point, see F. Copleston, [49], vol. 5, p. 2, p. 175. Copleston argues that Reid's ambiguity lies in his referring self-evident contingent truths to an "impulse to believe" and self-evident truths to the "meaning of terms." Grave, [80], p. 116, argues that there is no logical unity for the kinds of Reidian evidence.

86. *Works*, p. 230b; see also 329–b, 521a–b, 44a–b, 102b, 436b, 446a–451a, 795a–b. Notice that, for Reid, the most, simple, distinct, and accurate notions we have, even of sensible objects, are expressed by "term of art" where they are used in science [see Birkwood Collection, T. Reid, MSS 2131.6 (II), (2)]. See also, for the notion of defensibility, J. Hintikka, [92], pp. 31–33, 48–51. Another view is defended by C. MacLaurin, [121]; see also Davie, [58], pp. 105–200.

More important, however, is the *continuity* of these two dimensions which, for Reid, is assured by the reference to the "ultimate" laws of men's judgments. Our first principles are "ultimate laws" in that they are a set of facts concerning men's judgments beyond which philosophy cannot go except by means of speculative hypotheses. The immediate causal connection between a conception and an assent to the propositions Reid lists as self-evident is also ultimate in showing that it is a law of assent that characterizes our intellectual powers. These principles are ultimate because, beyond the natural laws of self-evidence, we cannot account for them. By virtue of the experimental method, this list of self-evident propositions may be compared to the laws of nature in natural sciences. Such laws constitute the utmost that we can know of the frame of the human mind. Thus self-evident principles are necessary, in being both unavoidable and unaccountable except *ultimately* by reference to our constitution, that is, by reference to the laws of natural evidence.[87]

Of course, Reid does not want to reduce necessary truths to contingent ones, or to elevate contingent principles into disguised necessary ones. His concern is that inasmuch as all first principles are natural to men's intellectual powers of judgment, they are all on the same footing: the assent to their evidence is as immediate as the apprehension is.[88]

Thus there is no confusion in Reid's codification of first principles between an appeal to description and an appeal to transcendental

---

87. *Works*, pp. 459a–469a, 83a, 416a, 185b–194b; see also I. Ross, [179], p. 62. Notice that in Reid's time, "Laws . . . had greater force than descriptive generalizations because they had acquired a fundamental systematic status in the scientific picture of the universe" (in A. R. Hall, [85], p. 173, cf p. 257). As Reid puts it, the attempt to overturn the principles of common sense is "no less ridiculous than if a mechanic should contrive an *axis in peritrochio* to remove the earth out of its place" (*Works*, p. 102b). For different interpretations on this point, see J. A. Laird, [111], p. 106; S. A. Grave, [80], p. 160; S. Rome, [177], p. 225; Bryson, [24], p. 23; Lyall, [119], pp. 42–48. For misinterpretations of this point, see supra, nn. 3, 9, 10, 22.

88. This was the point of Reid's distinction between a conception and a belief (assent or dissent) (see *Works*, pp. 447b, 154b, 224a, 277b, 292a, 298a ff., 368a, 376a ff., 430b). Notice that "Reason requires that the degree of our assent be proportioned to the evidence" [Birkwood Collection, T. Reid, MSS 2131.6 (II), (5) and (6)]. On the relationships between contingent and necessary principles, see *Works*, pp. 185b, 194b, 478a, 481b–484a, 442a, 442b, 468a, 468b.

arguments. Indeed, the originality of his understanding of the experimental method lies precisely in his conviction that reflection points
to certain facts which indicate that there are natural laws governing
men's assent to self-evident propositions. When it is time to show that
certain principles are self-evident to all men, Reid appeals to inductive
arguments. But when it is time to justify the status of his findings
(first principles of contingent and necessary truths), Reid, as Bracken
has argued, must use transcendental arguments.[89]

When properly used, the inductive-introspective method shows that
the human mind judges in accordance with *a priori* principles. To use
Kantian language, it is meant as a proof that the *quod facti* of human
judgment does include a set of *a priori* laws of belief concerning contingent and necessary truths. But while Kant understood Hume's
arguments as a *reductio ad absurdum* of empiricism, Reid understands
such attacks as a refutation of classical empiricism, and he tries to
reconstruct the experimental method. Finally, because reflection points
to the natural laws that govern men's assent to self-evident propositions, the experimental method points to a *quod facti* that is in itself a
quod juris.[90]

10. REID'S JUSTIFICATION OF THE APPEAL TO COMMON SENSE

As we have seen, the attempt to codify the dictates of common sense
was Reid's method for showing that there are self-evident propositions
to which all reasonable beings assent. His list of first principles concerning contingent and necessary truths is presented as the content
that truly makes the appeal to common sense an appeal to a final
court in matters of knowledge. Indeed, the common appeal to com-

89. H. M. Bracken, [22], pp. 334–46; see also P. Vernier, [12], p. 19.
90. For a clear example of the difference between Kant and Reid on this point, see
Kant, [105], pp. 318, 177–79, A 133–76, B 172–76; Reid, *Works*, pp. 263b, 444b, 445b.
In Reid's view philosophers also deny certain facts and not only their status or relevance,
as e.g., their "denial" that sensing activities are accompanied by all sorts of judgments,
necessary and contingent. "Reid was unconscious of the extent to which he was inferring
Hume's and Berkeley's principles from their conclusions and he was in fact unable to
exhibit this collapse purely as a consequence of the supposition of representative ideas"—
this is Grave's statement in his article on Reid in [81]. A similar point of view is expressed
by Frederick Copleston, [49], vol. 5, pt. 2, pp. 172–73.
For a discussion of the epistemological role the "way of ideas" has, in Reid's view of
common sense, see *infra*, Section 12.

mon sense is coextensive with the philosophical appeal to first principles inasmuch as Reid's method of dealing with the notion of self-
evidence can show that there are principles that are unavoidable and
indispensable in life as well as in science.[91]

In dealing with common sense, Reid appealed to induction, especially with reference to the generalization of particular cases, the treatment of self-evidence on the model of an efficient cause whose effects
are discernible in the way we assent to certain propositions, and the
refusal to accept a prioristic definitions of self-evidence. Concerning
the natural laws of operations of our mental powers, Reid has argued
that our choice is between the way of reflection (the name he gives
to the inductive procedure when applied to mental facts) and the way
of analogy (what results with any system of the mind that does not
submit itself to the strict and severe method of induction). Reid's
appeal to common sense is an appeal to induction. It is an attempt to
formulate the conditions of validity of an application of induction to
the realm of "mental facts."[92]

Let me insist on the general issue: Reid's systematic argument justifying an appeal to common sense is grounded on the view that there
is no possibility of giving a philosophical account of our intellectual
powers except by the use of the experimental method. Perhaps we
do not need induction when we make everyday or philosophical judgments. But in philosophy we need the inductive procedure in order
to follow carefully all judgments and reflect upon them.[93]

To this typically eighteenth-century faith in the experimental method,
Reid adds something that has passed unnoticed because of the interest
his doctrine has received at the expense of his method. Reid thinks
that the experimental method cannot be legitimately applied in the

---

91. In Reid's language, first principles do not stand alone and unconnected [see
Birkwood Collection, T. Reid, MSS 2131.6 (II), (6)].

92. On Reid's appeal to natural judgments given as an appeal to facts that cannot
be logically demonstrated, see *Works*, pp. 434b, 102a, 110a, 130a, 208a, 234a, 266a,
299b, 489b, 120b, 258a, 54b, 477a, 479b, 484b, 159–163b, 272a, 246a.

On Reid's insistence on the necessity of introducing reflections on conception, abstraction, etc., see *Works*, pp. 441a–443a, 501a, 74b–75b, 130a, 577a–579a, 594a–599a,
and I. Ross, [179], p. 47.

93. Reid's faith in the experimental method is not to be confused with his confidence
in his own use of it, as A. Rosmini-Serbati, [178], p. 70, no. 103, would have it (see
Works, pp. 455a, 102b; Birkwood Collection, T. Reid, MSS2131.6 (II), (5); see also
Hamilton, [87], p. 363; McCosh, 136], p. 10; Jouffroy, [104], 1:xxxii).

science of the mind unless it is recognized that, epistemologically speaking, common sense allows us to identify and respect our field of observation. In our attempts to discover the natural laws of intellectual operations, we must determine the boundaries of the territory in which the general laws will be said to hold true. We must, in other words, identify and respect the domain (1) in which men's intellectual operations find scope, and (2) within which they are naturally confined.

For Reid this epistemological domain of the science of the mind is quite broad, including all judgments, ordinary and philosophical, contingent and necessary, true and false, all judgments made by the learned and the unlearned, the skeptics and the dogmatists. To realize the importance of this domain is to explain why Reid used the term "common sense" throughout his writings even before he gave a more precise account of the notion. Whenever Reid refers to common sense it is always related to the facts that characterize men's judgments and thus is always within the field of inductive observation. It is also on the basis of his reflections on such facts that Reid gradually proceeds to his more precise account of the proper meaning of common sense as the tribunal of reason in self-evident propositions. What must be noticed here is that in referring to the scope of a science of the mind, Reid makes a general connection between common sense—which identifies the field of observation (judgment)—and induction—which provides means for investigating this field.

This connection explains why he based his investigation of common sense on an investigation of common judgments. It is not the prevalence of common sense among the unlearned that justifies the philosophical appeal to it, but instead it is Reid's commitment to the experimental method that requires that we consider common judgments. Such judgments constitute a large segment of the field of observation and reflection. Therefore they must be included if we are to claim that our inductive conclusions are general. In *this* context Reid argues that every man is a competent judge, for we must look for particular cases that can be generalized rather than for prototypes to be exemplified.[94] The first guarantee that the general laws that we

---

94. It is in this context that Reid argues that the "Few" philosophers who do proceed like scientists are *the only competent judges* (see *Works*, pp. 95a–b, 215b, 224b, 119b, 78b, 520a).

recognize as the basis of human knowledge are inductively true of human nature is provided by a reflection on actual judgments as they are performed. In other words, Reid's attempt to discover what kind of connection there is between ordinary beliefs and first principles of knowledge was derived from his attempt to respect the general scope of an inductive science of the mind while justifying the proper and more precise meaning of common sense.

Another important connection between common sense and induction is derived from Reid's view that, although our domain of investigation is broad, it is nonetheless naturally confined, especially when we deal with first principles. As Reid puts it, our faculties are our "sole engines." Because we have only the faculties we have and because we must use our faculties as they are, we must allow the laws of the operations of these faculties to be part of the materials we analyze. Furthermore, when we try to discover inductively which propositions are self-evident, our domain of investigation is, so to speak, self-contained. If our inductive conclusions on self-evident principles are valid, the reasoning by which we arrive at these conclusions is bound to include, at some point, the same sort of judgments we are studying: reasoning is valid inasmuch as it rests on self-evident premises. In this sense, Reid had said that Newton's rules concerning the experimental method are "maxims of common sense": all our inductive reasoning (including our reasoning on self-evident principles) is grounded on a self-evident principle of contingent truth.[95] Reid's argument, at this point, is not that common sense and induction are merely synonymous terms. His argument is that common sense and induction are necessarily connected by the most important limitation on our domain of investigation: our means of investigation concerning our faculties are our faculties themselves.

There are, therefore, two general connections between common sense and induction if we reflect on the scope of the science of the mind: (1) it is inductively invalid to exclude large segments from the domain of observation: the *extension* of our domain requires that the meaning of common sense be derived from reflections on the large segment of common judgments; (2) it is inductively naïve to pretend to overcome the fact that our faculties are our sole means of investigation, even when the subject of our inquiry is to discover the laws

95. *Works*, p. 97b.

of their operations: the *confinement* of our domain requires that we use the only faculties we have, as they are, in order to ascertain what the laws of our operations are.

These two general connections between common sense and induction are important but, in Reid's view, they are not sufficient to discover the laws of the operations of the mind. Indeed, we already know that he has presented his method of codification of first principles as a way to make sure that we do not confuse first principles and any sort of belief. We also know that Reid was anxious to show that his method of codification is inductively valid. What needs acknowledgment here is that even though Reid admits that we are bound at some point to reason by the same sort of judgment we are studying *when we deal with self-evident principles,* he also wants to make sure that we arrive at this point by an inductive process that is itself valid. His arguments may be summed up as follows: common sense and induction are connected because we can show that *only common-sense principles* satisfy the experimental conditions for discriminating between mere hypothesis and inductively grounded conclusions in self-evident propositions.[96] To make this last point clearer, we have to show why Reid thinks that, in the philosophy of the mind, the experimental method has been little followed, in spite of Bacon's earlier delineation of its features and, above all, in spite of Newton's assertion of its maxims, the *Regulae Philosophandi.*[97]

For Reid ancient philosophies were analogical because they materialized the mind, while modern philosophies are analogical because they spiritualize the body. Furthermore, even philosophers who have professed to use the experimental method—the most outstanding example is Hume—have fallen into analogical reasoning, and more importantly, into merely hypothetical accounts of our mental activities. Reid admits that in their attempt to establish a science of the mind, philosophers have not labored in vain. However, little has been done in this line because, even though philosophers claim to follow

---

96. For example, Grave argues against Reid that one can show that the doctrine of "representative ideas" is not empirically grounded without committing oneself to common sense. My analysis shows how the two questions are epistemologically related for Reid (see S. A. Grave, [80], p. 141). For other discussions on a science of the mind, see J. C. Robertson's analysis of a debate involving F. Jeffrey, D. Stewart, M. Napier, T. Brown [175].

97. *Works,* pp. 472b, 251a, 312b.

the great Newton and Bacon, they have missed the basic conditions according to which the great scientists have been successful.[98] In attempting to apply the experimental method without paying attention to its rules, philosophers not only have missed common sense as the epistemological domain of the science of the mind, but also have failed to see the specificity of the subject-matter of a science of first principles; and finally, they have failed to discover the natural laws governing men's assent to self-evident principles.

Reid, says L. L. Laudan, "was the first major British philosopher to take Newton's opinions on induction, causality and hypothesis seriously"; as a "well-read, capable physicist who knew Newton's work first hand," Reid "could see that there was more of methodological interest than the popularized works of Newtoniana could begin to suggest." As Stewart more generally put it, "the influence of the general views opened in the *New Organon* may be traced in almost every page of his [Reid's] writings, and indeed, the circumstances by which these are so strongly and characteristically distinguished is that they exhibit the first systematical attempt to exemplify in the study of human nature the same plan of investigation which conducted Newton to the properties of light and to the law of gravitation."[99]

11. REID'S UNDERSTANDING OF NEWTON'S METHODOLOGICAL RULES

Indeed, it is from Newton that Reid borrows the most important of his tenets concerning the experimental method. His arguments against philosophical systems are grounded on what he thinks is a better understanding of the *Regulae Philosophandi*—more specifically, his understanding of Newton's first rule: "What we take to account for many phenomena ought to be real and adequate to the effects."[100]

Newton's first rule is twofold. It states the reality condition (What we take to account for many phenomena ought to be real) and the adequacy condition (What we take to account for many phenomena ought to be adequate to the effects). It is with respect to the first

98. *Works*, pp. 251a, 312b.

99. D. Stewart, [194], pp. 259–61; L. L. Laudan, [40], pp. 106–7. This is contrary to the views of N. Daniels, [12], p. 40, and L. Turco, see my [126].

100. *Works*, pp. 250a, 236a–b, 57a, 271b. W. P. Krolikowski has missed the importance of Newton's rule in Reid's methodology (see [108], pp. 146 n. 1, 143, 146–47.

condition that Reid finds faults with all other philosophical systems of self-evidence. Explaining why philosophers are not real inductivists, Reid observes that they have been almost exclusively concerned with the adequacy condition, which is the result of their long-standing love for simplicity, a prejudice that not even the great Newton avoided. We deceive ourselves, argues Reid, if we think that the rule that "nature operates in the simplest and best way" is sufficient to discover and to understand the laws of nature. We deceive ourselves even further if, when we proceed from hypothesis whose validity is not tested, we feel that we have presented a true system of the mind by virtue of the cogent reasonings we derive from it. In Reid's view the urge toward adequacy is antiexperimental when the reality condition is not met.[101]

But what does it mean to say that our hypothesis concerning the human mind ought to satisfy the reality condition of the Newtonian rule? In the physical sciences, the law of attraction is not hypothetical as long as it expresses what really happens with physical bodies and their movements. Again, it is easy to see that "aether" can legally be used as a hypothesis only inasmuch as one tries to show that such aether exists and is adequate to account for various phenomena.[102] But in the case of self-evidence, how can we determine which conditions should be met in order to say of an explanation that it satisfies the reality condition of the Newtonian rule? For example, what would it mean to say that any reason given for a philosophical theory of evidence must be "real"?[103]

Precisely at this point Reid made a crucial request. Until the laws by which we assent to self-evident propositions are inductively established, we *cannot* say under which conditions a hypothesis could be legally used; under which conditions it could be shown to cope with the (real) laws of human beliefs. Only when reflection upon the most general phenomena of mental operations is completed do we know what it means, specifically, to satisfy the reality condition of the Newtonian rule and, in turn, what can be said to be merely hypothetical in our philosophical systems of evidence.

---

101. *Works*, pp. 234a–b, 470b–471; see also L. L. Laudan, [40], p. 114.

102. *Works*, pp. 261b, 234a; see also I. Ross, [179], pp. 52, 61.

103. For the "fifth" rule of philosophy, which Newton wrote about mental phenomena, see A. Koyré, [107], p. 272.

For Reid any reasons given as justification for a philosophical theory of truth are "real" if and only if they correspond to a natural law of belief. No philosophical theory can be said to respect the reality condition of the Newtonian rule if such a theory does not admit that common sense allows the identification of the field of our observations. Furthermore, no theory of self-evidence can be said to respect the Newtonian condition unless it admits the dictates of common sense as the *contents* of the reality condition in matters of self-evidence.

We have seen that in his codification of self-evident propositions, Reid insists on Newton's "second" most important discovery: our knowledge of the laws of nature is derived from our knowledge of the effects of natural causes. In this context, a philosophical theory of first principles is *real* inasmuch as it copes with the laws of men's assent to self-evident propositions (causes) and, more precisely, inasmuch as it establishes such laws by considering their (particular) effects in men's opinions, language, and conduct. However, in order to use the experimental method as Reid has used it in his codification, we should not consider the *effects* of men's intellectual powers along the model of causality that is used in physical sciences. Reid's codification of first principles is a systematic application of his distinction between two kinds of causality.[104]

In his letters to Kames and Gregory, Reid insists that the natural sciences deal with physical causes, with phenomena that are related to each other by priority and constant conjunctions. The science of the mind, on the other hand, deals with efficient causes, with a kind of causality which, in its relation to the effects, is analogous to voluntary and deliberate actions. In natural sciences, what we call a cause is simply the observable (antecedent) phenomenon always conjoined with another (consequent) phenomenon. The notion of a scientific law is that of the correlations between conjoined events; it is not a necessary connection or a knowledge of the nature of the so-called "causes and effects."[105]

104. *Works*, pp. 435a–437a, 56a–59a, 73a–76b, 65a, 76a–83b; see also pp. 132a, 97b, 235a, 396a–397b, 235a, 132a. Here Laudan's distinction of a scientific and an efficient cause in Reid's writings is misleading; see [40], p. 109; see also W. P. Krolikowski, [108], pp. 143–46; V. Cousin, [52], pp. 3, 303–15; V. Cousin, [50], pp. 369, 375–407. For related issues, see M. Bunge et al., [38].

105. *Works*, pp. 73a–74b, 64a–b. It is the unawareness of Reid's distinction that explains Krolikowski's misinterpretation of Reid; he says that the notions of causal relation and efficient cause became an obstacle that Reid tried to get rid of in referring to the relation between sign and thing signified (see [108], pp. 143–46). On this point,

In a science of the mind, we have another notion of causality, that of the efficient relation of a power to its effects, such as the relation of a power, in man, to direct his thoughts or his action in designed ways. In such cases, we cannot observe an antecedent cause, such as men's intentions or thoughts. This is to say that physical and efficient causes differ *toto genere*: physical causes correspond to the establishment of correlations between observable antecedent and consequent phenomena, while efficient causes correspond to the establishment of the efficacy of an intelligent cause that is not observable directly. The radical distinction between the two kinds of cause does not mean that the treatment of an efficient cause cannot be scientific. On the contrary, Reid thinks that his treatment of efficient causes is in accordance with Newton's rule: we know not the cause of anything but we can only ascertain the natural laws according to the effects they produce. Both physical and efficient causes are observable in their effects (consequent).

In distinguishing the physical and the efficient causes, Reid wants

---

see also Victor Cousin, who insists on the specificity of the inductive method when one applies its rules to mental facts. In this line Cousin argues that the Reidian method (which he calls "méthode réflexive-psychologique") is more aptly said to be Cartesian than Baconian or Newtonian. Against Stewart, Cousin maintains that an inductive science of the mind does not refuse to speculate about the nature and the essence of the soul but, on the contrary, the reflexive method "Atteint directement avec les phénomènes leurs causes efficientes, c'est-à-dire nos facultés et ainsi la connaissance certaine de la nature du sujet de ces facultés."

My interpretation of Reid's method in codifying the dictates of common sense does not go so far as Cousin's claim. In trying to take advantage of the scientific and the philosophical meaning of the word "cause," Reid is forced to admit that the knowledge we have of our faculties and of the thinking subject is determined, in its certainty, by the limits of induction itself or by the fact that a "law of nature" is known by the effects we can observe without knowing what the "cause" is in itself. Cousin seems to grant this point, at least, partially, for he goes on to say that it is "par l'intuition intime de ces facultés elle nous donne *sinon directement* au moins par l'induction *la moins éloignée* et la plus voisine de l'intuition elle-même la connaissance certaine de la nature du sujet de ces facultés" (italics added); see Cousin, [52], pp. 3, 303–15, and [50], Lesson 19, esp. pp. 369, 375–407).

For an interesting discussion of Reid's "metaphysical agnosticism," see M. F. Sciacca, [182], pp. 21–25, 67–74, 115. See also his articles on Reid and on the "Scottish School of Common Sense" in *The New Catholic Encyclopedia* (New York: McGraw Hill, 1966), 12: 211, 1246. Sciacca argues that one characteristic of the Scottish School is the conclusion that, because man's knowledge is limited to phenomena, man cannot know the substance.

us to apply the analogical principle (same effects, same causes) to the different kinds of causality. In the case of efficient causality, the initial conditions that allow us to determine the antecedent cause must be interpreted within a model where the antecedent is not observable in the same ways the antecedent physical phenomenon is. But a scientific treatment of efficient causality is possible if it proceeds from a knowledge of the effects of such causality in men's consciousness, language, opinions, and conduct. "We see not men's hearts nor the principles by which they are actuated; but there are external signs of their principles and dispositions, which, though not certain, may sometimes be more trusted than their profession."[106]

Reflection on the operations of the mind testifies to the immediate connection of, say, a conception and a belief, a natural assent to self-evident propositions. To look for an image in the brain or for a series of physical antecedents in order to explain the assent to self-evidence is to be an uncritical inductivist. To assume that a *latens processus* of such physical antecedents (what Reid takes to be Hume's version of custom) can explain our assent to self-evident propositions is clearly to confuse the two kinds of causality and to leave the real question open: if custom is a "second nature" we still have to know which original laws produced it and allowed it to gain strength.[107]

We are now in a position to understand the sense in which Reid claims that his theory of self-evidence respects Newton's motto, *hypotheses non fingo*. To do so, we must consider two difficulties raised by Reid's treatment of first principles: (1) the ambiguity of the meaning of "hypothesis" and (2) the sense in which Reid rejects the *reductio* method.

---

106. Notice that in neither case (physical and efficient causes), do we have a knowledge of the cause in itself. See *Works*, pp. 76a–b, 483b; see also Laudan, [40], p. 114.

107. See in the *Intellectual Powers*, Essay 2, chaps. 9 and 14; Essay 4, chaps. 2 and 3; also *Works*, pp. 128a, 374b, 107b, 198b–199a, 227b, 250b–251b, 263b, 272b, 276a, 305b, 373a–374b. Reid seems to identify the attempts to account for the "how" of mental activities with the Baconian attempts to show the *latens processus* that produces things. On the claim that the "how" escapes us, see *Works*, pp. 76a, 260b–262a, 280b, 302a, 309b, 323b, 329b. When philosophers confuse judgment and testimony, they confuse the accountability of the "how" of our judgments (which is impossible, it seems) with the obvious factuality of these judgments, which is an ultimate (*Works*, pp. 445a–448b, 452a, 152a ff., esp. p. 415a; also pp. 258a, 472b).

Ironically, when we deal with self-evident propositions we are dealing with hypotheses in the sense in which the term was used before the eighteenth century: hypotheses as assumed and unproved propositions. Reid is aware of this, as his manuscripts show when he tries to distinguish hypothesis and postulatum. The point of this distinction is to relate his use of the term "hypothesis" in the new eighteenth-century meaning: hypotheses as untestable propositions or uncorroborated explanatory assumptions. What Reid wanted to show was that although first principles cannot be proved true by means of reasoning—they must remain unproved and assumed proposition or hypothesis in the old sense of the word—there are experimental ways to make sure that they are not untestable or uncorroborated assumptions about the human mind; they are not hypotheses in the new meaning of the term.[108]

Let us now formulate the difficulty concerning the *reductio* method. As Laudan rightly pointed out, Reid does not think that the full force of inductive proof is gained by virtue of eliminating other hypotheses. This statement, however, needs the following qualification: when the reality condition is met, the elimination of a hypothesis surely strengthens the proof value of induction. In this sense, Reid's own eliminative procedure—in the codification of self-evident propositions—is consistent with his (qualified) rejection of the *reductio* method. Reid's point is that we must use different procedures to meet the two conditions of Newton's rule.[109]

This being said, we can understand the sense in which Reid's treatment of self-evidence derives its experimental validity from a systematic reflection on *hypotheses non fingo*. In his codification of self-evident

---

108. R. E. Butts, [40], pp. 74, 103; A. Koyré, [107], pp. 261–73. Although not very clear on the question of assumption and hypothesis, Reid surely realized that inductive evidence is absolutely essential; S. D. Schwarz denies this in [181], p. 228. In one of his manuscripts Reid clearly distinguishes hypothesis and postulate; talking of consciousness, Reid notes that "No Man as far as I know ever contrived an Hypothesis to explain how we get that immediate & certain Knowledge of the Operations of our own Minds which we call consciousness but how we remember things past, how we perceive external things; this has been considered as knot fit to be untied & therefore we find Hypothes about those operations ever since men began to Philosophize concerning their own Minds. In all these Hypotheses it is taken as a Postulatum that we are conscious of things in the Mind" [Birkwood Collection, T. Reid, 2131.6 (II) (8)].

109. Laudan, [40], pp. 111, 120, 108–16. See *Works*, pp. 57b, 234a ff., 56b, 96a, 131b, 132a, 132b, 251b, 150 ff. 248b ff.

propositions, Reid used *different* stratagems to satisfy the reality and the adequacy conditions of the Newtonian rule. The reality condition was met by referring to particular cases of assent and by sticking to such cases as much as possible in stating the general law from which they proceed. We were not dealing with what *could* happen in men's judicative operations, given this or that theory of self-evidence. We were dealing with actual examples of judgments and reflecting upon real assent. The adequacy condition was met by showing that the assent to self-evident propositions was self-sufficient, that it was immediately produced upon the apprehension or the conception of the proposition.

Reid's eliminative procedure was used to demonstrate that the alternative philosophical accounts of first principles satisfy neither the reality condition nor the adequacy condition of induction. He made this double point in arguing that reasoning and experience do not (reality condition) and cannot (adequacy condition) produce self-evident assent. In the case of self-evidence, we were not choosing among hypotheses but were attempting to state which (real) conceptions are immediately followed by an assent to the propositions called self-evident. Reid also tried to eliminate the hypotheses (such as those related to ideas, judgment, and self-evidence) that prevent philosophers from acknowledging the reality of such laws of assent to self-evident propositions as well as the inadequacy of their accounts of these (real) operations of the mind.

We are now in a position to understand that it is (1) Reid's assertion of the importance of the first rule of the Newtonian *Regulae*, (2) his attempt to distinguish physical and efficient causes, and (3) his attempt to show that in matters of self-evidence, common-sense principles satisfy both the reality and the adequacy conditions of this rule, which *grounds* his assurance that whatever contradicts common sense inevitably proceeds from false analogy, undue logical restriction, or hypothesis unsupported by facts. Because in an experimental philosophy of the mind there is no escape from facts, no theory holding that a general law of assent to self-evident propositions is "false" could be acceptable. If a fundamental law of evidence inductively established is said to be "false," it will be for extra-experimental reasons and, therefore, for Reid, for unacceptable reasons. The alternative would be to define "truth" not as the natural issues of our faculties, but as something unrelated to the laws of their operations. This would be hypothetical in one of the strongest senses of the word: outside the domain in which we can discover the natural laws of self-evidence.[110]

12. REID'S UNDERSTANDING OF FRANCIS BACON'S METHODOLOGICAL ADVICE

This being said, let us turn to the Baconian side of Reid's method. There is more to it than his language, which is often reminiscent of the *Great Instauration*. For example, Reid often refers to the "grammar of nature" and, as Bacon did, he often describes the situation of science (of the mind) as one of "perpetual agitation" for lack of inductive methods. Reid not only shares Bacon's view of the importance of "first philosophy" as a study of *axioms common to different sciences,* but he also follows much of Bacon's advice concerning the *experimenta lucifera* as distinct from the *experimenta fructifera.* Even though Reid does not explicitly refer to this advice, he surely agrees with Bacon that we need a different method in the induction of axioms; that we need a greater abundance of experiments than philosophers have realized; and that we also need, as Bacon puts it, "more than a natural impulse," that is, we must be "trained to syllogistic demonstrations."[111]

As Reid has argued, reflection on reasoning and on conception is necessary to achieve an accurate codification of self-evident propositions. The use of demonstration was not to prove self-evident propositions true but to provide—in Bacon's terms—a Table of Investigation. For Bacon, induction involves more than an enumeration of instances: it involves collection of data according to a Table of Affirmation (all instances that have the same characteristic, i.e., rule of presence), a Table of Negation (all instances that do not have the characteristic under investigation, i.e., the rule of absence), and a Table of Comparison (all instances of concomitant variations, i.e., the rule of different degree). In this context we can look at Reid's method of codification of self-evident propositions as follows: conception and belief (as affirmative instances) are in a Table of Affirmation; inductive

110. *Works,* p. 376b. Birkwood Collection, T. Reid, 2131.6 (II) (6). Reid's point is that there is no *aequilibrio* in nature between belief and disbelief: our statements are either real (coping with the fundamental laws of thought) or hypothetical (unrelated to such laws).
111. See in E. A. Burtt, [39], pp. 69–72; see also Laudan, [40], p. 121.

or deductive reasonings (as negative instances) are in a Table of Negation, and the immediate connection between the conception and the belief of a self-evident proposition, varying according to the accuracy, the clearness, the steadiness of our conceptions, is in a Table of Comparison.[112]

Another suggestion from the *experimenta lucifera* is that we must proceed from particulars and then "examine and try whether the axiom so established be framed to the measure of those particulars only from which it is derived, or whether it be larger and wider. And if it be larger and wider, we must observe whether by indicating to us new particulars it confirms that wideness and largeness as by a collateral security."[113] As we have mentioned, Reid has listed a series of "rational means" to be used in the codification of self-evident propositions (universal agreement, ridicule, opinions in infancy, *ad absurdum, ad hominem,* etc.). However, we have seen that these "rational means" were not presented as the main basis for an experimental codification of first principles, and one reason for this is that Reid has several reservations concerning their use. Nonetheless, Reid's "rational means" were clearly meant as "collateral" security for self-evident propositions in showing the *generality* of the law that we wanted to discover. These means were meant as "new particulars" (i.e., besides the immediate assent given to the apprehension of self-evident propositions) confirming the generality of men's recognition of certain beliefs as being irresistible.

In following Bacon's suggestion that it is necessary "to measure" the compatibility between the particular cases and the general axioms, Reid did not think that we need what Bacon had called "a just scale of ascent" from the lowest axioms through the middle to the highest axioms. Of course, one may look at Reid's distinction between contingent and necessary truths as a manner of stating middle and high axioms, but we have seen that Reid's contention concerning this distinction in self-evident principles is that, in both cases, we have fundamental laws of assent to certain propositions. We have also seen that Reid argues that it is very difficult to trace the line that divides perceptions, common understanding, and science. His main concern, therefore, was not to present a gradation of axioms by reference to

112. Bacon, [10], *Novum Organum* 2, 11–21 ff.
113. See in Burtt, [39], pp. 69–72.

the accuracy of men's knowledge, or by reference to the epistemological status (contingent or necessary) of first principles, or by reference to the kind of reasoning (probable or demonstrative) that first principles make possible; although Reid devotes several chapters to these questions.

In dealing with self-evident propositions, Reid's main concern was to show that such propositions, whether contingent or necessary, are on the same *natural* footing. They are, one would be inclined to say, what Bacon has called "prearogativae instantiarium"; they are instances that have nothing in common but their status as ultimate laws of men's constitution. At this point, however, Reid has departed from Bacon's suggestions: as we have seen, he has used Newton's first *Regulae* and his *own* distinction between efficient and physical causation as the methodological actualizations of Bacon's request that we assure the compatibility between particular instances and the general axioms (laws) deduced from them.

Quite central to Reid's understanding of the role of the inductivist philosopher is Bacon's advice:

... we have no authority arbitrarily to prescribe laws of man's intellect or the general nature of things. It is our office, as faithful secretaries, to receive and note down such as have been enacted by the voice of nature herself.[114]

In Reid's language:

... in all inquiries into the constitution of nature genius must act a subordinate part, ill suited for the superiority it boasts. It may combine, but it must not fabricate: it may collect evidence, but must not supply the want of it by conjectures; it may display its powers by putting nature to the question in well contrived experiments, but it must add nothing to her answers.[115]

114. Bacon, [10], p. 428.
115. *Works*, pp. 472b, 103b, 468b–469b, 199b. On this question, see *Works*, pp. 144a–b, 207b, 268b, 274a, 419a, 199a, 307a, 368b, 429a, 404a, 271b, 294a. Reid's own stronger statements on the necessity of reason to regulate our beliefs are to be found in his *Active Powers* and not in the *Intellectual Powers*. This suggests that it is in dealing with action and conduct that Reid sees a greater need to insist on a prescriptive dimension of reason itself. The prescriptive spirit Reid attacks is a speculative one, because what our laws of thought *naturally* prescribe ought to become the standard of philosophical systems.

In order to understand the full *methodological* meaning of the last point, we must acknowledge the importance of the analogy of the tribunal in Reid's conception of a science of the mind. Induction, as the proper method of philosophy, borrows more from a reflection on the practices of the courts than from the procedure of the logicians, that of philosophers, or even from the procedures of certain natural scientists.

The importance of this reference to the tribunal can be seen in Reid's language. He defined self-evidence in relation to the ways according to which "judges pass sentences" and he often referred to court practices as evidence for what we judge of man's understanding. He insisted, for example, that we reject in philosophy the same absurdities that we reject at the bar. Common sense was compared to a "tribunal of final appeal," the first principles were "dictates" of common sense, their list and their justification referred to a "codification of the laws" of natural evidence. Evoking a public trial, Reid wanted first principles to lay claim "openly" to that character and be "fairly exposed to the examination of those who may dispute their authority in an attempt to join an issue." Following jurists of his time, Reid referred to *mixed* evidence in the case of contingent truths—the conjunction of evidence from (internal and external) senses *and* understanding. As we have seen, Reid also asks that all hypotheses have a "legal" form—that of Newton's rule—and that we do not rule out exceptions or exclude what appears legal "without a hearing." Reid argues: "The analogy between a tribunal of justice and this inward tribunal of the mind is too obvious to escape the notice of any man who has ever appeared before a judge."[116]

---

116. *Works*, p. 413b. On the analogy of the tribunal, see T. Waldman, [200]. According to Waldman, the words "evidence is sufficient if it produces moral certainty to the exclusion of every reasonable doubt" were first stated by Thomas Starkie in 1824 in his work *A Practical Treatise of the Law of Evidence*. However, Waldman argues that Duncomb's *Trial Per Pais*, 8th ed. (1766), Baron Gilbert's posthumously published *The Law of Evidence* (1756), and John Morgan's *The Law of Evidence* (1789) show that the law of evidence appeared in the eighteenth century. In Reid's case the Aristotelian charge that one should admit evidence as the nature of the case permits certainly lies in the background, as well as the use of this maxim by, e.g., Bacon, Locke, Chillingworth, and Tillotson. See also W. Holdsworth, [94], pp. 287–335, 371–90.

The analogy of a tribunal has been noticed by Gavin Ardley: "the attempts of Buffier and Reid to lay down axioms of common sense are analogous to the recurrent attempts to lay down a code of precepts of natural laws" (in [6], pp. 115–16). McCosh also

But there is more to the reference to a tribunal than Reid's analogical language. By such a reference, Reid is able to detect and further
explain a basic mistake of noninductivist systems of self-evidence:
instead of judging of judgment as jurors judge of cases, to wit, hearing
witnesses and trying to base judgment on laws according to which
similar cases have been judged, philosophers are carried away by
confusion between consciousness and reflection, between judgment
and testimony and, ultimately, by confusion between a scientific account of the laws of self-evidence and a prescriptive attitude concerning the grammar of nature.

Reid, we have said, distinguishes consciousness of the operations
of the mind, which can give only a superficial view of such operations,
from reflection on such operations, which allows the precision possible
in an attentive and voluntary examination. However, philosophers
confuse consciousness and reflection when they ignore the correct
sense in which reflection is the prerogative of the very few. They are
right in thinking that only reflection can provide satisfactory accounts
of men's judgments and that not all men are capable of this kind of
reflection.[117] But they are wrong in assuming that the only operations

---

mentions the analogy of "natural law" in common-sense philosophy, quoting Hamilton,
who suggests an influence of G. Carmichael to this end (in [138], p. 41). S. A. Graves
notes that Hamilton spoke in the spirit of Reid and Stewart when he compared common
sense to common law, philosophers to jurists devoted to the assertion of the contents
of the rules, and common men to witnesses (in [80], p. 124). To the analogies I mentioned, we can add the following: Reid's understanding of evidence in relation to
procedures of proofs where we are asked to "make a virtue of necessity" in accepting
the best evidence we have in any domain certainly evokes the proving procedures used
by the jurists of his time. Reid's request that we avoid analogical reasoning evokes the
request in the courts to judge according to the nature of the case before the jury. His
preferences for features of assent exhibited in action can be seen within the legal
tradition: according to Waldman, a standard to judge of the degree of sincerity of, say,
the accused, implied a reference to the fact that the jurors themselves would act in
such-and-such a way according to such-and-such a conviction. Besides, by the end of
the seventeenth century, certain precautions were introduced so that the jury decided
from the evidence presented at the trial and not on the basis of private information.
This is interesting inasmuch as Reid shows a tendency to identify "ingenious systems"
with special and peculiar doctrines, as if philosophical theories worked like "private"
information about human nature. On this analogy and its influence on Russell, see R.
Beanblossom, in [74], p. 202.

117. On the limits of consciousness when compared to reflection, see *Works*, pp. 83a,
103b, 308b, 449a, 501a, 418b, 443b, 130a, 418a, 419a, 443b, 77b, 594a–599a. Reid

worthy of philosophical investigations are the operations of a few ingenious thinkers. This view precludes the possibility of discovering and understanding the *general* laws of beliefs.

We are not, Reid insists, in Bishop Berkeley's world, but in the world we *all* believe we inhabit. The tricky language in which philosophers have presented the issue of judgments seems to assume that the choice is between truth (the operations of philosophers) and error (the operations of the vulgar). For Reid the issue concerns the *general laws* of natural judgments, laws that provide the rules for our decision concerning self-evidence.[118] Thus the reason Reid has argued in his chapter on common sense that we must not assume that all men cannot agree on self-evident propositions must be related to his view of the inductive method along the analogy of a tribunal. More precisely, Reid's proceeding from particular cases of beliefs in order to assert general laws of assent to self-evidence suggests that the *truth* of a science of the mind should be like equity in a common-law system based on jurisprudence.

---

objects to philosophy as a "map of the intellectual operations of men of genius" (*Works*, p. 239a). To be conscious is merely to perform a mental activity. To perform judgment (therefore to assent to some proposition and thereby determine its truth) is to have consciousness. To *reflect* upon judgment is to attend to our judgments and distinguish their features and their minute differences, i.e., to testify to what we are conscious of in judging (see *Works*, pp. 83a, 130b). There is, insists Reid, no perception without consciousness (*Works*, p. 308b). "To analyze complex operations, distinguish their different ingredients, and combine them in distinct, accurate, and scientific notions which can be made the subject of reasoning is not the work of consciousness, nor can it be performed without reflection, recollecting and judging what we were conscious of and distinctly remember. Of all the powers of the mind, it seems to be the latest growth, whereas consciousness is coeval with the earliest" (*Works*, pp. 418a–419b). There is a "habit" of reflection (p. 77b). Reid insists on the difference in the accuracy in the knowledge of all men, according to their ability to reflect (see Laudan, [40], p. 128, n. 69; *Works*, pp. 120b, 258a, 483a, 369a; and I. Ross, [179], p. 15). In Reid's manuscripts one finds the same thesis reaffirmed: "few are capable of accurate Reflexion; it is one of the most difficult operations of the human understanding, and requires a natural capacity as well as much painfull practice to acquire it in any considerable Degree. This is the Reason why we are so ignorant of those operations of Mind of which we are conscious every day of our Lives, and this is the Reason why we are so easily imposed upon by false systems concerning the Powers of the Mind, and are capable of swallowing Theories which are contradicted by every days Experience" [Birkwood Collection, T. Reid, 2131.6 (II) (9)].

118. The references are numerous: see *Works*, pp. 258a, 413a–b, 196a, 244b; see also pp. 239a–240b, 450a–451b, 493a, 493b.

In order to use the inductive method accurately in questions related to self-evident propositions, it was not sufficient that the "discerning Few" look in the right direction, that of the general laws of assent to self-evidence. Another requirement—that our conclusions should rest on the touchstone of fact—gains further validity if we understand the experimental method in reflecting upon the practices of the courts: "Every man knows that to judge is not to testify and that a false testimony is a lie although a wrong judgment is an error." This distinction is crucial when we deal with self-evident principles. We assent to such principles immediately and therefore we cannot do more than testify to these facts. Of course, we have to evaluate whether the testimonies are accurate, whether they agree with available data. But when all testimonies point to the existence of a law of assent to self-evident principles, we must recognize that this testimony is sufficient because we have no access to other kinds of testimonies that would prove such principles to be either true or false. This is the reason why the unaccountability of first principles is, itself, a mark of their status. In such cases, the philosophical attempts to prove that self-evident principles are true are, in fact, illusory and circular attempts to testify to the testimony itself. "If a man's honesty were called in question, it would be ridiculous to refer it to the man's own word whether he be honest or not. The same absurdity there is in attempting to prove by any kind of reasoning, probable or demonstrative, that our reason is not fallacious, since the very point in question is whether reasoning may be trusted."[119] It is the philosophers' failure to recognize the limits of reasoning which prevents them from acknowledging that the testimonies used in the codification of self-evident propositions point to ultimate laws of the mind, to a *quod facti* that is a *quod juris*.

It appears that when philosophers consider judgment and self-evidence, they do use the analogy of the tribunal, but they have a very poor model of a tribunal in mind: their model seems to be one

---

119. See *Works*, p. 447b. To *account for* a phenomenon is to show that it is a necessary consequence of some known law of nature, says Reid (see Laudan, [40], p. 128, n. 69, and *Works*, pp. 120b, 258a, 483a). In this line, no account can be given beyond the laws of belief to whose generality testimonies are given (see *Works*, pp. 447b, 328b–329a, 309b, 415a, 258a). On the view that on first principles ordinary men may offer more accurate testimonies than philosophers (who try to account for testimonies by means of different theories), see Ross, [179], p. 15, and *Works*, pp. 369a, 76a–77b, 104a, 254b, 260b, 262a, 280b, 302a, 309b, 323b, 369b, 354b.

that history recalls with due contempt, the tribunal of the Inquisition. Instead of discovering the laws according to which the human mind judges, philosophers try to establish what men's natural operations must be, according to their theories of evidence. Having refused to pay attention to the general laws that govern men's assent to self-evidence, philosophers fabricate theories by virtue of which they finally refuse to accept that reality can be otherwise than *they* allow it to be. This spirit of Inquisition leads to terror, skepticism and represents mankind as "mere Yahoos" incapable of truth and certainty with regard to the most fundamental issues in life. How strange it is, thinks Reid, that a philosophical system should assume that all men are fools or mad.[120]

The origin of the spirit of Inquisition lies in the rules which, according to philosophers, our mental operations *must* use, as if the natural laws of self-evidence were not lawful enough. Thus philosophers insist that belief must be a function of reasoning and that what we can count as a genuine intellectual operation must follow some logical order: either the classical order of simple apprehension, judgment, reasoning or the logical atomistic model of association of ideas. In the same spirit they insist that existence must be derived from an idea or a conception, thereby following the same kind of prejudices that give rise to superstition. It is a prejudice to think that what we conceive must have existence or that in all the operations of the mind there must be an object that really exists while we think of it.[121]

Besides, philosophers build their theories of evidence upon a single hypothesis, that of a representative idea, a claimed "resembling picture of the mind" of the object of thought about which it judges. The "way of ideas," the doctrine grounded on the hypothesis above, claims that we can know nothing about anything outside the mind except by means of a representative substitute within the privacy of the mind (e.g., an image). This hypothesis, by virtue of which philosophers claim, for instance, that we do not know that the external world exists, is itself the result of reasoning from many untested analogies: that of sight, where to have an idea is presumed to be like seeing a (mental)

---

120. See *Works*, pp. 271b, 294a, 484a–b, 127a, 157b, 485a, 52b.
121. *Works*, see pp. 100a–103b, 243a ff., 107a, 375a, 375b, 368b, 267a, 292a, 237b, 368b ff., 205a ff., 470a ff., 254a ff., 210a. For a recent attack on the "Bucket theory of the mind," see K. R. Popper, [163], pp. 62–68, 341–63, 39, 145.

picture; that of spatial features of physical objects, where to have an idea is presumed to involve the locating of a picture in the mind in continuity with some part of the brain; that of consciousness, where to have an idea is presumed to refer to a universe existing from within, cut off from the external world; and that of the work of art and the artist, where to have an idea is presumed to resemble the reception of the action of an external object upon the mind (as if the mind were like the material of the artist) or where to have an idea is presumed to resemble the action of the mind upon an object (as if the mind were molding ideas).[122]

All these analogical devices culminate in what Reid calls, again by reference to the practices of the courts, the "error personae" and the "error juris." The *error personae* consists in supposing that if the material world exists, it must be the express image of our sensations; more formally, it is a confusion of the object of thought with the thought itself. The *error juris* consists in demanding of any idea worthy of philosophical analysis that it correspond to a sensation; more formally, it is a confusion about the tools we use in analyzing certain ideas. And when philosophers add a prescriptive spirit to such hypotheses, we have the Inquisition. Not only do we have a set of rules and criteria whose compatibility with the natural laws of self-evidence is never tested, but we arrive at a series of unyielding—if not terrifying—statements, condemning men's most natural beliefs as mere feelings of no philosophical value.[123]

In his examples of the philosophical problems resulting from the spirit of the Inquisition, Reid relies heavily on the philosophical system that he calls the "way of ideas" precisely because in his opinion the consistency of this doctrine exhibits the methodological failures that affect, to a more or less important degree, all philosophical systems. These are a fondness for hypotheses, for analogies, for simplicity in the form of reductionism; a substitution of logical models for a reflection upon the natural laws of self-evidence; and, finally, a prescriptive spirit, which does not respect human nature. This reference to the "way of ideas" is important also in that it permits Reid to offer a systematic explanation of his attitude toward philosophical systems

---

122. Numerous references: see *Works*, pp. 267a ff., 292a–b, 237b, 368b ff., 205a ff., 470a ff., 254a ff., 210a. On this, see R. C. Sleigh, [12], pp. 77 ff.

123. *Works*, pp. 278b, 274a, 419a, 199a, 307a, 144a–b, 207b, 128a ff.

by suggesting that the spirit of the Inquisition behind this theory is the *main* source of what Bacon has called the "idols of the theater." For Bacon, such idols are the false notions that have crept into men's mind from the various dogmas of philosophical systems such as the sophistical, the empirical, and the superstitious systems of philosophy. For Reid, when we use the experimental method, on the model of a fair tribunal, we can see the various systems of philosophy as various sects with their specific dogmas, which all share an *inquisitive* attitude concerning men's beliefs.[124]

It is in looking at the experimental method along the analogy of a fair tribunal rather than an Inquisition that Reid concludes: "the disorders of the understanding point out their own remedies so plainly that he who knows the one must know the other."[125] Instead of inventing rules that we use as universal prescriptions or dogmas, we must submit all philosophical claims about the judicative activities— however cogent, simple, logical, or ingenious—to a slow, patient, and strict verification: Is this claim about human judgments compatible with the laws of self-evidence that we have inductively established?

In a true science of the mind, a rather sketchy list of first principles composed of laws of assent to self-evident propositions arrived at through induction is better grounded than a better-articulated but inquisitionary system whose constituents and rules would be determined prior to or independent of experiments, that is, independent of the natural laws of assent to self-evident propositions. There was no agreement in natural philosophy before natural philosophers checked their theories against the laws of natural phenomena. Such agreement can also be expected in a philosophy of the mind if philosophers check their theories against the laws that govern men's assent to self-evidence. When he deals with self-evidence, the philosopher is not an inquisitive judge. He is at the least a witness and at the most one of the discerning few, a perceptive codifier.

13.   THE IMPACT OF REID'S METHOD ON HIS GENERAL DOCTRINE OF
FIRST PRINCIPLES

As Grave puts it, there is an "ambiguous revisionism" in Reid's doctrine of common sense.[126] On the one hand, Reid argues that the

---

124. *Works*, pp. 62b, 103a, 106a, 53a, 244b, 379b ff., 206a–208b, 474b; see also pp. 475a–b, 140a–b, 204b, 226a, 239a, 274a, 475a, 91b.
125. *Works*, pp. 468b, 91b, 450a–451b, 99a, 235b, 260b ff.
126. S. A. Grave, [80], pp. 138 ff.

dictates of common sense are ultimate laws of thought, which suggests that they are unrevisable. On the other hand, Reid admits that the inductive procedures are perfectible and that the generalizing process used in his codification of the dictates of common sense is not apodictical. Grave explains this ambiguity by saying that Reid's appeal to induction is only a negative argument against skeptical systems, permitting one to *re*discover the first principles of common sense under the rubbish of hypotheses.

However, as we have seen, the *positive* relationships that common sense and induction have in Reid's view of a science of first principles are too important and too precise to permit the ambivalent status of his view of common sense to be fully explained by a mere distinction between the Reidian method (directed against the skeptic) and the Reidian doctrine (a general theory of what Daniels has called "un-revisability").[127] On the contrary, I think that the tone of modesty one finds in Reid's methodological statements is also present in his doctrinal positions.

Concerning his own method, Reid admits at least one crucial limitation for every mark he uses in his codification of the dictates of common sense. He admits, for example, that self-evidence can wear a mask because of novelty, religion, solemnity, interest. He compares our reaction to self-evidence to the swallowing of our food, yet acknowledges the possibility for imperfect creatures to "swallow contradictions." Reasoning, he maintains, has nothing to do with men's natural assent to first principles. Yet reasoning can show that what we take without hesitation to be possible is impossible. Reid also thinks that many prejudices are natural to man, and he has a chapter on errors that, in a Baconian form, shows the necessity of careful analysis of men's opinions.[128]

However, the tentative tone in which Reid speaks of his undertaking concerns not only his method but also his doctrine, where one finds ambivalent if not contradictory statements. To use a striking example,

127. N. Daniels, [56], p. 165; see also J. H. Jacques, [96], p. 710. W. P. Krolikowski rightly insists on the "pre-demonstrative" meaning of "to conclude" in Reid; see [108], p. 146. For related issues, see T. C. Smout, [186]; for Reid's views on the danger (and sometimes necessity) of political innovation, see [172].

128. *Works*, pp. 434b, 82b, 102a, 110a, 130a, 208a, 234a, 266a, 299b, 489b, 443a, 363b–365a, 419a, 240a, 469a–470a, 438b–439a, 231a, 231b, 379a, 89b, 441a, 448b, 501a; see also I. Ross, [179], p. 47.

Reid says that we take it as a first principle that our faculties are reliable. But he also says that our faculties are *so obviously fallible* that "reason directs us as fallible creatures to carry along with us in all our judgments, a sense of our fallibility." He maintains that the reliability of our faculties, although a contingent principle, is *prior* to all others in the order of nature, but he also thinks that judgment cannot change the nature of the thing about which we judge, as in mathematics.[129]

To understand Reid's ambivalence, both methodological and doctrinal, we must acknowledge that, in his language, we cannot go beyond the natural laws of the mind, even though our knowledge of such laws is provisional. We assert as a law of nature the most general phenomena we can reach *until* further laws are discovered: "if we stop when we can trace it no farther and secure the ground we have gained, no harm is done and a quicker eye could go farther."[130] The problem is that he does not make clear in which sense a "quicker eye" would go further, concerned as he is with the question of the first steps of a new science.

However, Reid's statement indicates that although there is no end to further inductive investigation, certain facts are recognized as unquestionable. Concerning self-evident principles, the Reidian codification suggests that there *are* propositions which we immediately assent by an unavoidable law of our constitution. Provided that such cases are fairly established, given the strict and severe method of induction, they will remain unrevisable, *within their scope* and *given the human constitution.*[131]

The last statement, qualified as it is, suggests that, in the Reidian epistemology, the appeal to common sense could be falsifiable. Suppose we could show that this or that principle is not original, that

---

129. *Works*, pp. 485b–487a, 416a, 455a, 91b, 103b, 104a, 217b, 157a–b, 122a–b, 99b, 261b, 58a, 172a. On this question, see my article [126].

130. *Works*, pp. 99b, 261b, 58a, 172a, 157a–b, 122a–b; see also D. W. Robinson, [12], p. 49.

131. *Work,* pp. 484b. We must collect as many data as possible (*Works,* pp. 113a, 200a, 119a–121b, 482a ff., 693b). We should not rule out exceptions *(Works,* pp., 520a, 197a–b, 484a–b, 272a–b, 57b, 436a). We should design experiments in order to confirm the available data (*Works,* pp. 44a, 48a, 96b, 160a ff., 173a, 261b). So doing, Reid admits, we still ignore a lot of things (*Works,* pp. 364a–b, 367b, 392a, 472b, 488b, 693b, 455b), but, he argues, it is to misunderstand the possibilities and limits of induction to argue that "we do not know all phenomena" (*Works,* p. 461b). We know, as Reid puts it, "a little corner of God's dominion" (*Works,* pp. 217a, 693b, 688b, 712a).

reasoning, custom, experience, prejudice is the cause of our assent to
it; suppose we could show that the particular assent Reid considers
as the basis of one principle is subsumable under another proposition;
suppose that one shows that Reid's marks of first principles do not
point to what is immediately assented to by all men; again, suppose
one can show that the Reidian principles are not indispensable to life
and science. All these objections or refutations would be considered
seriously by Reid.

But to argue that induction is not the method of philosophizing,
or that common sense is not the epistemological domain of its applicability in a science of the mind, or that the Newtonian rule is not
valid in the case of self-evidence could not be accepted. For Reid there
is no question but that our natural beliefs, inductively established, are
part of the human constitution and the basis of any scientific account
of mental operations. Given the systematic status that laws have in
experimental philosophy, such accounts are the standard of philosophy; the alternative is to fall into hypothetical accounts of human
beliefs. Given the inductive establishment of such laws, they should
be treated as assumptions which no theory of knowledge could deny,
given their scope and *given our knowledge* of the constitution of the
mind.[132]

14. CONCLUSION

I have argued that Reid's explicit and consistent rationale for the
validity of an appeal to common sense in philosophy is his commitment
to induction and his identification of common sense as providing the
reality and adequacy conditions for the applicability of such a method
to self-evident propositions. I have shown that there is a continuity
in Reid's method on the question of common sense. In both the *Inquiry*
and the *Intellectual Powers*, Reid insists that we should reflect on mental
facts, mainly taken from perceptions, and the evolving order of his
investigation is determined by his proceeding from the sensing activities such as conceiving, judging, and reasoning.

I have shown that Reid distinguishes the common (unambiguous)
meaning of common sense (common understanding) and the common
(implicit) meaning of common sense (a part of reason by which we

---

132. On this, see Stewart, [194], pp. 270–73.

judge of self-evident truths). I have also shown that his main concern was to show that there is a *continuity* between these two meanings of common sense: his claim is that we can discover the principles that are self-evident to all men by reflecting upon ordinary judgments in an attempt to find out the general laws from which they proceed. This discovery is possible if we use the experimental method accurately, i.e., if we use the model of efficient causality. The continuity between the two meanings of common sense is established by a causal connection: the particular beliefs of ordinary life (common judgments) are effects of a self-evident cause, of a law of assent to self-evident propositions. First principles are *implicitly* recognized (in the same manner that common sense as a tribunal of truth is implicitly recognized) because they function as premises of particular judgments. Such principles are implicitly acknowledged because their analysis may be done only along the model of an efficient cause, a cause we know by knowing only its effects.

Because we use the experimental method, we know that it is necessary to reflect on the operations of the mind and their *contents* before we can conclude as to the existence of powers in man. We conclude that common understanding exists by reflecting on common judgments; we conclude that an intuitive function of reason exists because of our ability to codify principles that are self-evident to all men. We also conclude that there is a fundamental connection between these two *powers* of the mind, common understanding and intuitive reason—although we acknowledge differences in accuracy between common understanding and science—because we can show that our first principles are the grounds (the cause) of particular beliefs in ordinary life as well as in science.

In considering Reid's method seriously, we see not only the distinctions and relationships he sees between ordinary beliefs and self-evident propositions, but we are able to understand in what sense the undemonstrability of first principles is a *mark* of first principles, which the inductive method permits one to check by the eliminative procedure. This eliminative procedure permits one to see whether a proposition is self-evident, that is, self-sufficient to produce our belief. If we add to this eliminative procedure Reid's reference to a fair tribunal, we realize that the self-sufficiency of self-evident propositions is a matter on which testimonies (but no proof) could be given.

Finally, in considering Reid's systematic understanding of the inductive method in its relation to common sense, we can see that his first principles are assumptions that must be admitted in theories of knowledge inasmuch as these principles have the status that laws have in natural philosophy. The recognition of such assumptions does not imply that a science of the mind is static. It only shows that a creative use of experiments and hypotheses is valid under certain conditions. In using the experimental method, we must determine the scope of our investigation. But when we put nature to the question, we cannot deny the facts that were inductively established and we cannot deny the laws that were inductively drawn from these facts.

Thus if one asks, "Why common sense?" Reid's consistent answer is: because induction is the only way to philosophize accurately and because common sense embodies many epistemological conditions of induction in a science of the mind, especially in a science of first principles. But if one asks further, "Why induction?" Reid's *teleological* answer would seem so apparent that we cannot conclude our analysis of his doctrine of common sense without making a few critical remarks on this point.

There is hardly one page of his works without a mention of God. In Reid's view, nature is the work of God, and its laws are the rules according to which the Supreme Being governs the world, and can only be changed by him who established them. Our natural judgments are God-given as well. If they are neither got nor lost by any "use or abuse of our faculties," it is evidently necessary for our preservation that it should be so, adds Reid, concluding that they are "therefore unconditionally given to all men by the Author of nature."[133]

In this sense, induction is *guaranteed* by the Good Maker who created the world, and who governs it by certain laws, including the laws of the mind. God has given us faculties upon which we must rely in order to find the natural laws of his work. All this is God's work, and therefore it is good and well ordained. Any attempt to substitute for facts, which are the voices of God, conjectures of man's imagination is not only vain but also doomed to failure. On the contrary, a "genuine spirit of philosophy" convinces one that it is "an impiety to contaminate the divine workmanship by mixing it with those fictions of human fancies." In our choice between the way of analogy and the way of reflection, theories and hypotheses "will always bear the signature

133. *Works*, pp. 416a, 484a–b, 209b, 330b.

of human folly," while an attention to the laws of nature bears the "signature of divine wisdom."[134]

Hence for Reid induction becomes a form of worship: it "humbles the pride of man" and reminds him that his most ingenious conjectures are "pitiful and childish" compared to the works of God. In interpreting nature, which is God's work, induction permits one to use a rewarding and gratifying approach: by induction, one discovers more and more regularities in the course of nature and thereby one confirms the assumption of a well-ordained world.

At this point the crucial question is the following: To what extent does Reid's belief in the existence of a Good Maker and his well-ordained work present a condition without which Reid's appeal to common sense would not be inductively possible? My answer to the question goes along the lines of the accounts of Ueberweg, Norton, and Grave, all of whom think that the reliance on a Deity is a basic presupposition of Reid's epistemology and doctrine.[135] I think that it is impossible to understand Reid's views of induction, and more specifically his assurance that it is *the* proper method for philosophizing, without recognizing that he assumes we inhabit a well-ordained world whose laws are God-given and thereby good, true, and wholesome. On the other hand, I think that, inductively speaking, Reid's appeal to common sense would still be possible even without his reliance on a Deity. In other words, Reid has *many* reasons for appealing to induction, and while he does appeal to God, the reasons he gives for induction can hardly be claimed to be *only* a set of theological deductions from this belief.

Clearly the reference to a Deity is a crucial item to consider in analyzing Reid's appeal to common sense. Usually Reid *adds* such references to the kind of considerations that we have previously analyzed. For example, having argued that we must take as a self-evident principle of contingent truth that "the natural faculties by which we distinguish truth from error are not fallacious"—in using the model and the procedures that we have analyzed in his codification—Reid adds the following comment: we must trust our natural faculties im-

---

134. *Works*, pp. 236a, 472a, 470b, 218b, 460b, 127a, 330b.

135. Ueberweg, [197], 2:135; D. F. Norton, [148], p. 58; [149], and his article in [150]; S. A. Grave, [81]; see also J. Collins, [47], p. 424; B. Brody, [12], p. 13; N. Daniels, [12], pp. 35–44; P. Vernier, [12], pp. 14–16; K. Lehrer, [74], p. 190.

plicitly, "until God give us new faculties to sit in judgment upon the old."

Surely these theistic references add something to the meaning of Reid's method and doctrine. For example, in describing knowledge obtained by reasoning as a "kind of crutch to a limited understanding"—a limitation Reid thinks we do not ascribe to God—the Reidian appeal to intuitive knowledge resembles an attempt to partake of a divine understanding. Reid's preference for the reality condition of the Newtonian rule and his systematic concern to make sure that the motto *hypotheses non fingo* will apply to his work can be seen in the light of his conviction that men's conjectures are *contamination* of the work of a perfect Being. His serenity in talking of a "safe side of error"—errors that proceed from insufficient or excessive application of the natural laws of beliefs—can be seen in the light of his conviction that ultimately the use and abuse of our faculties will turn to the advantage of truth: an application, if not a knowledge, of God's laws. More importantly, Reid's conviction that the *rationality* of men's assent to self-evidence can be defended on the model of an efficient cause may be explained by his belief in the existence of an intelligent Designer. If there can be voluntary production of such effects as men's *involuntary* assent to self-evidence, it is because the latter is the work of an intelligent Designer: God, says Reid, intended that we believe instinctively.

This being said, we must acknowledge that Reid never questioned the value or the importance of his theistic assumptions *in their general relations to his method*. That is to say, Reid never seriously considered the objections that Hume had raised concerning the tricky kinds of circularity that characterize many arguments from induction. At this point it has been argued that the reason for this attitude lies in the fact that Reid is a naïve and doctrinal realist who appeals to God as a final guarantee for his argument, while Hume is a critical inductivist who refuses such appeals.

I think that Reid, in never discussing the connection between his method and the assumption of a God-given order in nature, shows that he is, on this general issue, a naïve inductivist rather than a naïve realist.[136] I also think that *this* general question aside, Reid's very care-

---

136. *Works*, pp. 447b, 463a–464b, 441a, 442a, 430a, 198a. On the general issue, see also Feyerabend, [40], pp. 150–70, and Probst, [165].

ful and original understanding of the conditions of an experimental science of the mind makes him an inductivist critical enough to argue with Hume and other inductivists of his time. Finally, I think that it would be false to think that Reid has no critical reflection whatsoever on the question of the existence of a Deity.

To make this point clearer, we must look briefly at a second feature of Reid's numerous references to God. In crucial issues, Reid clearly rejects certain arguments based on a Deity, suggesting that any appeal to God should be justified on the basis of common sense and not conversely. Indeed, Reid thinks that his way of looking at the experimental method offers a new way of treating the problem of the existence of a Deity. Moreover, his concern is to develop a method of codification of self-evident propositions that would avoid the circularity which, in his view, characterizes the Cartesian appeal to a nondeceiving God in order to prove the veracity of our faculties.

It must be emphasized that Reid does not demand (either directly or methodologically) that one believe in the existence of God in order to undertake the codification of self-evident propositions. On the contrary, he insists that our beliefs in first principles (such as the reliability of the senses) depend on no authority, not even the authority of God. Furthermore, his (methodological) treatment of particular cases of belief implies that our faculties are trustworthy but does not acknowledge God's role. Consistent with this view, Reid uses an eliminative procedure, which shows that our understanding of self-evident propositions is self-sufficient to produce our belief and that no reason, no proof, no inference can have produced it, not even reason, proof, or inference based on the Deity. In other words, in his codification of self-evident propositions, Reid is quite careful never to use the appeal to God as a proof that his first principles are true. Reid is a critical inductivist to the extent that his method does avoid the circularity that plagued Descartes, the circularity that consists in using our faculties in trying to prove that they are reliable by appealing to a nondeceiving God.[137]

Surely Reid grants that God is the source of our constitution. However, the *proof* of the existence of God is, in his opinion, guaranteed by his way of using the experimental method. The inductive-introspective approach to self-evidence shows that there are self-evident

---

137. On this question, see my article [122].

principles from which we can derive a proof of the existence of a Deity. For Reid, therefore, the existence of a Deity can be proved true as a *result* of his approach to self-evident principles, an approach, we have said, that does (methodologically) avoid an appeal to God as a proof.

But, while the existence of a Designer is demonstrated on the *basis* of the dictates of common sense, and in this sense, Reid's treatment of a Deity is critical, the assumption (theistic in Reid's works) that there is an order in nature is not given a systematic treatment. For Reid the assumption of an order in nature is necessary for the experimental method—at least, in making it possible for us to discover the laws of nature, which we could not do if we were sure that nature is chaos—and this assumption is gradually confirmed by the experimental method. In turn, the experimental method shows that there is an intelligent Designer, which guarantees such an order. On this general question, we do not find a set of methodological provisions that would parallel Reid's alternative to the Cartesian method. For example, Reid offers no methodological means to make sure that the general *cycle* of his argument is not circular: we can prove that God exists on the basis of natural laws of self-evidence, which we discover in assuming that there is an order in nature and in respecting such order which is guaranteed by the existence of a Designer. And, I think, it is on these kinds of *general* issues that Reid is a naïve inductivist.

However, as I suggested earlier, even though we cannot understand Reid's appeal to induction without acknowledging the importance of his theistic assumption, it would be false to conclude that his appeal to common sense is a case of disguised prayers or clumsy teleological deductions. We have seen that Reid had many reasons to relate common sense and induction, and that these reasons were not teleological. Besides, Reid had many reasons to appeal to induction itself, and these reasons were not all teleological. For the sake of brevity, we can summarize these reasons as being historical, practical, polemical, and doctrinal.

Obviously, the *historical* reason for Reid's appeal to induction is the understandable desire to emulate Newton in a science of the mind. The importance of Newton's achievements certainly creates Reid's conviction that no harm could be done in using a method elsewhere so successful and fruitful. The historical reason becomes *practical* inasmuch as Reid argues that no other method has shown equivalent merits, and that any philosopher hopeful of progress should try the same steps, especially given the backward state of the science of the mind. Reid also has *polemical* reasons to refer to induction: his target is the Humean system, and Hume also professes to apply the experimental method. Using the weapons thus provided, Reid's hope is to refute Hume on his own grounds. More positively, Reid's hope is to use the Humean understanding of the experimental method as a *reductio ad absurdum* of classical empiricism and the remarkable consistency of his system as a clue to the discovery of an alternative.

There is also a *doctrinal* reason for Reid's preference for induction. Given his desire to rehabilitate natural human beliefs, it is easy to guess how Reid could have thought of induction. This method allows him to give a central epistemological role to the particular cases of assent, where, as we have seen, he argues that everyone agrees, the learned and the unlearned, the skeptic and the dogmatist. Induction enables Reid to treat the distinction between such particular cases of assent and the skeptical treatments of mankind's beliefs as invalid. What the skeptic does in particular cases and what he says about general issues cannot be irreconcilable, for our practice exhibits particular cases of assent, the most obvious features of which must be formulated in terms of general laws that are the substantiation of the reality condition of our speculations upon the mind. Speculation and practice cannot be irreconcilable in a model where conduct is the effect of a belief.

Induction permits Reid to give a theoretical dimension to the continuity he claims to be necessary between common understanding and science, and at the same time it gives him a ground to reject as hypothetical any prescriptive account of mental activities. When the aim of the codification of the dictates of common sense is to show that philosophers are misled in their understanding of self-evidence, induction is again useful, permitting us to treat self-evidence on the model of an efficient cause whose effects are discernible in the ways man assents to certain propositions. Self-evident common-sense propositions exemplify a scientific and accepted treatment of the laws of nature.

Finally, in his doctrinal pursuits Reid could have preferred induction to any other approach because it permits him to argue on the basis of his "inductive findings" while leaving many issues open on the grounds that new information gradually enables us to enlarge our theories. It permits him to argue for the kind of stability, itself a condition of growth, which, in his opinion, natural philosophy has.

Thus if we consider Reid's understanding of the experimental method and the originality of his suggestions for a science of the mind, we see that, besides teleological reasons, he had practical, historical, polemical, and doctrinal reasons for defending his method. If we further consider his careful reflections on the conditions and models we can use in order to apply such a method to the difficult problem of first principles, we see that he is a critical inductivist. Finally, in considering Reid's version of common sense from the point of view of his method, I hope I have shown that the real problem with his notion is not that his use of the term is confusing. It is the challenging complexity of a quite systematic attempt to determine inductively the extent to which common understanding and science are continuous in their *respective* subordination to principles that are naturally self-evident.

IV

General Conclusion

IN THIS CONCLUSION, I want to provide an answer to the questions raised in the introduction of this book: (1) the specific question of whether or not Reid's theory was plagiarized from Buffier (the extent to which Buffier and Reid differ in substantial issues), and (2) the question of whether or not common-sense philosophers offer legitimate philosophic arguments to support their positions (the extent to which Buffier and Reid can be used as counterexamples to the caricatures of common-sense doctrines).

I propose to treat these two questions together. Instead of providing a list of detailed differences as a refutation of the charge that most of Reid's theory is taken directly from Buffier, I shall show that Buffier and Reid offer substantially different solutions to the precise problem that common-sense philosophers are held to ignore: that of providing a justification for the appeal to common sense in philosophy. In focusing on these different justifications, I shall demonstrate the basis for my conclusion that not only is the charge of plagiarism refuted by internal evidence, but also that we must abandon the caricatures of common-sense doctrines. The analysis of the positive philosophical suggestions made by Buffier and Reid shows that common-sense philosophers did offer legitimate philosophical arguments in support of their position and suggests that it would be philosophically important to analyze other common-sense doctrines from a new and philosophical perspective.

At the outset, one must realize that a general discussion of the most striking similarities between the philosophies of Buffier and Reid shows that, despite important differences, they had the same *general* reasons for appealing to common sense. In more critical terms, however, this assessment also suggests that we should not uncritically assume that, because two philosophers defend the appeal to common sense in philosophy, they are bound to offer duplicate doctrines.

For both Buffier and Reid, common sense has an important place in philosophical argument and an important epistemological status. Common sense is the root and standard of philosophy because it is the area of basic truth that expresses "natural reason." Natural reason is particularly crucial in the doctrines of both men because it refers to the immediate assent to self-evident propositions. By insisting on the importance of self-evident propositions, Buffier and Reid want to criticize the attempt to judge the validity of the grounds of reasoning by means of reasoning itself, a circular attempt that, they think, characterizes other philosophical theories.

Both Buffier and Reid react against skepticism and refer to common sense as the standard against which we can measure the untenability of absurd philosophical claims. They seek to provide a solid grounding for a philosophy that would remain perennial amid diversity and relativity while avoiding the dogmatic features of other philosophical systems, and they argue that this grounding must be derived from a better knowledge of the nature of the human mind, because they both think that all knowledge is faculty-laden. Both see consciousness and introspection as fruitful means of philosophical investigations and as intrinsically related to logic and grammar. Each presents a list of first principles of common sense, which neither claims to be either perfect or exhaustive—and their two lists offer interesting similarities.

At this point one may argue that more detailed descriptions would suggest that the comparisons above are misleadingly general. Common sense, for one thing, is not a "tribunal" in Buffier's doctrine, as it is in Reid's. Recall that Buffier holds the analogy of the tribunal as a good example of dogmatism and contradictions, while Reid takes it to be more accurate than the logicians' models. As to their appeal to immediacy, Buffier considers that what we feel from within is always clearest, while Reid argues that the primary qualities of external objects are as clear as one could desire. Buffier insists that we avoid arbitrary first steps by suspending judgment, while Reid insists that men's natural judgments are lawful enough to guarantee that our first steps are not arbitrary. Buffier thinks that we must separate common sense and common opinions, while Reid sees common opinions as the direct effects of the first principles of common sense. Language expresses the relativity of human opinions for Buffier, and it expresses the basic structures of human thought for Reid.

However, in piling up detailed descriptions of the two doctrines, the danger is that we shall lose sight of the similarity of patterns that are present in these philosophies. Buffier and Reid not only agree in their final conclusions about the value of common-sense principles, but their general arguments in favor of their doctrines also have a similar formal structure. We can summarize this general argument in four points:

1. We cannot prove the validity of first principles by means of a deductive proof of their truth.
2. We must find an alternative to deductive reasoning.
3. This alternative will be discovered by using introspection as a means of philosophical investigation.
4. The validity of this alternative is based on knowledge of what is essential to the human mind.

In considering the structure of this general argument, it is tempting to argue that the doctrines of Buffier and Reid are basically the same in substantial issues, and differ only in details that could be explained by historical factors. For example, we have seen the influence of Descartes's philosophy on Buffier's defense of common sense, and the influence of Newton's *Regulae* on Reid. However, I think that an analysis of their theories leads to the conclusion that however similar the structure of the general argument offered by Buffier and Reid appears, there are substantial differences between their views on the philosophical conditions for the justification of common sense and, accordingly, quite important differences between their doctrines.

My claim is that we cannot accurately evaluate the four steps of the argument mentioned above if we do not analyze them from the point of view of the *alternative* to deductive reasoning, which Buffier and Reid are proposing. We cannot accurately assess the nature of this argument if we do not focus on its third and fourth steps where this alternative is delineated. But in analyzing the characteristics of the alternatives defended by these philosophers, we can demonstrate that it is impossible to conclude that they offer the same argument in order to defend the same doctrine. Indeed, while Buffier and Reid share the view that an alternative to deductive reasoning in matters of first principles must be grounded on a better knowledge of the nature of the human mind arrived at through introspection, they agree in almost nothing about what such a better knowledge should be or what it does reveal.

I propose to discuss this general conclusion in three sections:

1. Buffier and Reid have quite different views on introspection as a means of philosophical investigation—as their ways of defining common sense show.
2. These different views on introspection are systematically related to quite different views on what is essential to the human mind— as their respective views of the main source of justification for an appeal to common sense demonstrate.
3. Such differences in epistemology have important consequences for the tenor of their *doctrines* of common sense—as the different status given to first principles in the two doctrines reveals and as the different basic presuppositions of these doctrines (together with the difficulties such presuppositions create) will further confirm.

1. THE DIFFERENT VIEWS OF BUFFIER AND REID ON INTROSPECTION

Whereas for Buffier common sense can be delineated by a precise and technical definition, the validity of which is determined by the value of his distinction between two kinds of self-evidence provided by two rational dispositions (the internal sentiment and common sense), Reid holds that we cannot provide a valid definition of self-evidence and of common sense if we base our approach on the attempt to determine the specific differences between many sorts of self-evidence, many sorts of truths, or many sorts of judgments. Buffier maintains that common sense must be distinguished from the Aristotelian faculty, innate ideas, feelings, vulgar prejudices, and uniform judgments. It is only in reference to a specific distinction between common sense and the internal sentiment as dispositions of the mind that Buffier thinks it possible to validate the principles of common sense. For Reid, on the other hand, there is no philosophical meaning of common sense outside an appeal to it, and no philosophical appeal to common sense outside a codification of its dictates. For him common sense has no meaning outside its contents: it is composed of a set of self-evident principles, which can be acknowledged if we reflect on all sorts of judgments in order to discover the principles from which all men judge. In other words, while for Buffier the notion of self-evidence requires the determination of as many distinctions as necessary to avoid confusion, for Reid the notion of self-evidence must be broad and flexible enough in order to make sure that we do not exclude relevant data from reflection.

These attitudes toward the definition of common sense are so far from being interchangeable that they are in many ways incompatible. Because of the arbitrariness and relativity of mankind's opinions, the methodological openness that Reid considers necessary would not be acceptable to Buffier, whose conviction is that vulgar and philosophical errors on common sense can be solved only by accurate and precise definition. From Buffier's point of view the further danger of elevating mere prejudices into the status of first principles renders Reid's implicit reference to the self-evident clearness of first principles greatly insufficient and ultimately inadequate: the only way to show the plausibility of first principles of common sense is to explicitly weigh the comparative degree of clearness of many propositions, including proofs and disproofs of self-evident propositions. Buffier also holds that, especially concerning the implications of common-sense principles, we must use a logic of paradoxes that is a result of an analysis of the many distinctions in kind, in degree, in mode, in meaning of the notion of evidence. Finally, Buffier would not be satisfied with any definition of common sense that depended on an analysis of the way our senses operate. In his view the justification of common-sense principles is required before we can evaluate the rules of sensory perception. Buffier is not only convinced that the senses have no role in justifying common sense, but he also holds that common-sense principles do not guarantee the truth of sensory perception: our senses do not reach more than mere appearances, and the truths they afford are related to practical needs but not to speculative issues. Accordingly, Buffier argues that the natural sciences afford a low degree of probability, even a "species of romance," a series of tenets Reid could not accept.

On the other hand, Reid does not think that the problem of common sense can be solved by means of definitions determining the genus and species of all operations of the mind or of all sorts of truths. For him, the Buffierian distinction between two dispositions of the mind (common sense and internal sentiment) would not take us very far toward an understanding of the proper meaning of common sense. For him, the whole point is to discover the real and even semantic continuity between common understanding and science in matters of judgments. Thus it is necessary to treat the notion of self-evidence inductively because only a reflection on all judgments will show that there is a philosophically valid continuity between the common appeal to common sense and the philosophical appeal to first principles. Besides, in Reid's view, all self-evident propositions (contingent or necessary) are on the same footing. This is so because of their epistemological status: they are the natural laws that ultimately govern men's beliefs. In other words, Reid's view of common sense is too broad to be satisfied with a technical definition that refers to the kind of object upon which a common-sense disposition passes judgments. Besides, his view of the experimental method is too precise to be satisfied with Buffier's way of avoiding confusion, by restricting the meaning of the terms he uses. In Reid's view, the problem is to give a general account of all the relevant facts related to judgments, and in this context the more precise our preliminary definitions the more inadequate they could be in narrowing the field of our inductive reflections on judgments. Finally, Reid would not be satisfied with Buffier's central focus on the clearness of common-sense principles, for he does not think that any criteria related exclusively to the characteristics of our conceptions would be sufficient to overcome our disagreements on first principles. In fact, the focus on the clearness of first principles can confuse the very issue Reid's set of marks is meant to clarify: that to believe that a proposition is true and to conceive a proposition is to perform two specifically distinct acts of the mind, even though both acts must be present in the complex act of the mind that we call a judgment.

Thus, in discussing the proper ways of defining common sense in philosophy, Buffier and Reid are not only attempting to be clear about their notion, they are also delineating their conceptions of introspection as a philosophical means of investigation. Both Buffier and Reid argue that reflection on what passes in our minds leads to a justification of the principles of common sense. But while they both appeal to introspection in this general sense, they have quite different purposes in mind. Accordingly, they understand introspection and its relation to logic and grammar in quite different terms.

Indeed, Buffier wants to show that men's internal impressions of truths are compatible with one another. Introspection for him is a complement to logic, the science of consistent reasoning, because it allows us to introduce rules by which we detect the similarities among ideas in order to complement the (logical) rules of identity and non-contradiction. Reid, on the other hand, appeals to introspection as a means of investigation in order to show that philosophical systems do not systematically bear the touchstone of facts. Introspection for him is a means of investigation by which we can determine when and how general theories (however consistent) must be rejected as hypothetical.

Because Buffier understands introspection as a complement to logic, he relates this means of investigation to grammar in a normative sense. It is by a logical type of introspection that we analyze the ambiguities and the confusions that the relativity of men's ways of speaking create for philosophical analysis and conclusions. On the basis of this analysis, we determine whether we should accept or reject different propositions, given their multiple aspects, which introspection permits us to identify. It is also by a logical type of introspection that we understand the presence and the importance of those propositions on which the impressions of all men converge.

Because Reid understands introspection as a means of providing testimony on mental facts, he does not reduce it to a logical analysis. He thinks that philosophers usually overlook the importance of the discoveries we can make by an experimental reflection. He thus opposes introspection and deductive logic when he reaches his conclusions concerning the most general phenomena we can reach (the natural laws of beliefs, self-evident propositions, cannot be rejected for extra-experimental reasons). On the other hand, Reid makes important connections between inductive logic and the structures of language when he engages in the generalizing process. It is by an experimental use of introspection that Reid can show that the particular facts he analyzes have at once more complexity and more authority than deductive logic could allow.

2. THE VIEWS OF BUFFIER AND REID ON THE MOST IMPORTANT
FEATURES OF THE HUMAN MIND

The different views held by Buffier and Reid concerning introspection as a means of philosophical investigation have important consequences for their justification of common sense because their views on both introspection and justification are systematically related to what Buffier and Reid deem essential to the human mind. In assessing the sort of argument that Buffier and Reid present as a rational alternative to deductive reasoning in the justification of self-evident propositions, I shall relate their claim for the rationality of their alternative argument with their views of what is most essential in a valid account of the human mind. In so doing, we shall see that while both argue that knowledge is faculty-laden and that a valid definition of truth must be compatible with the human mind, they propose quite different justifications for an appeal to common sense.

Buffier thinks it possible to deduce the value of the appeal to common sense from the value and limitations of the internal sentiment as the rule of all truths. In denying that we can prove self-evident propositions to be true by means of deductive reasoning, Buffier does not maintain that no deductive argument could be used in favor of common-sense principles. He, rather, denies the possibility of proving the truth of these principles by means of a restricted form of deductive reasoning, that form of deductive reasoning which would derive consequences by means of tautologies only. This restricted form of deductive reasoning is, in Buffier's opinion, the form of reasoning used by the solipsist in order to reach the conclusion that we cannot make sure that other beings and things exist.

The basic logical model that Buffier opposes to the solipsist system is thereby one of conjunctive truths whose validity is discovered when we analyze and evaluate the differences and similarities among our ideas (our immediate sentiments), and our rational dispositions (the internal sentiment and common sense). Buffier's argument for common-sense principles runs as follows: (1) Our common-sense disposition is employed in assertions concerning the existence of other beings and things. (2) In order to recognize the validity of these assertions, it is necessary to complement the rule of identity by other rules, which permit us to judge of nonidentical statements. (3) This new set of rules is possible if we introduce many distinctions among our ideas in our reasoning and if we evaluate these distinctions in order to see whether we have cases of identical, similar, ambivalent, or incompatible statements. (4) The validity of this new set of rules is guaranteed by a more complete account of the features of the principle of the internal sentiment (I think, I feel, I exist), especially the conjunctive feature of this principle. (5) Common-sense principles are guaranteed by their similarity to the principle of the internal sentiment.

For Buffier therefore to offer a rational argument in favor of common sense is to offer an argument whose compatibility with and similarity to the *cogito* are guaranteed. An argument is rational to the extent that it has the clarity and distinctness of the *cogito* itself, notwithstanding the conjunctive feature of the propositions, which are thus clear and distinct. In other words, Buffier claims that in order to admit the rationality of his argument for common-sense principles, we must reappraise the concept of identity as an exclusive criterion and as an exclusive rule of truth. This he does by enlarging the notion of consistency so that it can include compatible but nonidentical judgments. The limit of rationality is not determined by the field of tautological judgments: it is determined by the field of conjunctive judgments whose similarity with the *cogito* is guaranteed: those are the judgments that are certain for human beings. Buffier's reappraisal of the concept of identity and its resulting enlarged notion of consistency leads him to claim that all statements whose compatibility with the *cogito* is *not* clear and distinct—most statements made by human beings—will produce a legitimately ambivalent feeling in our mind. The most rational attitude concerning such statements will then be an analysis of the paradoxes to which they lead (the analysis of the many points of view from which they could be asserted) and most often the suspension of judgment.

For Reid the justification of the appeal to common sense derives from an accurate understanding of the only method we should use in philosophy, the inductive method. Accordingly, the main Reidian argument for the validity of the appeal to common sense lies in showing that the principles of common sense have epistemologically crucial relations with the conditions for valid procedures of induction: (1) Common sense permits the identification and respect of the field of observation that must be studied in order to understand both common understanding and science. (2) Common sense also embodies a set of propositions that are self-evident to all men and that may be shown to be self-evident by virtue of the fact that they satisfy both the reality condition and the adequacy condition of Newton's first rule when this is applied to the notion of self-evidence. (3) In order to show the last point, we must interpret the analogical principle (same effect, same cause) in distinguishing efficient and physical causes. (4) When we thus determine the specificity of a science of the mind as compared to a science of physical objects, we can demonstrate that the natural laws of human beliefs (self-evident propositions) are as important (constitutive, ultimate) as the natural laws discovered by natural scientists in the field of physical causality.

In other words, Reid claims that a rational argument in favor of common-sense principles is an argument whose compatibility with the experimental method and its rules is guaranteed, taking into account the specificity of the object of a science of the mind. For Reid we can show the rationality of this argument for common sense if we introduce, in the philosophy of the mind, the experimental condition of reality: we want to make sure that we assert what is really natural to the human mind. However, in introducing this notion of "real beliefs" as an important notion in theories of knowledge, we also have to reappraise the concept of reality, because what is real for the human mind must not be seen in terms of the model that is used to ascribe reality to physical objects. Besides, we not only want to determine what is "really" a belief: we want to determine what really is a "natural" belief, namely, a belief whose validity must be admitted because it is a law of our intellectual constitution. In other words, when we analyze men's beliefs, it is important to have an *experimentum crucis* by which we can determine whether the reality condition and the adequacy condition of Newton's rule have been met. When these conditions are met, as they are with the principles of common sense, we realize that the most rational attitude is not to doubt but to test our beliefs in the attempt to ascertain accurately and fully the natural laws from which human beliefs proceed, and in the hope of further refinements of our knowledge of these laws and of their numerous implications.

If we now compare the sort of rational argument used by Buffier and Reid in favor of common sense, we realize not only that they are in many ways incompatible, but that they hint at quite different views of what is most essential to the human mind. Indeed, while both Buffier and Reid defend their main argument for common sense as an alternative to the monopoly of deductive reasoning in matters of philosophical proofs, they neither agree on what this alternative should be nor agree on the sense in which deductive reasoning is a target. For Buffier, we have seen, the target is deductive reasoning restricted to the derivation of tautologies. For Reid the target is deductive reasoning as opposed to experimental method and inductive logic. Buffier thinks that he can deduce the value of his argument for common sense from the validity of the *cogito*, provided we enlarge our notion of logical consistency. Reid thinks that we can show the validity of his argument for common sense if we better understand the rules of the inductive method, provided we determine the specificity of a science of the mind. Reid does not think that any deductive approach—be it enlarged—could offer more than a (Baconian) Table of Investigation when we deal with first principles. Buffier is convinced that no empirical or inductive procedure—if one were possible and methodically applied—could be self-justifying and could serve as a demonstration of the truth of principles of common sense. Buffier certainly thinks that a description of what passes within the mind of all men would confirm his position, and Reid is willing to use reasoning in order to show that we can meet the adequacy condition of Newton's first rule. However, in Buffier's view no inductive description could answer the skeptical challenge raised by the solipsist—the skeptical challenge is logical—while in Reid's view no deduction could convince a skeptic (the model is David Hume) to abandon his stronghold—the skeptical challenge is epistemological.

I think that Buffier and Reid defend the rationality of quite different types of arguments in favor of common-sense principles because they do not agree on what a study of the human mind reveals as the most important basis for a philosophically valid account of the truth. When they argue that our philosophical systems must be compatible with the human mind (because knowledge is faculty-laden), they do not have the same reference in mind. This is strikingly clear from their attitude concerning the *cogito*: for Buffier the *cogito* is the paradigm of truth, and a better reading of its features reveals that it guarantees more than tautological truths. For Reid the *cogito* is an outstanding example of the fact that philosophers disagree the most when they seem to have the surest means of agreement, a self-evident proposition. For Buffier, in other words, the most important feature of the human mind is the fact that it includes one belief, the *cogito*, which is the best example of knowledge we have. It is on the basis of this example that we assess the possibilities and limits of knowledge in general and of knowledge of the human mind in particular. In our attempt to propose a philosophical system that is compatible with human faculties, we start with what is already *given* and we proceed to our philosophical elucidations by always comparing our new developments to our paradigm.

For Reid, on the other hand, we cannot make sure that our systems are compatible with the human mind if we rest our analysis on one example of belief, however unquestionable it appears. Indeed, there is no example of belief that could not be challenged, and our problem is to overcome our disagreements as to what is self-evident to all men. In other words, for Reid nothing could be considered as "given" unless we develop a method by which we can scientifically ascertain the natural laws of intellectual operations. We are so far from having one paradigmatic example of knowledge that the most urgent task of philosophy is to discover, inductively, what the nature of the human mind is. It is this knowledge that we can use as the basis for determining which examples of beliefs are valid. In brief, the attempt to discover inductively the laws of intellectual operations is the very basis of any valid definition of truth.

Thus, while Buffier argues that his argument for common sense is rational because we do have a given *example* of knowledge from which we can determine what is most essential to the human mind, Reid argues that his argument for common-sense principles is rational because it is urgent to realize that only an inductive attempt to *determine* what is most essential to the human mind (the natural laws of beliefs or self-evident propositions) could provide a valid basis for evaluating all philosophical systems and conclusions.

3. THE DIFFERENT COMMON-SENSE DOCTRINES OF BUFFIER AND REID

The differences between Buffier and Reid concerning introspection and the most important feature of the human mind have important consequences in their respective doctrines, as may be shown in focusing on the epistemological status they give to the principles of common sense they defend. Buffier's first principles of common sense are admittedly better than alternative or counterpropositions, but they claim no more than the "highest probability," an evidence inferior in degree and mode to the evidence of the internal sentiment. For Reid also we can claim only probability for the dictates of common sense, but because this probability is determined through a systematic use of induction, it is presented as the "utmost" that a philosophy of the mind can reach: *all* principles of common sense, whether contingent or necessary, and (in Buffier's language) whether internal or external truths, have the *same* systematic status and they have the *same* value as natural laws in natural sciences.

Thus it is important to realize that even though Buffier and Reid agree on the general content of some principles of common sense, their doctrines give these principles quite different status. In general terms Buffier's examples of first principles of common sense are given as propositions whose *denials* are more difficult to maintain than their assertion. Buffier also holds that it is crucial to distinguish first principles and their implications, because in the final case we must proceed to an elucidation of legitimate paradoxes. Accordingly, Buffier usually prefers to give a *negative* formulation to his principles of common sense (we cannot deny that other beings exist). This kind of formulation is important because the aim of his philosophy is to refute skeptical extremes (we cannot go so far as denying that the other exists) while defending a mitigated form of skepticism (for most beliefs, the most rational attitude is the analysis of paradoxes and the suspension of judgment).

For Reid, on the other hand, the codification of first principles of contingent and necessary truths includes propositions whose *affirmation* is naturally lawful. Reid prefers a *positive* formulation of principles of common sense because his aim is not only to show that there *are* propositions that are self-evident to all men, but to show that such propositions have an identifiable content that can serve as the basis for *all* valid reasoning. Reid is so far from maintaining, as Buffier did, that we must distinguish first principles from their implications that he makes it a methodological rule that we connect these. We must see the implications of first principles as the many effects of first principles in men's opinions, conduct, and action, and we must consider these effects as crucial because it is from their presence and their importance that we can proceed to an inductive enunciation of the laws from which they proceed. The positive formulation of first principles is so important for Reid that it grounds his hope that his philosophy can delineate the foundation of an entire superstructure of natural philosophy.

The different status of first principles of common sense in the doctrines of Buffier and Reid may be illustrated in more specific terms. First, the existence of mental operations is not a principle of common sense for Buffier but it is for Reid. External things exist and are what we perceive them to be, says Reid. Other beings and things exist but we cannot be sure of their intrinsic nature, says Buffier. For Buffier, common sense *only* assures us that we should not go so far as to deny that other beings and things exist and that some of their properties are striking if we compare them to the properties of what we call our soul. In the Reidian doctrine, human veracity is a first principle of contingent truths, while such veracity is subject to many subsidiary rules in the Buffierian doctrine. For Buffier common sense permits one *only* to deny that people's utterances are completely arbitrary and extravagant. According to Reid there are necessary first principles in morals and in taste. For Buffier the question of good and evil is highly ambiguous (common sense assures us *only* that it would be extremism to identify free will and the necessity to act) and if there were first principles concerning beauty, they would be highly paradoxical. In fact, the examples that Buffier presents as first principles of common sense are, in Reid's own list, examples of first principles of contingent truths, with the exception of the assertion of an intelligent cause of order, which corresponds in Reid's list to both a contingent and a necessary (first) principle.

In brief, in the discussion of the status and meaning of first principles of common sense, Buffier thinks that by restricting their meaning and extending the number of qualifications we should use in discussing their evidence we provide the best guarantee that their (restricted) status is defendable. The complexity of the analysis of the meaning of the principles of common sense is, for Buffier, a good way to show that common sense, as a disposition, is a *general* source of truth, even though it is a *restricted* source of truth. We cannot deny that the internal sentiment is the best source of truth, but in general terms we cannot deny that common sense as a disposition is another source of truth. The restriction of common sense to a few propositions presented with qualifications is the best way to show that in general terms it is false to hold that we can expect no truth whatsoever from our common-sense disposition: we do have qualified counterexamples to this assertion.

For Reid, on the other hand, we must focus on the content of the examples of beliefs we analyze, because our problem is to derive inductive conclusions from data related to judgments. The value of our generalizations concerning the examples of beliefs depends on the nature of the connection between particular cases of belief (effects) and first principles of knowledge (cause). For Reid, we can significantly conclude that faculties exist (or in Buffier's terms, that dispositions exist) only if we have a precise and scientific knowledge of the effects that our faculties have when they are used. These effects are particular beliefs from which we inductively discover the laws of our intellectual operations. When this is done, we have shown what it means to say precisely and specifically that men have intellectual faculties. Thus, while Buffier prefers a negative formulation of first principles of common sense because he holds that the issue concerns the validity of a rational disposition (common sense) properly qualified, Reid prefers a positive formulation of first principles of common sense because he holds that the issue concerns the scientific validity of a significant assessment of the laws of human beliefs, which must be derived from particular examples.

The doctrines of Buffier and Reid are not only substantially different if we consider the status they give to their first principles of common sense, they are also quite different if we consider the basic presuppositions from which they defend their doctrines and the resulting difficulties we find in their defense of common sense. In presenting this element of difference between the two doctrines, we shall have the opportunity to make a few critical remarks and to discuss briefly the problem of presuppositions in common-sense doctrines.

Buffier's basic assumption is that rational sentiments are means to truth. Accordingly, he is much more concerned with elucidating the status of rational sentiments than he is with showing how these sentiments are actually applied. This accounts for a certain vagueness in Buffier's discussion of specific logical rules. Buffier holds that it is more important and more difficult to defend the status of first principles of common sense than to delineate the rules of deductive reasoning or to apply such rules when we reason on the basis of first principles. Because Buffier makes the assumption that rational sentiments are means to truths, he is sure he can convince the solipsist by arguing from the *cogito*. This assurance is possible because he uses the same premises as the solipsist and because he agrees with a mitigated form of skepticism. However, even though Buffier insists that it is important to recognize the complexities of the issues involved in his defense of common sense, he sometimes weakens his claim to offer an alternative to the theoretical views of the solipsist by oversimplifying the solipsist argument. One example of this is his interpretation of the rules of deductive reasoning on the basis of simple mathematical rules, such as two quantities equal to a third are equal.

Reid's basic assumption is that there is a God-given order in nature and that this order guarantees the validity of an inductive method which is faithful to a well-ordained world. In other words, even though Reid rejects the appeal to a Deity as guaranteeing the reliability of our faculties, he thinks that the aim of induction is to discover an order that does exist, and that induction is guaranteed when, in a step-by-step process, we discover the regularities and laws that exist. Reid is more concerned with the discovery of the specific order that characterizes the intellectual operations of men (Newton's discovery of the law of attraction being the configuration that there is an order in nature) than he is with general objections to the experimental method. In discovering this "mental" order, Reid is more concerned with the effects of what he sees as rational factors than he is with such factors as custom or education whose variety is, in his opinion, too great to allow a general (inductive) conclusion.

Because of his assumption that there is an order characterizing men's intellectual operations, Reid has a tendency to identify non-immediate causes of assent to self-evident propositions (such as custom and education) with nonoperative factors. Reid does not automatically discount such factors when he decides that certain propositions are self-evident due to immediate assent. As we have seen, his more subtle argument is that we cannot invoke these factors as adequate causes of our assent to self-evident propositions. But in showing this, Reid seems sometimes to overlook the very *presence* of these factors (they are treated as absent because inadequate) and accordingly to minimize the difficulty of choosing among hypotheses when we look for the most adequate account of the role played by many real factors.

Buffier and Reid, it must be acknowledged, do not offer many arguments in support of their basic assumptions—at least, if we compare their treatment of common sense and their treatment of these assumptions. Accordingly, the difficulties raised by their doctrines are not solved. At this point one may be inclined to argue that, in most cases, it is in the function of an assumption to remain only implicit or to become explicit only when a whole system has been developed and is analyzed. However, this explanation is puzzling when applied to common-sense philosophers, because their own doctrines were made possible by detection of the role played by assumptions (such as the status of the rule of identity or the role played by the hypothesis of representative ideas) in philosophy. Thus common-sense philosophers can hardly miss the importance of assumptions in philosophical theories, nor can they forget the skeptical challenge to their own assumptions.

Another way to look at this difficulty would be to say that neither Buffier nor Reid argues against making assumptions. Instead, they argue against specific assumptions that they see as false. In arguing that we cannot reason, theorize, or philosophize without admitting first principles, common-sense philosophers may be said to be arguing that we should make only those assumptions that are compatible with a set of self-evident beliefs. In this sense common-sense philosophers argue for their own assumptions because their basic assumptions are compatible with the self-evident propositions they wish to defend. It remains to be shown, however, that Buffier's more complex assessment of the features of the *cogito* as the best example of rational sentiments is compatible with a more rigorous account of the rules of deductive reasoning. And it remains to be shown that Reid's view of what constitutes a better understanding of the experimental method as it applies to conclusions about the existence of an intelligent Designer can avoid circular conclusions concerning the order of nature. In a similar manner it remains to be shown that a commitment to the inductive method does not restrict the creative use of hypothesis, or the meaning of the adequacy condition, because the assumption of a natural order would lead to confusion between this order and the reality condition.

4. TWO COUNTEREXAMPLES TO THE CARICATURES OF COMMON-SENSE DOCTRINES

Despite these criticisms, I do not think that we should conclude that Buffier and Reid are silent on the justification of the appeal to common sense in philosophy, or that they have nothing interesting to say on the question of human rationality. On the contrary, I think that we should see the common-sense doctrines of Buffier and Reid as interesting counterexamples to the caricatures of common-sense philosophies. First, Buffier and Reid have much more to offer in support of their theories than the argument *ad risum*. When they both say that it is absurd to deny the truth of common-sense principles, they do not mean to say that laughing at the absurdity will be sufficient to overcome the skeptical attacks. On the contrary, their entire attempt to defend common-sense principles is an attempt to show that there is a genuine philosophical issue behind the feeling of absurdity that a denial of the principles of common sense produces.

In the case of Buffier, the issue is a philosophical reappraisal of the concept of identity, a reappraisal that requires a new reading of the *cogito*. This new reading is not an attempt to show that the rule of the mob must serve as a philosophical standard. It is an attempt to show that philosophy must be consistent with natural reason, while acknowledging that the term "natural" has a normative meaning because it refers to that which, amid considerable diversity, unites human beings. In the case of Reid, the issue is a reappraisal of the concepts of reality and adequacy when we apply these concepts to the field of "natural" human beliefs. This issue is so far from being settled by an appeal to the rule of the mob that Reid's most important question is *whether* men agree about self-evident principles or not, and *whether* we can develop a method and valid criterion for determining whether they do, or not.

In a similar manner it is incorrect to present the common-sense doctrines of Buffier and Reid as the result of confusion concerning the distinction between speculative and practical issues. Buffier's view of the necessity of this distinction is not original, except for his interesting connection between vulgar prejudices and philosophical reductionism. In fact, Buffier is willing to admit that a justification of common sense is not very important in ordinary life—where it is not questioned—but that such a justification becomes important in relation to the philosophical and speculative problem raised by the solipsist's conclusion. The main danger of the solipsist doctrine for the common man is that it may reinforce people's identification of philosophy with irrelevance, a danger that touches metaphysics in its educational function of improving our ways of judging. Thus, where the practical use of reason is concerned, Buffier usually thinks it better to distinguish practical reason from the speculative and theoretical issues of philosophy. Such is his attitude toward ordinary language and ordinary opinions.

However, and this is, I think, the original aspect of his views, Buffier shows that there is a negative connection between ordinary opinions and philosophical opinions in that they both illustrate the same sort of mistake. At the root of dogmatism, either popular or philosophical, he finds the reduction of the rules of argument to the rules of identity and noncontradiction, rules that cannot sufficiently account for most judgments, including logical judgments. His point is that the Yes-or-No prejudice in matters of opinion (one of two opinions must be true) has a parallel (and perhaps a cause) in the binary logic based exclusively on the laws on identity and noncontradiction. What Buffier says is that no one is immune from critical analysis and that there is no philosophical ground for dogmatism, either popular or philosophical. In turn, Buffier's view of the negative connection between vulgar prejudices and philosophical reductionism (as with the solipsist system) suggests that, far from being an approval of dogmatism, the philosophical defense of common sense is truly a defense of paradoxes.

Reid's view of the connection between theoretical and practical issues is different from that of Buffier: Reid holds that the very distinction between theory and practice, speculative reason and practical reason, is an error. This is not to say that Reid merely confuses the issues but to recognize that for him philosophy must try to depict human nature as it is. The distinction between theories of mental activities and the practice or the real performance of perception, conception, abstraction, judgment, and reasoning is possible if, and only if, one does not submit oneself to the conditions of induction. Inasmuch as the skeptical systems rely upon this distinction, the only tenable position is to cut the knot we cannot untie and refuse to allow prescription to take the place of description, or more precisely, to allow descriptive accounts of mental laws to be rejected for extra-experimental reasons.

The originality of Reid's view of the connections between theoretical and practical issues in matters of truths lies in the ways in which the experimental method permits him to determine the theoretical and systematic value of "practical" reason. In treating self-evidence on the model of an efficient cause whose effects are discernible in men's language, opinions, and conduct, Reid gives these effects a theoretical status assured by the validity of Newton's rules. In treating particular cases of beliefs as the basis of a codification of first principles, Reid gives ordinary beliefs the status of scientific data and gives the dictates of common sense the status of laws in natural philosophy.

Reid's argument for the connection between speculative and practical issues is philosophical in that his aim is to discover inductively the nature of human mind. Because there are many connections between the intellectual and the active powers of the mind, it is philosophically important to treat the distinction between speculation and practice as a methodological distinction. In brief, if by practical issues one means a valid description of the ways in which both thought and action are connected in the activities of rational beings, then Reid's doctrine of common sense is meant as a defense of practical issues. But this is not to say that his doctrine is a case of speculative inability. For Reid the very connection between speculation and practice is the ground of a revolutionary attempt to account inductively for the notion of truth.

Finally, it is quite incorrect to represent the common-sense philosophies of Buffier and Reid as cases of a lack of understanding of the skeptical argument. Clearly Buffier and Reid object to some skeptical arguments and try to refute them. But they do take the skeptical challenge seriously, and it is incorrect to present their reaction to skepticism as mere emotional distaste or as the unqualified rebuttals of dogmatists whose most cherished beliefs are questioned.

Buffier and Reid do not have the same reaction toward skepticism. For Buffier, we have seen, the main problem is to overcome skeptical extremes. Such extremes as the solipsist conclusion must be rejected because, in admitting the truth of his own existence and of the existence of his thought, the solipsist must also admit the truth of the existence of other beings and things. This he will do if he realizes that the valid skeptical conclusion he draws from the *cogito* is not warranted because it overlooks the conjunctive features of this principle. By recognizing the conjunctive feature of the *cogito*, the skeptic will improve the validity of philosophical systems, in particular in unfolding the implications of the criteria of clearness and distinctness. By means of a mitigated form of skepticism, Buffier's common-sense doctrine is an attack against dogmatism in its ordinary and philosophical forms. Dogmatism, for Buffier, always derives from a failure to consider all perspectives on a proposition. But skeptical extremes aside; the skeptical arguments remain the test of rational certainty, which for human beings is restricted to a limited number of self-evident truths. In other words, Buffier's common-sense doctrine is so far from emotional distaste for skeptical arguments that it is itself a defense of a mitigated form of skepticism.

For Reid the main problem is to overcome a quite general form of skepticism, the form of skepticism that questions the very validity of men's natural beliefs. This form of skepticism, which he describes as the result of a philosophical Inquisition, must be rejected because once philosophers seriously attempt to establish the truth of human beliefs, they must acknowledge that the validity of their system must be grounded on a scientific account of the natural laws that govern men's beliefs and thus must acknowledge self-evident propositions. This acknowledgment is possible if philosophers realize that skeptical systems draw their conclusions concerning the truth of human beliefs from a series of incorrect hypotheses about the ways in which the human mind performs the operations of perceiving, conceiving, judging, and reasoning. If, however, philosophers become genuine inductivists, in particular by applying inductive rules compatible with the specificity of their object, mental facts, they will improve philosophical theories. Reid's doctrine of common sense is a revolutionary philosophical procedure in which the test of rational arguments will be provided by the experimental discovery of the natural laws of self-evidence and by further experimental discoveries of their implications.

However different their reactions toward skepticism, it is clear that the reactions of Buffier and Reid are important counterexamples to the caricatures of common-sense doctrines. In the process of their reflections on common sense, both Buffier and Reid are willing to admit the subtlety of many skeptical arguments and the unanswerability of some of them. For example, when Buffier and Reid argue that it is impossible to prove self-evident propositions to be true by means of deductive reasoning, they both see this argument as an admission of an important limit of human rationality, the limit of deductive reasoning. For Buffier and for Reid the problem is: How can we offer a guarantee that the first steps of our reasoning are not arbitrarily determined, given the fact that we cannot offer a deductive proof of their truth and given the fact that we must take this limit of human rationality seriously?

Usually, however, this admission that it is impossible to prove all propositions to be true by means of reasoning is not taken seriously by their critics. The reason for this is, I think, that their critics see in this admission the exact inversion of Kant's reaction to Hume's *Treatise*. These critics hold that rather than awakening common-sense philosophers from their dogmatic slumber, skeptical denials would only awaken them from a low (ordinary) form of dogmatism (they never thought of doubting, and they never thought that one could doubt) to a high (philosophical) form of dogmatism (a system of philosophy based on principles that must be admitted without argument or evidence).

I think that this view of common-sense philosophies rests on an incorrect interpretation. It must be emphasized that common-sense philosophers such as Buffier and Reid do not see deductive reasoning as the only source that could guarantee a belief. They do think that we must look for other kinds of guarantee, while admitting that these alternatives will not have and cannot have the halo attached to deductive reasoning. This admission of the limits of human rationality, the limits of deductive reasoning, is in my opinion an important critical admission made by common-sense philosophers.

I also think that there is another sense in which the common-sense doctrines of Buffier and Reid must be seen as critical analysis. Buffier and Reid not only admit that it is difficult to find a justification for self-evident propositions whose truths cannot be demonstrated by means of deductive reasoning, but they also admit that their alternative argument in favor of common-sense principles is involved in the difficult problem of dealing with a *nonobvious* notion of self-evidence, either in ordinary or in philosophical terms. Buffier and Reid are seriously concerned with the question of diversity in opinions, and their concern on this point is a strong indication of their doubts concerning the ways in which universality could be used as the criterion of the truth of a proposition or of a theory. For them both, whenever we have a valid claim for the universality of a belief, it has to be the result of a difficult process of detection and evaluation. Furthermore, Buffier and Reid insist on the necessity of a closer analysis of the nature of self-evident propositions, restricting their meaning in the case of Buffier, and broadening our domain of investigation in the case of Reid. This insistence on a close analysis of self-evident propositions is a strong indication of their doubts concerning the ways in which we can make sure that we have cases of immediate, natural beliefs. Finally, the very attempt made by Buffier and Reid to provide means, criteria, models, and arguments by which one can recognize, define, and defend self-evident propositions shows that these common-sense philosophers are quite critical of this notion. Many of their critics, again, mistake these attempts. Often they ironically point out that common-sense philosophies would not need to be justified were self-evidence self-evident! But, I think, common-sense philosophers are quite right in arguing that the notion of self-evidence is not obvious.

The issue at this point is whether there is a standard by which we can rationally determine that statements like "It is evident that . . . " are philosophically valid. What both Buffier and Reid point out is that even though many philosophers deny that they do—or that they should—appeal to self-evident principles, there is no philosophical system in which the argument that a proposition is evident is never used. They further acknowledge that if we want to claim that a proposition is true, that is, universally true, we must subject this claim to critical analysis, for the basis of any such claim is the attempt to represent human reason and this, they argue, is not an easy matter. The attempt to avoid confusing popular or philosophical idiosyncrasies with a valid general claim about human reason—the attempt that characterizes the doctrines of Buffier and Reid—is surely very far from a dogmatic appeal to the rule of the mob or to unquestioned belief.

When common-sense philosophers ask other philosophers to come "down to earth," they do so on the basis of a set of doubts concerning the validity of the philosophical meaning given to universality. Their argument is that human nature is not to be defined through a form of epistemological elitism, that is, through judgments claimed to be universal by virtue of the consent of philosophers. The issues raised by this critical attitude concerning universality must be taken seriously. Philosophical skepticism should not be restricted to the kind of doubts that philosophers may raise concerning ordinary beliefs. It must also include the kind of doubts that philosophers may raise concerning philosophical beliefs and assumptions, including the beliefs and assumptions that philosophers have concerning *all* men's beliefs.

At this point Buffier and Reid argue that the philosophical solution to this enlarged set of doubts can only be found in common sense. By this, they mean that no universal theory about human beliefs can be valid unless the nature of human rationality (its grounds, its limits) is taken seriously. However, if we take this question seriously, it is not easy to get to what is truly essential (or in their terms "natural") to human reason. In order to discover this, Buffier and Reid both argue that it is vital to go beyond the superficial dichotomy of the rule of the mob and the rule of philosophy.

To conclude, not only is it the case that Buffier and Reid have much more to offer than the argument *ad risum* in favor of common-sense principles, but their quite different views on the nature of a rational argument raise important philosophical issues. These issues, I think, must be critically discussed as we discuss other sorts of philosophical doctrines. Clearly we cannot have a philosophically valid opinion on the importance and value of common-sense doctrines if we uncritically assume that all such doctrines are covered by simplistic explanations such as kicking the stone, laughing at the skeptic, rule of the mob, speculative ability, and so forth. Before we can accurately assess the segment of the history of ideas represented by the history of common-sense doctrines, it is important to analyze the kind of doctrine, the kind of argument, the kind of justification proposed by common-sense philosophers in favor of their theories. It is important, in brief, to treat these philosophies as genuine philosophies, which raise interesting philosophical issues.

In analyzing the doctrines of Buffier and Reid, we have seen that among the issues involved in the search for truth, the question of the nature of a rational argument is important, as well as the idea that our suggestions should be grounded on important features of the human mind. For both Buffier and Reid the question of *who* is allowed to determine the nature of truth for human beings is an essential part of the questions raised about the criterion of truth. When they say that we should turn to common sense for information about the nature of truth, it is because they hold that the attempt to represent human reason is both serious and difficult. It is also because they are concerned to avoid a special version of what we would call today the problem of ideology. For common-sense philosophers such as Buffier and Reid a definition of truth that would be based on the exclusive notions and criteria of a single class of human beings is self-refuting. For them a philosophical system is bound to fail if it denies the relevance of the evaluation of *who* talks on behalf of all men in matters of true beliefs and on *what grounds* one thus claims to represent human reason. It may be that in the history of ideas the common-sense philosophies represent the most serious and concerned attempts to make sure that philosophy itself is neither a systematic form of elitism nor a systematic ground for elitism of other kinds. It may also be true that these attempts were not successful. But the only way to know whether this is the case is to analyze specific common-sense doctrines as genuine philosophies that raise important and yet unsettled philosophical issues.

In showing that Buffier and Reid do raise important philosophical issues while defending quite different views on the nature of an appeal to common sense in philosophy, I have shown that the charge of plagiarism raised against Reid is clearly refuted by internal evidence. In considering the substantial differences between these common-sense doctrines, we can only conclude that the most probable explanation for the fact that the question of Reid's originality has not received a substantial answer based on internal evidence before now is to be found in general caricatures of common-sense doctrines, views that have provided ready-made but incorrect explanations of common-sense philosophies. In turn, in showing that the doctrines of Buffier and Reid are two clear and significantly different counter-examples to such caricatures, I have shown that it is time to abandon these distorted views of common-sense doctrines and that it is due time to assess this segment of the history of ideas by analyzing other common-sense doctrines with a more philosophical perspective.

Further work on common-sense philosophies will not only indicate, I suggest, that there are many quite different sorts of appeal to common sense in philosophy but also, I predict, that the different views of common-sense philosophers on the compatibility between universal philosophical claims and the nature of human rationality, and on the relationships between speculative and practical issues in the determination of valid beliefs, constitute a rich and still relevant segment of the history of ideas.

Appendix: Thomas Reid's Curâ Primâ *on Common Sense*

Edited by David Fate Norton

THOMAS REID'S SELF-STYLED *curâ primâ* on the topic of common sense was apparently written in late 1768 or very early 1769.[1] This conjecture derives from evidence of two sorts: entries in a copy of "the original Minute Book" of the Literary Society of Glasgow[2] and indications found within Reid's manuscripts themselves. The Minute Book in question, or at least the existing copy of it, reports the topics discussed at the weekly meetings of the Society. The entry for February 10, 1769, is "Dr. Reid on Common Sense." That it was this *curâ primâ* that Reid presented is made likely by the fact that the minutes of the Society give no indication of an earlier performance on common sense, while an entry for the following February reads, "Dr. Reid gave a

1. This previously unpublished paper is item 2/III/7 of the Birkwood Collection (MS. 2131), King's College, University of Aberdeen. For a brief description of the collection see D. F. Norton, "Reid's Abstract of the *Inquiry into the Human Mind*," in *Thomas Reid: Critical Interpretations*, ed. S. D. Barker and T. L. Beauchamp (Philadelphia: Philosophical Monographs, 1976), p. 125. Further Reid manuscripts including at least some of those published or discussed in J. McCosh, *The Scottish Philosophy* (New York: Carter, 1875), pp. 473–76, were deposited in the King's College Library during 1980 (Ref. Mss. 3061/1–26).

2. Glasgow University Library MS. Murray 505. This effort to date the *curâ primâ* has been substantially aided by Mr. J. Baldwin and Professors R. Emerson and J. C. Stewart-Robertson. David Murray's copy of the Minute Book includes entries for the years 1764–79, or all but the last of Reid's active teaching years at Glasgow. Glasgow University Library MS. Gen. 4 includes entries for meetings of the Society held from 1794–1800.

discourse on common sense." This second paper on the topic is likely to have been manuscript 2/III/8 of the Birkwood Manuscripts, a paper which begins:

In a former discourse *which I had the honour to read before this society*, I inquired into the meaning of the word *common sense* by an induction of instances wherein this word is commonly used, and endeavoured to show by the authority of good writers that we mean by it that natural power of the understanding by which men that are adult and sound in their mind are distinguished from brutes, from idiots, and from infants.[3]

Certainly this is an apt summary of ms. 2/III/7, and as such constitutes grounds for thinking that the label *curâ primâ* is correctly applied to it insofar as it indicates that ms. 2/III/7 is the first of a series of discourses on common sense. Furthermore, although Reid deleted the phrase, "which I had the honour to read before this society," I believe he did so not because it was mistaken, but for stylistic reasons. I take it to be possible, then, that ms. 2/III/7 is not the precise text that Reid spoke from on February 10, 1769—it may not be, literally, his *curâ primâ* on common sense. On the other hand, I am entirely satisfied that ms. 2/III/7 represents the starting point from which began Reid's efforts to clarify common sense itself, a task he had not attempted in the *Inquiry into the Human Mind, on the Principles of Common Sense,* first published in 1764.

As the reader will see, the *curâ primâ* begins by noting that despite the frequency with which the term "common sense" is used, there is

---

3. The italicized portion of this citation has been stroked out. The first version of the paragraph read, it appears, as follows: "In the last discourse which I had the honour to read before this society, I inquired into the meaning of the word *common sense* in the English language and the corresponding word in French and from the authority of good writers as well as by an induction of instances wherein this word is commonly used, endeavoured to show that we mean by it that nature [and?] power of the understanding by which men that are adult and sound in their intellect are distinguished from brutes, from idiots, and from infants." The fact that Reid first indicated that his earlier paper included consideration of the use of the corresponding word in French tells against the suggestion that the *curâ primâ* is precisely the paper read to the Society on February 10, 1769.

It should be noted that in all citations from Reid's manuscripts, capitalization, punctuation, and spelling have been modernized and editorial interpolations placed in square brackets. The complete text of the *curâ primâ* is also modernized in the three respects mentioned.

a disinclination to pursue its precise meaning. Everyone supposes himself "possessed of this faculty," Reid says, and consequently asks for no definition of it: for any individual to do so would suggest that he is in fact unacquainted with common sense. No indefensible concern of this sort deters Reid. The word, he assumes, must have some specifiable sense which can be elicited from the "use of it in common discourse." He immediately notes that we do not attribute common sense to animals, or to infants or the mentally defective. It is only to "persons of mature age who have no natural defect" that we attribute that "degree of discernment and of understanding which we call common sense." Furthermore, we suppose such a "talent" to be "the gift of nature." It can only be improved, never be acquired, by education or training. Indeed, education and training presuppose common sense; without it a man cannot be trained "to any art or science, or even to prudence in the ordinary conduct of life."

Assuming, then, that "common sense" is the term by which we refer to "those natural powers of the understanding which distinguish men from brutes and idiots," Reid attempts to specify some of these powers as well as "the notions and principles of belief we acquire by means of them." Without intending that his survey be taken as complete he suggests:

1. That though animals have sensory experiences akin to man's, they lack important powers of memory and imagination, powers that permit us to attend to the order, composition, and connection of parts, and to have distinct notions of the past and future, both in a manner not apparently found in animals. Furthermore, man has the power to reflect upon past experience, a power lacking in animals, mental defectives, and infants—although these last develop this ability as they progress through childhood.
2. That man has a conception of number or proportion that is never found in animals. An animal may see all that I see, but will not perceive the number of things seen.

Having proceeded in this general way for several pages, Reid's approach rather abruptly changes. At about the mid-point of page eight of the manuscript (p. 196 below) he adds, following a discussion of certain differences between children and adults, a seemingly gratuitous remark about the nature of number, and leaves the remainder of the page blank. At the top of page nine he has written:

The operations of mind which fall under the province of common sense are chiefly these:

1. The perceiving the obvious relations of things.
2. Distinguishing in the same object things that are different.
3. Observing in different objects things that are common.
4. Our natural and intuitive judgments about things which are not grounded upon reasoning but must be the foundation of all reasoning.
5. Reflecting about what has passed in our own minds.

However, the discussion which follows in the remaining pages of the discourse is not arranged according to these five heads. Rather, it follows one of two overlapping outlines added to the lefthand margin of page nine. This addition reads:

1. Distinguishing. 2. Generalizing. 3. Discovering.
   4. Reflection 5. Judging. Reasoning.
2. Comparing. Numbering.
3. Classing $\left\{ \begin{array}{l} \text{Dividing} \\ \text{Defining} \end{array} \right.$ Compounding.
4. Judging.

Attending to the discussion that ensues, we find that Reid follows the second of these outlines. That is, the operations of the mind that he discusses are, in order, distinguishing, comparing, classing, and judging. It appears, then, that Reid discarded two outlines before settling on the one actually followed. In fact he may have settled on his outline—the correctly ordered list of four operations of the mind—only after completing his essay. Realizing that he had proceeded from distinguishing to comparing, classing, and judging, he then made further additions to the marginalia of manuscript page nine. Be that as it may, it should be noted that although Reid actually numbers only his discussion of the first two operations, namely, distinguishing and comparing, one can nonetheless detect where the discussions of classing and judging begin.

Two features—deficiencies, perhaps one should say—of Reid's published work make this manuscript of particular interest. First, there is the fact, already noted, that Reid's *Inquiry into the Human Mind, on the Principles of Common Sense* contains so little discussion of common sense per se. Reid may have based his inquiry on the principles of common sense, but it must be said that the principles themselves are left implicit. They are presupposed, but not articulated. When he says in his *curâ primâ* that the "first principles upon which the various branches" of human knowledge are grounded have not been "pointed out and ascertained" save in mathematics and natural philosophy, he is criticizing himself as much as other philosophers. In sharp contrast to the *Inquiry*, however, Reid's *Essays on the Intellectual Powers of Man* (published in 1785) includes extensive and detailed discussions of common sense and the principles thereof. It seems safe to say that this manuscript represents Reid's earliest attempt to remedy what he perceived to be a deficiency in his *Inquiry* and in philosophy in general. The *curâ primâ* is, in other words, Reid's initial effort at a larger project, a general account (a clarification, not a justification) of the principles on which all sound philosophy rests.

Secondly, despite the attention given to common sense in the *Intellectual Powers*, there appears to be no sustained discussion of the differences between animals, infants, and the mentally deficient (all of whom fail to have common sense) and those normal, adult humans who appear to have it. Neither is Reid in the *Intellectual Powers* nearly so insistent upon maintaining that common sense is a "natural power of the understanding" in the sense of being a faculty, while the *curâ primâ* highlights just this view and leads one to realize how fundamental it is in the later published work. At the outset of the *Intellectual Powers*, for example, Reid indicates that every operation of the mind implies a power, and that "those powers of the mind which are original and natural" are most properly denominated faculties.[4] Further, what Reid on one occasion calls the "power of judging in self-evident propositions" he had earlier in the *Intellectual Powers* described as the first office or degree of reason:

We ascribe to reason two offices, or two degrees. The first is to judge of things self-evident; the second to draw conclusions that are not self-evident from

---

4. *Essays on the Intellectual Powers of Man*, in *The Works of Thomas Reid*, ed. Sir Wm. Hamilton, 2 vols. (7th ed., Edinburgh, 1872), 1:221.

those that are. The first of these is the province, and the sole province, of common sense; and, therefore, it coincides with reason in its whole extent, and is only another name for one branch or one degree of reason. Perhaps it may be said, Why then should you give it a particular name, since it is acknowledged to be only a degree of reason? It would be a sufficient answer to this, Why do you abolish a name which is to be found in the language of all civilized nations, and has acquired a right by prescription? Such an attempt is equally foolish and ineffectual. Every wise man will be apt to think that a name which is found in all languages as far back as we can trace them, is not without some use.

But there is an obvious reason why this degree of reason should have a name appropriated to it; and that is, that, in the greatest part of mankind, no other degree of reason is to be found. It is this degree that entitles them to the denomination of reasonable creatures. It is this degree of reason, and this only, that makes a man capable of managing his own affairs, and answerable for his conduct towards others. There is therefore the best reason why it should have a name appropriated to it.[5]

Nonetheless, the discussion of *Intellectual Powers* so often gives the impression that common sense is constituted of first principles in the form of propositions—self-evident truths, axioms, judgments of nature—that it is easy to overlook the fact that Reid's is a faculty psychology, and that common sense is the most fundamental of our faculties. The *curâ primâ* suggests nothing that is inconsistent with the *Intellectual Powers,* nor does it champion a view that is not to be found in this later work. But it does offer a simpler, if only because briefer, account of common sense. It unequivocally describes common sense as a faculty or power, and adding it to the corpus of Reid's published works will serve to remind us that this is Reid's view.

I have mentioned that ms. 2/III/8 is a sequel to Reid's *curâ primâ.* So too are mss. 2/III/9 and 2/III/10. There are, then, four of these manuscript discourses on common sense; some brief remarks about the later three may be helpful.

Ms. 2/III/8. This manuscript is nearly the length and size of 2/III/7. 16 pages, each approximately 15 × 19 cm, and each with a vertical margin of about 3 cm in which Reid has more often than not made additions or corrections. Each page contains between 350 and 625 words, depending on whether Reid's script is small or very small, and

5. *Intellectual Powers,* 1: 434, 425.

upon the number of interlineations and marginal additions. I estimate the manuscript to be about 8000 words long.

Reid has himself, in the opening paragraph of the third discourse (ms. 2/III/9), aptly summarized the content of this second paper:

In a former discourse I explained what I understand by principles of common sense or first principles, namely propositions which have their evidence in themselves and which do not derive their evidence from some other proposition upon which they rest and from which they are deduced or inferred. We have endeavoured to show that all knowledge got by reasoning whether probable or demonstrative must be grounded upon such principles. That it would contribute greatly to the stability and to the improvement of human knowledge, if the first principles upon which the various branches of it are grounded were pointed out and ascertained, which has not been done as far as I know in any branch of science but mathematics and natural philosophy. That although first principles do not admit of direct proof, being self evident, yet as we may by education or prejudice be led into errors concerning them, so nature has not left us destitute of means by which we may correct such errors.

Much of what Reid has to say in 2/III/8 he has repeated in Essay VI ("Of Judgment") of the *Intellectual Powers,* especially Chapter IV ("Of First Principles in General").

Ms. 2/III/9. This manuscript is approximately the same dimensions as the previous two (15 × 19 cm), but in its present incomplete form is only eight pages, or about 4000 words long. In the second paragraph of the manuscript Reid indicates that his intention is "to reduce to certain general heads or classes the principles of common sense upon which the various branches of human knowledge are built." His remarks on this topic correspond in large part to *Intellectual Powers,* Essay VI, Chapter V ("The First Principles of Contingent Truths"), so much so, in fact, that it seems likely that this manuscript was a first or early draft of the chapter.

Ms. 2/III/10. Although incomplete (Reid by a marginal note calls for a three-page insertion that has not been located) this paper is nearly as long as the *curâ primâ.* It is of the same general dimensions as are mss. 2/III/7, 8, and 9. Reid begins this fourth discourse, titled "Common Sense," by saying:

I come now to that which I conceive the most important branch of this subject, to attempt some enumeration of those principles of common sense which I conceive to be the chief foundations of science. This may seem a humble task.

This suggests an aim very much like that of ms. 2/III/9, and there is indeed a sense in which the two manuscripts duplicate one another—2/III/9 offers as first principles three contingent truths, while 2/III/10 offers these same three plus two others. There is little further similarity, however. Ms. 2/III/10 begins with a discussion of the difference between necessary and contingent truths that is quite unlike that of the third discourse of Essay VI, Chapter V of the *Intellectual Powers*. Furthermore, the manuscript version of the fifth contingent truth ("The existence of those bodies which we perceive by our senses and of their sensible qualities, is another first principle, which we may ascribe to those powers of the mind which we call our external senses.") differs significantly from that found in the *Intellectual Powers*. The two discussions of the principle are also significantly different. In the manuscript Reid is concerned with the operation of the senses insofar as these give us "immediate intelligence" of both the "sensible qualities of bodies" and of "the existence of the body of which these are qualities," and his discussion ranges over sensations, primary and secondary qualities, and disorders of the body known by means of painful sensations, topics taken up under different headings in the *Intellectual Powers*. It is hoped that this important manuscript can be published in the near future.

In preparing the *curâ primâ* for publication I have sought to provide a substantially accurate and easily readable version of Reid's manuscript—a working text, one might hazard to call it. To this end, all substantive alterations, however minor, are clearly marked, either by the customary square brackets or by an explanatory note. Further, Reid's deletions of potential philosophical significance have been recorded. Fortunately, although the manuscript is not a fair copy, there are, except for marginal and interlined additions, relatively few alterations of any sort, and only a handful that may be thought of philosophical interest. On the other hand, I have freely and silently modernized Reid's spelling, and silently added or modernized punctuation whenever this seemed justified by my concern to provide a text of use to the growing number of Reid interpreters, but I have not altered such apparently arbitrary inconsistencies as "reflection" and "reflexion" or "connection" and "connexion." A microfilm copy of the manuscript may be consulted through Mr. Colin McLaren, Archivist, King's College Library, University of Aberdeen.

Curâ primâ

Of Common Sense

There is no word more frequently used than *common sense* or whose meaning seems to be more generally understood. Every man conceives himself to be possessed of this faculty and therefore asks no definition of it. He thinks it would be an imputation on his understanding, to suppose him unacquainted with it.

A word so much used must have a meaning, though perhaps not so precise and well defined as a philosopher would desire. We may in some measure collect the meaning of this word from the use of it in common discourse.[6]

We do not attribute common sense to brutes nor do we expect to find it in infants or idiots; but in persons of mature age who have no natural defect we always expect that degree of discernment and of understanding which we call common sense.

We conceive this talent to be the gift of nature, and that it can never be acquired by education or training where nature has not bestowed it. It is indeed the ground work of education and it is impossible to train a man destitute of common sense to any art or science, or even to prudence in the ordinary conduct of life. And every man according to the degree of his natural understanding is capable by his own industry and by proper education, of making improvement in speculation or in the arts of life.

We conceive various degrees in what we call common sense. It fills up all the interval between idiocy on one hand and uncommon discernment and penetration on the other. And it is hardly possible to ascertain the line where one of these ends and the other begins.[7]

6. Following here is a further sentence, "*Common sense* seems to denote a certain degree of natural understanding that is intermediate between idiocy on one hand and an uncommon quickness and penetration on the other." This sentence is circled, probably to indicate deletion, for essentially the same claim is made in the fifth paragraph of the manuscript.

7. The paragraph which follows is circled, perhaps to indicate Reid intended it to be deleted. However, as it is not found elsewhere in the essay, I have included it in the main body of the text.

The province we assign to common sense is to perceive the obvious agreements and differences and relations of things and to judge in matters of common life that require no refinement or subtle[8] reasoning. Gross impropriety in conduct or absurdity in opinion shocks common sense.[9]

When men differ in opinion and enter into debate with one another, if there is no other authority in which both parties acquiese, the last appeal is always to common sense. Every one acknowledges the authority of this tribunal; and if any man were so impudent as to decline its authority, in any matter either of opinion or of conduct, every man of sense disdains to reason with him any farther. Nay it is impossible if he were ever so willing to carry reasoning farther. For all reasoning must be built upon first principles or axioms, and what are axioms but the dictates of common sense. "Amidst the different opinions started and maintained by several of the parties with great life and ingenuity, (says Lord Shaftesbury alluding to a conversation with some of his learned friends) one or other would every now and then take the liberty to appeal to common sense. Every one allowed the appeal and was willing to stand the trial. No one but was assured common sense would justify him. But when issue was joined, and the cause examined at the bar, there could be no judgment given. The parties however were no less forward in renewing their appeal, on the very next occasion which presented. No one would offer to call the authority of the court in question; till a gentleman whose good understanding was never yet brought in doubt desired the company very gravely that they would tell him what common sense was."[10]

8. Reid originally wrote "intricate," then stroked this out and wrote "subtle" above it. Further changes of this sort are indicated in the following manner: subtle] intricate.

9. In the margin of the first page of the manuscript (which here ends) Reid writes: "Omnes tacito quodam sensu, sine arte aut ratione, in artibus et rationibus rula et prava dijudicant. Cicero, *De Oratore*, Lib. 3." He is apparently citing from memory a portion of 3.50.195 which reads, "Omnes enim tacito quodam sensu sine ulla arte aut ratione quae sint in artibus ac rationibus recta ac prava dijudicant." (For everybody is able to discriminate between what is right and wrong in matters of art and proportion without having any theory of art or proportion of their own. Trans. E. W. Sutton and H. Rackham for the Loeb Classical Library edition of *De Oratore*, Cambridge, Mass., 1959–60.)

10. Anthony Ashley Cooper, Third Earl of Shaftesbury, in *Sensus Communis: An Essay on the Freedom of Wit and Humour in a Letter to a Friend*, Part I, Sec. VI. See *Characteristics of Men, Manners, Opinions, Times*, ed. J. M. Robertson, 2 vols. in 1 (Indianapolis: The Bobbs-Merrill Co., 1964), 1: 54–55. This work was first published in 1711. Reid has altered Shaftesbury's text and punctuation in entirely insignificant ways.

This ingenious author is the only one I remember to have met with who has seriously proposed the question, what common sense is? It were to be wished that he had entered more fully into this inquiry than he has done. He has indeed given some reasons and collected authorities of able critics to show that *sensus communis* in Juvenal and Horace signifies humanity, natural affection, or a just sense of the common rights of men. But if these poets made their *sensus communis* relate only to the qualities of the heart, it is most certain *common sense* in English writers is rather applied to the understanding. The passage I have quoted from this same author is sufficient to show this. His friends would not have appealed to common sense in their differences of opinion if they had not conceived that by common sense men might judge of opinions and distinguish what is true from what is false.[11]

Aristotle observed that the faculty by which we distinguish the objects of different senses, e.g., white from sweet, must be a faculty distinct both from sight and taste. Some of his followers gave the name of common sense to this faculty; some of them made it to be the intellectual faculty. They thought vision imperfect without this faculty. See Aguilonij *Opticorum*, Lib. 1, Prop. 91: Externus visus sine ope sensus communis perfectam visionem non producit.[12] This book of Aguilonius is well wrote for the time. The manner of vision is very fully explained according to the peripatetic doctrine. The fallacies of vision are treated more fully and judiciously than in any book I have

11. Reid by a marginal note instructs the reader to proceed to p. 18 of his manuscript. This page contains one line from a paragraph beginning on ms. p. 17, printed below as the final line of this essay, and the two paragraphs that follow immediately after the reference to this note.

12. Reid has placed an X after 91, and a corresponding X before a marginal entry of the cited sentence. Aquilonius is François Aguillon, Aiguillon, or Alguillon. He is said to have begun, in 1586, at the age of 20, to study theology and philosophy with the Jesuits at Douay and Antwerp, and to have been the first important Jesuit mathematician in the Low Countries, and the first writer to use the term "stereographic projection," although this concept dates from Hipparchus. There are brief articles on Aguillon in several early biographical dictionaries. See, for example, *The General and Biographical Dictionary*, ed. A. Chambers (vol. 1, 1812), or *Biographie Universelle*, ed. L. G. Michaud (vol. 1, 1811).

Reid is referring to Aguillon's *Opticorum ... philosophis iuxtà ac mathematicis vtiles* (Antverpiae, Ex officina Plantiniana, apud viduam et filios I. Moretti, 1613). That Reid refers to what must have been a very obscure work even in 1769 is not surprising given his life-long interest in mathematical topics and his close connection to the family of David Gregory, Savilian Professor of Astronomy at Oxford after 1691.

seen. The whole is in a mathematical form, after the manner of Gregory's *Astronomy*,[13] and contains a great number of lemmata purely mathematical, the rules of perspective demonstrated, and the orthographic and stereographic projection of the spherical great length. Elliptical compasses of the author's invention are described. The doctrine of sensible species is more fully handled and defended than in any book I have seen.

The generality of the peripatetics gave the name of common sense both to that power of the mind by which we distinguish the objects of different senses as white from sweet, but also to that power of the mind by which we know that we perceive. The last is by the moderns sometimes called consciousness, sometimes reflection.

Taking it for granted then that common sense signifies those natural powers of the understanding which distinguish men from brutes and idiots, we shall endeavour to point out some of these, together with the notions and principles of belief we acquire by means of them. I will not pretend to a complete enumeration. To make a full inventory of the furniture of the human understanding far exceeds my abilities. And those who have attempted this have so far fallen short in the execution that their successors ought to take warning from their example, not to make such bold pretences.

I take it for granted that brutes see and hear and feel and taste and smell much in the same manner that men do. There is not one of these senses which some other animal does not seem to have in greater perfection than man. They have *acquired* as well as *original* perceptions by the senses. It is more difficult to determine in what sense or in what degree they possess memory and imagination. That many ani-

---

13. Reid's reference is to David Gregory's *Astronomiae physicae et geometricae elementa*. Gregory (1661–1708), who taught mathematics at Edinburgh before becoming Savilian Professor of Astronomy at Oxford in 1691, was Reid's maternal uncle. Two other uncles, James and Charles, were Professors of Mathematics at, respectively, Edinburgh and St. Andrews, while his great-uncle James (1638–75), Professor of Mathematics at St. Andrews, is credited with inventing the reflecting telescope and with introducing Newton's physics into Scotland. These family connections may help to explain Reid's not inconsiderable mathematical interest and ability. A. Campbell Fraser, *Thomas Reid*, Famous Scots Series (Edinburgh, c. 1898), pp. 12–15, makes much of the connection. Among the manuscripts of Reid currently in possession of King's College, Aberdeen, there is one (ms. 3061/25), dated June 24, 1788, which begins "Some account of the family, of the Gregorys at Aberdeen . . ." This manuscript has only recently been added to the collection at Aberdeen.

mals know their own places of abode and become familiar with men who have been kind to them, that they avoid places where they have met with bad accidents, and learn in some degree from experience to distinguish their friends from their enemies, cannot I think be doubted. At the same time I see no reason to think that they have any distinct remembrance of the series of past events and of the order in which they happened. Events that have been conjoined in time or place come to be associated in their minds, so that when one occurs again they expect the other. Thus a dog once disciplined with a whip, expects the same discipline when he sees the whip presented again. A pointer knows when his master dresses himself for hunting, and shows his impatience for the game. If memory implied nothing more than a series of thoughts and passions similar to what had happened before, going on in a train when any one of them is excited by some present object, I cannot have any doubt of something of this kind in brutes. Thus a horse that is rid a dozen miles from home in a road he was formerly unacquainted with, will take the same road in his return without any direction, and seems to know that he is going home.[14] But it does not appear that he has any distinct remembrance of what is past or the interval of time since it happened. It produces its effect without reflexion, in the same manner as habits do with us. I suspect that brutes have not such distinct notions of the past, the present, and the future as men have, that those past events which have made a lasting impression upon their minds are not arranged according [to] the order of time in which they happened; I see no reason to think that they have any notions of priority or posteriority in past events, although it is evident that where events that are interesting have been conjoined in their experience, the appearance of one gives them an expectation of that which usually attends it.

But it is not my intention to determine with precision what degree

14. Reid apparently intended that the following marginal comment be inserted here as a note: "The sagacity of a horse in returning by the road he came is very remarkable. If he returns the same day or within a day or two, he will know his road as well as most men would do in day light and much better in the dark. Yet objects do not succeed each other in this case in the order they did before but in the reverse. I suspect smell is a great aid to horses in finding the road and could mention some stories to confirm this. Although the horse may be directed partly by smell when it is dark, yet I cannot think but that he is also directed by sight in returning by the road he came. Is there not here a power of tracing the preceeding events in an inverted order?"

of these faculties is to be found in brutes; nor indeed is it in my power. It is enough to observe in general that it does not appear to us that either brutes or infants distinguish intervals of time or apply any measure to it like that of hours, days, or months: And if this be really the case, what we call memory in them must be far inferior and very different from memory in men.

Men could have but very confused and imperfect notions even of the objects of sense without recollection and reflection upon what their senses have presented to them. Objects that are complex cannot be presented to the senses all at once. We must by reflexion and memory put together the parts that are seen or heard successively in order to have a distinct notion of the whole, and of the parts of which it is made up, and their relations and connections. A dog may be taught to turn a jack, but it is probable he has no distinct notion of the machine, nor is ever capable of acquiring it. A child is in the same state in infancy, though he can see and handle every part of the machine, he has no distinct notion of the whole till his rational faculties begin to open; then it becomes a new subject of study to him and he gets a notion of it quite different from that which he had when a child, and a notion which the dog is never capable of acquiring.

From this instance and innumerable others of the same kind which might be given I apprehend that the notions that men have even of the objects of sense are extremely different from those which brutes acquire of the same objects. The order, composition, and connexion of the parts is not discerned by brutes or infants; these are not objects of sense, though they are commonly taken to be so, but of higher powers of the mind, which brutes never acquire, and which children have not in infancy.

I conceive therefore that brutes do not measure time, nor view past events in a connected series and order as men do. That in complex objects of sense they do not perceive order, connexion, and composition in the parts nor any relation to an end.

In the next place it does not appear that brutes have any notions of number or proportion. Those who have endeavoured to trace our ideas to the two sources of sensation and reflexion have considered number as an idea both of sensation and reflexion. That number belongs to objects of sense is very true. There are twelve windows in the front of the house which I just now look at, and these are all objects of sight but I think it may be truly said that their number is not an object of sight. A dog or a child can see them all as well as I and yet cannot number them nor form any notion of the number twelve. A number is a whole made up of parts. And it is impossible to conceive a number without conceiving the relation that the parts have to the whole and to each other. All the objects numbered may be perceived without perceiving these relations of whole and parts, but their number cannot. Children proceed very slowly in acquiring the notion of number and even after they have learned to distinguish the singular from the plural it is commonly a long time before they can go beyond three. We are told that some nations are so rude as to have no names for numbers beyond three. And it is pretty remarkable that in all languages, the flexion of words with regard to number is extremely limited. We find a singular and a plural in all languages; in many we find a singular, a dual, and a plural, but in none as far as I know have we any more numbers. It is probable that in the origin of language unity and number were distinguished by the flexion of words before they were distinguished by the abstract names *one, two, three, etc.,* for the abstract names would have made such flexion altogether unnecessary. Yet this flexion, which was probably the earliest way of distinguishing numbers goes no farther than three, so that when this flexion was contrived mankind seem to have been in the same state as we would be if we had only three names to express number, to wit *one, two, many.*

Whatever may be in this the distinguishing of numbers and having a distinct notion of them requires an effort of understanding in children which is much later than the perfect use of all their external senses; and I do not see that the idea of number can with any propriety be called an idea of sensation. I hear the clock strike ten, and perhaps I attend not to the number of strokes but to some unusual sound in the bell; in this case although my ears are intent I do not perceive the number struck; that is a kind of perception different from mere hearing, and the faculty of hearing may be where this faculty of numbering is not.

As the objects of sense perception must go before bare conception, no man could conceive colour or sound if he had never before perceived these things.[15] It is so likewise with regard to number; we first perceive number in objects; afterwards we can conceive it when we do not perceive it. And as number is capable of endless composition, when we have perceived a small number in objects we can in imagination add to it and conceive a greater and a greater still, until we learn to comprehend great numbers.

I see four men conversing together upon the street, a dog sees all that I see, he sees the men as I do, his eyes are as good as mine but he perceives not their number as I do, nor has he that faculty by which I perceive their number. I see the men therefore with my eyes. I perceive their number by my understanding or common sense. If there are 50 or an hundred men I perceive a multitude, but I do not perceive their number. It is necessary in this case to count them one by one; this is an operation that requires memory as well as immediate perception; and probably our memory would hardly serve us to count such a number, until we affix names or signs to that number and all that are below it.

The perception we have of number in objects seems to be confined within very narrow bounds. When I see a company of soldiers in a rank, I do not see their number. To find their number I must count them one by one; or perhaps I count them by threes, fours, or fives and sum up the whole. This is an operation that requires some time. It is not bare perception. But when I see only two, three, four, or five men I perceive their number immediately. I am not conscious in this case that I count them. The number is perceived instantaneously. Men immediately perceive number in objects when their number does not exceed four or five; they can count their number when it is great. Brutes can do neither. There is hardly any idea more abstract than that of number. *Number* being an adjective some substantive must be understood, and when it is used abstractly the substantive is [a] thing.

---

15. Reid first wrote: "As objects of sense perception must go before conception, and no man could conceive colour or sound if he had never perceived these things by his senses." He makes several insertions (italicized in what follows) and one deletion, leaving: "As *in the* objects of sense perception must go before *bare* conception, and no man could conceive colour or sound if he had never *before* perceived these things." The text I have prepared omits "in" and "and."

Two, three, that is, two things, three things; what is more abstract than this?[16]

The greatest degree of idiocy in men is no way better discerned than by the want of this power of numbering. If a man can count the number of halfpence in a shilling and divide them into two, three, or four equal parts, he is not a changeling. On the other hand a man come to years of understanding, and living among civilized men who cannot do this, must be accounted an idiot or next thing to it. Yet I doubt if a single instance can be given of any brute animal that does so much.

Unity has such a necessary relation to number that it seems to be impossible to conceive one without conceiving the other. When I see three men together the notion of unity and number is suggested at the same time, nor does it seem possible that one of these can go before the other. Yet neither unity nor [the] number three can with any propriety be called an idea of sensation.

Mr. Locke conceives that every object of sense and every idea our understanding is employed about brings the idea of unity along with it, and that it is by repeating the idea of unity that we get the idea of number. This may be true in some sense with regard to those who are grown up and in whom the ideas of unity and number are familiar. But that we have the idea of unity before we have the idea of number does not appear evident to me. I beg the reader to attend to his notion of unity and reflect a little upon it. For my part when I attend to it most carefully it appears to have such a relation to number, that as number cannot be conceived without unity so neither can unity be conceived by one who has no conception of number. Unity and number like little and great are relative to each other. It cannot be said that the idea of little is before the idea of great or that the idea of great is before the idea of little. In like manner the notion of simplicity cannot go before the notion of composition or the notion of cause

16. This paragraph is found in the margin between pages six and seven of Reid's manuscript. There is no indication as to where it should be placed or whether it should be treated as text or note. I have located it here as part of the text on the debatable grounds that it seems to fit best here. Page six of the manuscript ends about two-thirds of the way through the preceding paragraph: ". . . this is an operation that requires memory/as well as immediate perception . . ."

before that of effect.[17] A number is that which is made by the repetition of units and a unit is that whose repetition makes a number. This is the simplest notion I can form of a unit and this notion supposes that of number.

One may have the idea of a simple object without having any idea of its simplicity. And it may truly be said that the idea of simplicity is not prior to that of composition. The notions of simplicity and composition are relatively opposed; each implies a negation of the other, and one cannot be conceived without the other.

The same thing may be said with regard to the notions of unity and number.[18] One may have the idea of an individual object without having any idea of its unity. The notion of unity and that of number are relatively opposed and the conception of one involves that of the other.

Locke says that the idea of unity is brought to us along with every idea whether of sensation or reflexion. If this is so one would think it should neither be an idea of sensation nor of reflexion, but an idea which accompanies other ideas of both kinds. This however is inconsistent with a fundamental principle of Locke's system that all our ideas are reducible to these two kinds of sensation and of reflexion. If he had said that our ideas are either those of sensation or reflexion or such as accompany ideas of sensation and reflexion he would have come nearer the truth. It is plain that children have the same ideas of sensation unaccompanied with the notions of unity and number, but after they are grown to years of understanding they perceive number in sensible objects which they did not perceive before.

Number is a thing *sui generis*. It is neither mode, substance, nor relation. Were there no universals there could be no such thing as number; an individual can never make a number. We therefore generalize as soon as we have any notion of number.

The operations of mind which fall under the province of common sense are chiefly these:

---

17. Following this sentence but stroked out: "The conception of unity excludes the conception of number."

18. Reid has inserted "the notions of" interlineally, but so as to make this sentence read: ". . . with regard the notions of to unity and number."

1. Distinguishing. 2. Generalizing. 3. Discovering. 4. Reflection.
   5. Judging. Reasoning.
2. Comparing. Numbering.
3. Classing $\left\{ \begin{array}{l} \text{Dividing} \\ \text{Defining} \end{array} \right.$ Compounding.
4. Judging.[19]

    1. Distinguishing in the same object things that are different. There is hardly any object either of the senses or understanding which we may not perceive to have various attributes, affections, or things belonging to it, which we can distinguish from one another and from the whole object. Thus in the page upon which I write I distinguish four sides, four corners, a certain length and breadth, and a certain colour; I have a clear conception of each of these as things belonging to this page. I distinguish them easily from each other and from the object to which they belong. This distinction of objects into the various attributes that belong to them is a kind of intellectual analysis, and is the foundation of most of the operations that are proper to us as rational and intelligent beings. When we attend to any object we enumerate as it were in our own minds the various attributes which we perceive to belong to it, and while we remember these we have a distinct[20] notion of it. We can then think and speak and reason concerning it clearly and distinctly.[21]

    It is only by means of such an analysis of objects that we can describe them to others. For what is description but an enumeration of the obvious attributes of the thing described. Brutes, idiots, and children

---

    19. This summary of the operations of the mind is found in the margin of page nine of the manuscript. As I have already indicated, Reid's discussion is of distinguishing, comparing, classing, and judging, in just that order. The text initially read:
    1. The perceiving the obvious relations of things.
    2. Distinguishing in the same object things that are different.
    3. Observing in different objects things that are common.
    4. Our natural and intuitive judgments about things which are not grounded upon reasoning but must be the foundation of all reasoning.
    5. Reflection upon what has past in our own minds.
    20. a distinct] a clear and distinct.
    21. Following this paragraph is another that Reid has apparently marked for deletion by inscribing a large X through it. The deleted text reads: "There are some objects of the mind that have certain attributes from which all the rest may be deduced by reasoning. A triangle, for instance, or any other mathematical figure has certain attributes that are included in its definition. All the other attributes or properties belonging to it follow necessarily from those that are contained in the definition."

are incapable either of describing objects that have been presented to them or of understanding any description that is given of them. They have a gross conception of the whole but cannot distinguish the parts and take them in detail. The first effect of a new object is much the same upon a man of sense and an idiot. This effect naturally expresses itself by an unmeaning stare. They feel some uncommon effect from the whole object but give no attention to particulars. The idiot continues in this state and makes no farther progress. But in the other the powers of common sense are immediately roused. The object is surveyed with an active and prying attention. The very features of the fact now discover a great difference between the idiot and the man. In the first we see only the surprise that was occasioned by the new object dying away gradually as it becomes more familiar. In the last we see this surprise quickly succeeded [by] an eager and active effort of the understanding to examine and analyze the strange object, to survey every part separately and to discover its relation to the other parts and to the whole. There is hardly any object so simple that it has not various parts, or ingredients or various attributes or relations to other things that are obvious [to] the human understanding. These are not discerned and distinguished at once, and in the twinkling of an eye as objects of sense are. It takes time to unravel them, and requires the exercise of a power superior to the outwards senses; a power which we do not find in brutes or infants,[22] and to which I think we give the name of common sense. There is an intelligent attention to objects and survey of them, which is necessary to our having a distinct and accurate notion of them. This attention is not found in brutes. This cool intellectual attention must be distinguished from that which is produced by some passion or affection regarding the object. A man in love may stare at his mistress for an hour together without discerning blemishes which an indifferent spectator will per-

---

22. The remainder of this sentence and the next are partially circled, though for what purpose Reid does not indicate. Given his practice of using a part of one manuscript when preparing another or when giving lectures, he may only mean to make this text easily noticeable when so used. The situation is complicated by the fact that most of this long paragraph (from the top of manuscript page 10, ". . . the parts and take them in detail," to mid-page 11, ". . . to each other and to the whole.") is marked by a vertical line in the margin, and twice labelled "A." This clearly suggests an intention to use the material elsewhere, but I am unable to conjecture where this might be.

ceive in half a minute.[23] A man who has not thrown off the prejudices of the nursery and who thinks he sees a spectre in the dark gives great attention to it, but it is not a cool intellectual attention. His attention serves only to feed his panic, not to enlighten his understanding. His intellectual powers lie dormant, and therefore when he has stared ever so long he has got no clearer or more distinct notion of the object. If he can lay aside his fear the intellectual powers immediately step forth and examine its length and breadth, its colour and figure and distance, of which while his panic lasted he could form no distinct judgment though his eyes were open all the time, and gave him all the information that the mere external sense could give. When the eye of sense is open but that of common sense shut by a panic or any violent passion that engrosses the mind, we then see things confusedly and probably much in the same manner as brutes, idiots and children do. We observed that this operation of distinguishing in the same object things that are different requires time. Hence objects whose appearance is instantaneous and of no continuance, leave a very confused and indistinct notion of themselves in the mind. A flash of lightning for instance gives us no time to attend to it and therefore we can seldom tell whence it comes or whither it goes. The mere perceptions of the external sense are as complete in the first instant of their existence as ever, nor do they receive any perfection by being continued. But a distinct and accurate notion even of a sensible object is never got alone; it is the effect of continued calm attention and survey, by which we observe its various parts and attributes and their relations to each other and to the whole. I conceive for this reason that brutes and children have no distinct and accurate notions even of the simplest figures, such as of a triangle, square, or circle, or of a right line. We never see brutes attempt to delineate figures or to use tools. And when children do this, it discovers the dawn of reason.

All our distinct and accurate notions seem to be formed by means of this power of distinguishing the several things belonging to an object and collecting them into one whole.[24]

---

23. half a minute.] at a glance.
24. An "X" here refers to a marginal addition: "Many of these Locke has not touched. Some of them he has obscured and distorted by endeavouring to reduce them to ideas of sensation and reflection." Before this remark is another, now stroked out: "Such as subject and accident, whole and parts, genus and species."

2. By that faculty which we call common sense we compare objects that are presented to us and discern various affections and relations belonging to them, things concerning them, such as identity or diversity, number, similitude, contrariety, proportion, sum, difference, quantity, quality, time, place, genus and species, subject and accident, whole and parts and innumerable other relations.[25] We have an immediate conviction of our own identity as far back as we remember, but we cannot prove it. It is a first truth which we must take upon trust. Identity supposes continued existence, and no man can prove his continued existence. The notion of identity is various according to the subjects to which it is applied. It is then taken most strictly when applied to substances that are indivisible, as to men or thinking substances. In these there seems to be no medium between perfect identity and perfect diversity nor any different degrees of one or of the other. But in material substances which are in a constant flux the limits between identity and diversity cannot be fixed but by the custom of language. A regiment that has never been broke may be called the same after a century, but it may also be called different.

Locke seems to have been led into some strange paradoxes concerning personal identity, by not distinguishing between what constitutes personal identity, and what proves or evidences it.[26] Men are

---

25. At the end of this sentence Reid expands his list, and also repeats himself: "causes and effects and means and end, matter, form, action, passion, subject and accident, whole and parts." The text here is exceptionally small and difficult to decipher as it is interlined thus:

> such as identity or diversity, number, similitude, contrariety, proportion, sum, difference, quantity, quality, time, place, genus and species, subject and accident,
>
> We have an immediate conviction of our own identity as far back as we
>
> whole and parts and innumerable other relations. Causes and effects and means and end,
>
> remember, but we cannot prove it. It is a first truth which we must take
>
> matter, form, action, passion, subject and accident, whole and parts
>
> upon trust. Identity supposes continuous existence, and no man can
>
> prove his continued existence. The notion of identity is various.

Such interlining is to be found in other of Reid's manuscripts, and seldom presents any great difficulty of interpretation provided the text can be made out.

26. between personal identity, and what proves or evidences it.] between personal identity considered in itself, and the way in which men judge of it.

led to conceive the thinking principle in man to be one and the same from his birth to his grave. The identity of the body is not that which constitutes the identity of the man, but that which shows it. If it is the same body we think it certainly follows that it is the same man because we have never any suspicion that the thinking principle belonging to the same body is changed and another put in its place. But if we should be desired to suppose for argument's sake that the thinking principle in Socrates' body was annihilated or removed and another thinking principle substituted in its place to animate the body, I conceive no man would conceive Socrates before and after this change to be the same person, or that the actions done by the first Socrates should or could in equity be imputed to the second. Supposing the second thinking principle to be inspired with a fallacious conviction, such as Mr. Locke calls consciousness of his having done all the good and bad actions that the first did, no man can show this to be impossible. Would this make him really guilty of those bad actions or give him the merit of the good? By no means. This is like *Crede quod habes et habes.*[27] A fallacious consciousness or memory is only a fallacious opinion. And nothing seems more absurd than that a man's having a false opinion of his having been guilty of a crime twenty years ago should really make him guilty.

When a man speaks of his own identity or self no doubt he attributes to himself what ever he remembers to have done; he has a full conviction that the person that remembers and the person that did the thing remembered is one and the same, but this conviction when it is false does not make them to be the same person.

What proof does a judge require of the identity of a person? No other than that which proves the identity of his body. Can we infer from this that human laws make personal identity to consist in the identity of the body? By no means; human laws only suppose that the body and the person or moral agent are conjoined for life and that where one is the other is also, although they be not one and the same thing. ———How does a man satisfy himself that he is the same identical person, who at such a time was whipped at school? He is conscious of it (to use Locke's phrase), that is he remembers that he got this very whipping. This is all the evidence he asks and he thinks it absurd to ask any other. Does it follow from this that his identity

27. "Believe that you have it, and you have it."

really lies in this consciousness? By no means. It follows only that he thinks this consciousness or memory cannot deceive him, that this consciousness and identity are never separated, not that they are one and the same thing. We often infer identity from similitude. When I prove my property in a horse by the oaths of my neighbours, they swear this is the horse that was stolen from me. How do they know this? Because he has all the marks of him, that is, is perfectly like him. Does it follow from this that the identity of the horse consists, or is believed to consist in perfect similitude? By no means. It is only believed that no two horses are so like but that one may be distinguished from the other. Therefore perfect similitude, though it by no means constitutes identity, yet in horses and other domestic animals as well as in men it is thought a sufficient proof of it.

Identity supposes continued and uninterrupted existence; nor is it possible to conceive the one without the other. What is once annihilated, cannot be recreated, though something perfectly like to it may.

The notions of identity and diversity are simple and not to be defined but they are perfectly clear and distinct. Philosophers have perplexed themselves only by endeavouring to resolve and analyze them, when they are incapable of any analysis. Had not Locke attempted to resolve identity into ideas of sensation and reflection he would have found no difficulty in it, nor would he have run into such paradoxes concerning it.

When a man compares an object that now exists with an object that existed some time ago, and the question is put whether they are one and the same or different, every man of common understanding perfectly comprehends the meaning of this question. By attempting to explain it you only darken it. And you may as well attempt to explain what is meant by one quantity being equal to another or being greater or less. Every man has these notions from common sense. Not from sensation or reflexion. Neither of these can give us the notion of continued existence, consequently not [that] of identity.

There is indeed another application of the word *identity* which is not so plain. That is when it is applied not to the same individual existing at different periods, but to some attribute of different individuals that are affirmed to have the same nature, the same properties or any thing in common. As when we say, the natural rights of all men are the same.

I will not undertake to determine whether brutes may have some confused notion of identity or of similitude. I think it more probable that they have not and that they never think either of similitude or identity. But I think we may affirm that every man of common understanding has distinct notions of both, that they are simple notions and cannot with any propriety be called ideas either of sensation or of reflection.

We may I think affirm that brutes have not the notion of contrariety which is a simple notion of a very peculiar nature. One substance cannot be contrary to another as Aristotle long ago observed. All contrariety therefore is in accidents. And the things that are contrary must be of the same genus. Love is contrary to hatred, but both are affections of the mind. Pleasure is contrary to pain but both are sensations of the mind. Virtue is contrary to vice but both are habits. Giving to taking away both actions. Truth and falsehood, the genus predication, but both must be propositions.[28] Propositions that are contrary have always the same subject and predicate. East is contrary to west, time past to time future, debt to riches,[29] addition to subtraction, multiplication to division. Contrariety in sensible qualities is not so manifest. Heat and cold seem to be contrary only in so far as one is an agreeable, the other a disagreeable, sensation, or in so far as they produce contrary effects. Moist and dry are not properly contraries, but as they produce contrary effects. Between most contraries there is, as it were, a middle point where one begins and the other ends. And the extremes may be more or less removed from this limit. Yet this is not the case in truth and falsehood, for every proposition is either true or false and there are no degrees in truth and falsehood.

These are axioms with regard to contrariety which every man of common sense discerns, and of which brutes and idiots seem to have no knowledge. Are there not some things that are not contrary in their own nature but only in some relation they bear to a third which lies as it were between them? To one who lives between London and York those cities have a contrary position. But to one who lives to the

28. Some of this material is added interlineally, which no doubt accounts for its incompleteness and awkwardness. Reid seems clearly to mean: "Giving is contrary to taking away, but both are actions. Truth and falsehood are contrary, but both of the genus predication, and both must be propositions."

29. Reid has added "credit" above "riches" but has not stroked out the latter.

south or to the north of both they have the same position. To an inhabitant of the earth Venus is an inferior planet and Mars a superior. But to an inhabitant of Mercury both Venus and Mars are superior planets. A cave that feels cold in summer may feel warm in winter, things being cold or hot not absolutely in their own nature but in relation [to] something that is of a middle temperature.

The attributes and relations of things of which every man of common understanding can easily obtain a clear and distinct discernment are innumerable.[30] To enumerate them would be impossible; even to reduce them to general heads and classes would be very difficult; and should any man attempt this there would probably be a great many left out of the account. Let us however take notice of some general classes that may show what a prodigious variety of furniture is to be found in the human mind which the brutes do not share in.

The first class we may call grammatical, [and] contains such as these: noun, pronoun, preposition, and all the other parts of speech with their subdivisions; the numbers and cases of nouns and participles; the voices, moods, tenses, numbers and persons of verbs; [the] sentence with all the divisions and subdivisions of it. In a word, the whole materials of grammar, which men of common sense easily comprehend when they are explained to them, but infants and brutes have not the least conception of them. Grammar comprehends a vast number of notions so simple that they admit of no logical definition, so abstract and spiritual, if I may use that term, that there is no reason to think that brutes or idiots have the least conception of them.

We might easily show that there is in like manner a large class of notions in every other science easily comprehended by common sense. There are notions rhetorical, poetical, logical, metaphysical, political, economical, physical, mathematical, medical, chemical, theological, commercial, nautical. There are notions proper to every art and manufacture.[31] We shall find the terms of art, in each of these sciences and professions, to express some quality, attribute or relation of the things they are severally conversant about, which is founded in the nature of the things and is easily discovered by those whose attention is turned to that subject. We shall find many of these notions so simple as not to admit of a logical definition. There is I believe no science

---

30. The discussion of classing appears to begin with this sentence.
31. every art and manufacture.] every mechanical art and mystery.

wherein so few terms are used that admit not of definition as mathematics; yet we may find several terms even in that science which no mathematician attempts to define—such as quantity or magnitude, greater, less, equal, sum, difference, unity, number. Other terms they have attempted to define with bad success such as a right line, an angle, ratio.

Perhaps it may be thought that the notions of a line, angle, triangle, square and the like are ideas which we have directly by our senses, and consequently, which brutes or infants may have as well as we.[32] We shall consider carefully how far this is true, and that will enable us in other like cases to distinguish between those notions which we have by the bare external senses and those which require the exercise of some higher power.

First then I acknowledge that it is by sense that we have our first notions of extension and figure, and that if we had not the senses of sight and touch we could never by all our other faculties acquire the least notion of extension or any of its modifications. Extended and figured bodies are immediate objects of sight and touch. They may be seen and felt as clearly by brutes and infants as by men. And if such objects had never been seen and felt by men, they could never have formed to themselves the notions of lines, angles, triangles and the other notions of a geometrician. All this I think must be acknowledged. And if no more be meant by Locke and other philosophers when they affirm that all our simple notions concerning extension and matter, their modifications, attributes and relations, are ideas of sensation presented by our senses, their meaning may be true. But it is very improperly expressed. For we must observe in the second place, that the notions which we have immediately by our senses are neither simple nor are they accurate and well defined. They are gross and indistinct, a *rudis indigestaque moles*,[33] which in the furnace of common sense is[34] digested, analysed, the heterogeneous parts separated and the simple ingredients which before lay hid in the common mass are distinctly discerned.

In the notions of a geometrician we may distinguish between the matter and the form of those notions. The materials are supplied by

32. The discussion of judging appears to begin with this sentence.
33. "A coarse mass, void of order." The phrase is from Ovid, *Metamorphosis* 1.7.
34. which in the furnace of common sense is] which being by our rational powers

the senses but in a rude unformed state. By our rational powers we educe from these rude materials many elegant and accurate forms, some simple, others more complex. Geometrical[35] ideas may be said to be derived from the ideas of sense much in the same way as the Venus de Medicis might be said to be derived from the block of marble which the artist used in that elegant statue. The matter indeed was derived from the block but the form in which all the elegance and beauty dwells was derived from the artist. If any man should affirm that the man who possessed[36] this block before it came into the artisan's[37] hand was possessed of the statue,[38] there is some kind of truth in this, but it is a very improper way of speaking. And I conceive the impropriety is no less when we affirm that the ideas of a geometrician are presented to[39] us by the senses.[40] Geometrical[41] notions are modifications of extension, as the Venus de Medicis is a modification of marble. But as one who has the marble may yet be incapable of producing this modification of it, so brutes and infants may have a notion of extension while they are incapable of giving it those modifications which the geometrician does. Mr. Hume has not attended to this in what he has said against mathematical notions. We shall endeavour to illustrate all this by a particular instance.

A tetrahedron or a cube may be seen and felt by a child as well as by a man. Both have the senses of seeing and of touch in equal perfection and therefore the man can neither see nor feel more in these bodies than the child does, and consequently if upon contemplating these bodies he discerns any thing in them which the child does not discern nor is capable of discerning, this must be done by some faculty which the child cannot yet exercise.[42]

35. Geometrical] Mathematical

36. Reid has added "man who possessed" above "proprietor of" but has not lined out the latter.

37. This word is added between lines and is unclear. From what can be made out "artisans" seems more likely than "artists."

38. Reid has written "was possessed of the statue" twice.

39. presented to] Reid first wrote "included in," then "derived" (for "derived from"?), then "presented to."

40. The remainder of this paragraph is a marginal addition which seems intended as part of the text.

41. Reid here first wrote, it appears, "The ideas of a geometrician." He then deleted "The ideas of a" and altered "geometrician" to "geometrical."

42. child cannot yet exercise.] child has not yet acquired.

First then the man when he considers attentively the cube for instance will easily distinguish the body from the surface which terminates it. The child can make no such distinction. Secondly, the man can perceive that this surface is made up of six planes all equal to one another. The child does not perceive this. 3. The man perceives that each of these plane surfaces has four sides and four angles, that all the sides are equal and all the angles are equal. The opposite sides of the several planes and the opposite planes are parallel. It will surely be granted that common sense will enable a man to discern all this in a cube which is presented to him and which he makes an object of contemplation; and that by the same faculty he may give a general name such as that of a square to all planes that are terminated by four equal sides and four equal angles; that he may likewise give a general name such as that of a cube to every solid figure that is terminated by six equal squares. It will likewise be granted that the child even when he can see and feel perfectly is not capable of any of these operations about the cube which we have attributed to the man. There is not the least reason to think that a child of a year old has the mathematical notions of a surface, a solid, of lines and angles, of a square and a cube, of parallelism and equality. Yet he has the notion of a cube which the senses give, and from which the man by his common sense educes all the mathematical notions I have mentioned, in like manner as Phidias from a block of marble would educe a statue. In the idea of the child lines, planes and angles, surface and solid lie mingled, as it were, in one indistinguished heap. The idea of the child may be clear in some sense, and it is so when the object is seen in a good light and with a good eye, but it is neither simple nor distinct; it is not simple because it has many ingredients of different natures such as lines, surfaces and solid, and various positions of these lines and surfaces. It is not distinct because the different ingredients of which it is made up are not distinguished from one another, so that he cannot with any propriety be said to have a notion of any one of them but only of a certain medley that is made up of the whole. Such is the notion that the child has of the cube and such is the notion that the senses give of it. If we consider on the other hand the notion which the man has of it after working upon it by his intellectual powers it will appear to be far different. He separates the different ingredients that lay confused and forms a distinct notion of each. Thus he obtains the simple notions of a line, a plane,[43] a solid, an angle, a square. And his idea or notion of the cube is a certain regular composition of these known ingredients put together in a known order. So that he has a perfectly distinct notion of the whole and of the simple ingredients that compound it, and he can convey this notion to another person who has the same faculties with himself.

There are notions of sensible objects which are gross and indistinct; there are others that are distinct and scientific. The former may be had from sense but the last cannot be attained even in objects of sense without that degree of understanding which we call common sense.

43. a plane] a surface.

Bibliography

1. Aguilar, J. A. Ventosa. *El Sentido Común en las Obras Filosóficas del P. Claude Buffier, S.I.* Barcelona: Seminario Conciliar, 1957.
2. d'Alembert. *Sur la destruction des Jésuites en France.* Par un auteur désintéressé. Paris: 1765.
3. Allard, E. "Die Angriffe gegen Descartes und Malebranche im Journal de Trévoux 1701–1715." *Abhanlungen zur Philosophie und ihrer Geschichte,* 43 (1914): 1–58.
4. Alletz, Pons Augustin. *L'esprit des Journalistes de Trévoux ou Morceaux précieux de littérature répandus dans les Mémoires pour l'Avancement des Sciences et des Beaux-Arts depuis leur origine en 1701 jusqu'en 1762.* 3 vols. Paris: de Hansy, 1771.
5. Angelis, Enrico de. *L'idea di buon senso, Osservazioni su alcuni scritti comparsi tra il 1584 ed il 1960.* Rome: Edizioni dell'Ateneo, 1964.
6. Ardley, Gavin. *Berkeley's Renovation of Philosophy.* The Hague: Martinus Nijhoff, 1968.
7. d'Argens (Jean-Baptiste), Marquis. *La philosophie du bon sens ou Réflexions philosophiques sur l'incertitude des connaissances humaines à l'usage des cavaliers et du beau sexe.* London: Aux dépens de la compagnie, 1737.
8. Armogathe, Jean-Robert. *Une secte-fantôme au dix-huitième siècle: les égoïstes,* Mémoire de Maîtrise. Paris: La Sorbonne, 1970.
9. Bachman, Albert. *Censorship in France from 1715 to 1750: Voltaire's Opposition.* Institute of French Studies. New York: Columbia University, 1934.
10. Bacon, Francis. *The Works of Francis Bacon,* edited by Basil Montagu. New ed., vol. 14. London: William Pickering, 1831.
11. Bailly, A. *Grammaire générale et raisonnée de Port-Royal suivie de la partie de la logique de Port-Royal qui traite des propositions, des remarques de Duclos de l'Académie Française, du supplément à la grammaire générale de Port-Royal, par l'Abbé Fromant et publié sur la meilleure édition originale, avec une introduction historique.* Geneva: Slatkine Reprints, 1968.
12. Barker, S. F., and Beauchamp, T. L., eds. *Thomas Reid: Critical Interpretations.* Philadelphia: Philosophical Monographs, 1976.
13. Beausobre, Louis de. *Le pyrrhonisme raisonnable.* Berlin: 1755.

14. Belaval, Yvon. *Histoire de la philosophie. De la Renaissance à la révolution kantienne.* Paris: Encyclopédie de la Pléiade, 1973.

15. Bernard, H. "Diderot et l'Encyclopédie." *Archivium Historicum Societatis Jesu,* 21 (1952): 176–81.

16. Bernard, P. "Claude Buffier." *Dictionnaire de théologie catholique.* Paris: Letouzey & Ané, 1924.

17. Bertrand, A. "Claude Buffier." *Biographie universelle ancienne et moderne,* edited by J.F. Michaud. New ed. Graz: Akademische Druck & Verlagsanstalt, 1966–70.

18. Bouillier, Francisque. *Histoire de la philosophie cartésienne.* 3rd ed., vol. 7. Paris: Delagrave, 1868.

19. Boutroux, Emile. *De l'influence de la philosophie écossaise sur la philosophie française, extrait de la Revue Française d'Edinbourg.* Edinburgh: Williams & Norgate, 1897.

20. Boutwood, Arthur. "Reid and the Philosophy of Common Sense." *Proceedings of the Aristotelian Society for the Systematic Study of Philosophy,* 3, (1895–96): 154–71.

21. Bracken, H. M. *Early Reactions to Berkeley's Immaterialism 1710–1733.* Rev. ed. The Hague: Martinus Nijhoff, 1965.

22. – "Innate Ideas—Then and Now." *Dialogue* 4, no. 3 (December 1967): 334–46.

23. Bréhier, Emile. *Histoire de la philosophie.* Vol. 2, *Philosophie moderne.* Paris: Presses Universitaires de France, 1950.

24. Bryson, Gladys. *Man and Society: The Scottish Inquiry of the Eighteenth Century.* Princeton: Princeton University Press, 1945.

25. Buffier, Claude. *Cours de sciences, sur des principes nouveaux et simples; pour former le langage, l'esprit et le coeur, dans l'usage ordinaire de la vie.* Paris: Guillaume Cavalier et P.F. Giffart, 1732.

26. – *Difficultez proposées à M. l'Archevêque de Rouen par un ecclésiastique de son diocèse, sur divers endroits des livres, et surtout de la théologie dogmatique du P. Alexandre, dont il recommande la lecture à ses curez.* 1696.

27. – *Elemens de métaphisique a la portée de tout le monde.* Paris: Pierre François Giffart, 1725.

28. – *Examen des préjugez vulgaires, pour disposer l'esprit à juger sainement de tout.* Paris: Chez Mariette, 1704.

29. – *Examen des préjugez vulgaires, pour disposer l'esprit à juger sainement et précisément de tout, nlle edition considérablement augmentée avec l'Analise et l'Usage Moral ou Litéraire de chaque sujet.* Imprimé à Evreux. Paris: Chez Pierre François Giffart et la Veuve Mongé, 1725.

30. – *First truths, and the origin of our opinions explained with an inquiry into the sentiments of moral philosophers relative to our primary notions of things to which is prefixed a detection of the Plagiarism, Concealment and Ingratitude of Doctors Reid, Beattie, Oswald.* London: Johnson, 1780.

31. – *La doctrine du sens commun, ou traité des premières vérités et de la source de nos jugements suivi d'une exposition des preuves les plus sensibles de la véritable religion.* Par le P.B.D.L.C.D.J. *Ouvrage qui contient le développement primitif du principe de l'autorité générale adopté par M. de La Mennais comme l'unique fondement de la certitude. Pour servir d'appendice au Tome II de l'Essai sur l'Indifference en matière de religion.* Avignon: Chez Séguin aîné, 1822.

32. – *Les principes du raisonnement Exposez en deux Logiques nouvèles. Avec des remarques sur les Logiques qui ont eu le plus de réputation de notre temps.* Paris: Chez Pierre Witte, 1714.

33. – *Oeuvres philosophiques du Père Buffier de la compagnie de Jésus avec notes et introduction par Francisque Bouillier.* Paris: Adolphe Delahay, 1843.

34. – *Pratique de la mémoire artificielle, pour apprendre et pour retenir aisément la chronologie, et l'histoire universelle. Par le Père Buffier, de la Compagnie de Jésus.* Paris: Chez Nicolas le Clerc, Edme Couterot et Michel Brunet, 1705.

35. – *Sentimens chrétiens, sur les principales véritez de la Religion; Exposez en Proses, en Vers, et en Estampes.* Paris: Joseph Mongé, 1718.

36. – *Suites du traité des premières véritez, ou des véritez de conséquence.* Paris: Chez François Didot, 1724.

37. – *Traité des premières véritez et de la source de nos jugements, où l'on examine le sentiment des philosophes sur les premières notions des choses.* Paris: Veuve Mongé, 1724.

38. Bunge, M., et al. *Les théories de la causalité.* Paris: Presses Universitaires de France, 1971.

39. Burtt, Edwin A., ed., *The English Philosophers from Bacon to Mill.* New York: Random House, Modern Library, 1939.

40. Butts, R. E., and Davie, J. W., eds. *The Methodological Heritage of Newton.* Oxford: Basil Blackwell, 1970.

41. Cassirer, E. *La philosophie des Lumières.* Paris: Fayard, 1932.

42. Chastaing, Maxime. "Reid, la philosophie du sens commun et le problème de la connaissance d'autrui." *Revue Philosophique de la France et de l'Etranger* 144 (1954): 352–99.

43. Chevalier, Jean Claude. *Histoire de la syntaxe. Naissance de la notion de complément dans la grammaire française (1530–1750).* Geneva: Droz, 1968.

44. Chisholm, Roderick M. *The Problem of the Criterion* (The Aquinas Lecture, 1973). Milwaukee: Marquette University Press, 1973.

45. – *Theory of Knowledge.* Foundations of Philosophy Series. Englewood Cliffs, N.J.: Prentice-Hall, 1966.

46. Cohen, Morris R. *Reason and Nature, An Essay on the Meaning of Scientific Method.* London: Kegan Paul, 1931.

47. Collins, James. *God in Modern Philosophy.* Chicago: H. Regnery Company, 1959.

48. Compayré, Gabriel. *Histoire critique des doctrines de l'éducation en France depuis le seizième siècle.* Vol. 2. Paris: Hachette, 1879.

49. Copleston, Frederick. *A History of Philosophy.* Vols. 4, 5, 6. New York: Doubleday, Image Books, 1960.

50. Cousin, Victor. *Cours de l'histoire de la philosophie moderne.* Vol. 4. Paris: Lagrange-Didier, 1848.

51. – *Introduction aux oeuvres du Père André.* Paris: Imprimerie du Crapelet, 1843.

52. – *Philosophie écossaise.* 3rd ed. Paris: Librairie Nouvelle, 1857.

53. Crousaz, Monsieur J. P. de. *Examen de l'Essay de Monsieur Pope sur l'Homme.* Lausanne: Bousquet & Company, 1737.

54. – *Examen du pyrrhonisme ancien et moderne.* The Hague: Pierre de Hondt, 1733.

55. – *La logique ou systèmes de réflexions qui peuvent contribuer à la netteté et à l'étendue de nos Connoissances.* 3 vols. 2nd ed. revue et augmentée. Amsterdam: l'Honoré & Chatelain, 1720.

56. Daniels, Norman. *Thomas Reid's Discovery of an Non-Euclidian Geometry: A Case Study in the Relation between Theory and Practice.* Thesis, Harvard University, 1970.

57. Dauriac, Lionel. *Sens commun et raison pratique, recherches de méthode générale.* Paris: Alcan, 1887.

58. Davie, George E. *The Democratic Intellect; Scotland and Her Universities in the XIX Century.* Edinburgh: Edinburgh University Press, 1961.

59. Denyse, Jean. *La vérité de la religion chrétienne démontrée par ordre géométrique.* Paris: Jean Delaulne et Jacques Quillau, 1717.

60. Désautels, Alfred R. *Les Mémoires de Trévoux et le mouvement des idées au dix-huitième siècle 1701–1734.* Rome: Institutum Historicum Societatis Iesu, 1956.

61. Destutt de Tracy, A. L. C. *Eléments d'idéologie.* Pt. 3. Paris: Courcier, 1804.

62. *Dictionnaire des ouvrages anonymes et pseudonymes dans la Société de Jésus.* Paris: Librairie de la Société, 1884.

63. Diderot, Denis. *Déclaration du clergé de France de 1682 (Bossuet) suivi des édits d'Henri IV, de la Bulle de Clément XIV contre les Jésuites, et de leur histoire abrégée.* Paris: Ponthieu, 1826.

64. Dreyfus, Ginette. "Notes & Discussions: le Cogito et l'axiome 'Pour penser il faut être'." *Revue Internationale de Philosophie,* no. 19 (1952), pp. 117–21.

65. Dumas, Gustave. *Histoire du Journal de Trévoux depuis 1701 jusqu'en 1762.* Paris: Boivin, 1936.

66. Dupont-Ferrier, M. G. *L'ancien Louis-le-Grand, Discours prononcé à la distribution des prix, 30 juillet 1908.* Paris: A. Munier, 1908.

67. Faurot, Jean H. "Common Sense in the Philosophy of Thomas Reid." *The Modern Schoolman*, 33, (March 1956): 182–89.

68. – "The Development of Reid's Theory of Knowledge." *University of Toronto Quarterly* 21, no. 3 (April 1952).

69. Faux, Jean M. "La fondation et les premiers rédacteurs des Mémoires de Trévoux (1701-1739) d'après quelques documents inédits." *Archivium Historicum Societatis Iesu*, no. 23 (1954), pp. 131–51.

70. Fearn, John. *First Lines of the Human Mind*. London: A. J. Valpy, Red Lion Court, 1820.

71. – *A Manual of the Physiology of Mind, Comprehending the First Principles of Physical Theology: Which with are laid out the Crucial Objections to the Reidian Theory*. London: Red Lion Court, 1829.

72. Foxe, Arthur N. *The Common Sense from Heraclitus to Peirce: The Sources, Substance and Possibilities of Common Sense*. New York: Tunbridge Press, 1962.

73. Franquesnay, de la Sarraz. *Essay sur l'esprit, sur divers caractères et ses différentes opérations*. Paris: André Cailleau, 1731.

74. Freeman, E., ed. "The Philosophy of Thomas Reid." *The Monist* 61, no. 2 (April 1978).

75. Garnier, Adolphe. *Critique de la philosophie de Thomas Reid*. Paris: Hachette, 1840.

76. Genest, Abbé. *Principes de la philosophie ou preuves naturelles de l'existence de Dieu et de l'immortalité de l'âme*. Amsterdam: Emanuel de Villard, 1717.

77. Gilson, Etienne. *Réalisme thomiste et critique de la connaissance*. Paris: Vrin, 1939.

78. Gorini, Corio de, M. le Marquis. *L'anthropologie, traité métaphysique traduit de l'italien*. 2 vols. Paris: Marc-Aurèle Bousquet & Compagnie, 1771.

79. Gouhier, Henri. *La pensée métaphysique de Descartes*. Paris: Vrin, 1962.

80. Grave, S. A. *The Scottish Philosophy of Common Sense*. Oxford: Clarendon Press, 1960.

81. – "Thomas Reid." *The Encyclopedia of Philosophy*, edited by Paul Edwards. New York: Macmillan, 1967.

82. Greig, J. Y. T., ed. *The Letters of David Hume*. 2 vols. Oxford: Clarendon Press, 1960.

83. Griffin-Collart, E. "Les croyances naturelles de Hume et les principes de sens commun de Reid." *Revue Internationale de Philosophie*, nos. 115–116 (1976), pp. 126–42.

84. – "Perception et sens commun: L'immatérialisme de Berkeley et le réalisme de Reid." *Annales de l'Institut de Philosophie* (1977), pp. 63–85.

85. Hall, A. R. *The Scientific Revolution 1500–1800. The Formation of the Modern Scientific Attitude*. London: Longmans Green & Co., 1954.

86. Hamilton, Sir William. *Fragments de philosophie.* Traduits par Louis Peisse, avec préface, note, appendice. Paris: Lagrange, 1840.

87. – *Lectures on Metaphysics and Logic,* edited by Henry Longueville Mansel and John Veitch. Vol. 2. Edinburgh and London: Blackwood & Sons, 1859.

88. Hazard, Paul. *La pensée européenne au dix-huitième siècle de Montesquieu à Lessing.* 2 vols. Notes et références. Paris: Ancienne Librairie Furne, Boivin & Cie, 1946.

89. – "Les origines philosophiques de l'homme de sentiment." *The Romanic Review* 28, no. 4 (December 1937): 318–42.

90. – *The European Mind 1680–1715* ("La crise de la conscience européenne"), translated by J. L. May. Baltimore: Pelican Books, 1964.

91. Hermand, Pierre. *Les idées morales de Diderot.* Paris: Presses Universitaires de France, 1923. Reprinted Hildesheim: Georg Olms Verlag, 1972.

92. Hintikka, Jaakko. *Knowledge and Belief: An Introduction to the Logic of the Two Notions.* Ithaca, N.Y.: Cornell University Press, 1962.

93. Hippeau, M. C. *Histoire de la philosophie ancienne et moderne.* 2nd ed. Paris: Hachette, 1838.

94 Holdsworth, William. *A History of English Law.* 3rd ed., vol. 9. London: Methuen & Co., 1966.

95. Hume, David. *Enquiries concerning the Human Understanding and concerning the Principles of Morals,* edited by Selby-Bigge. 2nd ed. Oxford: Clarendon Press, 1902.

96. Jacques, J. H. "The Appeal to Common Sense." *The Listener* 63, no. 1621 (April 1960): 709–10, 715.

97. Jansen, Bernard, S. J. *Die Pflege der Philosophie im Jesuitenorden während des 17./18. Jahrhunderts.* Fulda: Druck von Parzeller & Co., 1938.

98. – "Philosophen katholischen Bekenntnisse in inhrer Stellung zur Philosophie der Aufklärung." *Scholastik* II, no. 1 (1936): 1–52.

99. *Jésuite (Le) défroqué ou les Ruses de la société.* Rome: aux dépens de la société.

100. *Jésuites (Les) condamnés par leurs maximes et leurs actions.* Paris: Martinet, 1825.

101. *Jésuites (Les) criminels de lèze-majesté dans la théorie et dans la pratique.* 5th ed. The Hague: Chez les frères Vaillant, 1760.

102. *Jésuites (Les) ennemis de l'ordre social, de la morale, et de la religion, par leur probabilisme, leur doctrine régicide et leur conduite dans les missions et leur système de calomnie le tout prouvé par des pièces authentiques, & par des lettres originales déposées aux Archives du Vatican.* Paris: Delaunay, 1828.

103. Jones, Olin McKendree. *Empiricism and Intuitionism in Reid's Common Sense Philosophy.* Princeton: Princeton University Press, 1972.

104. Jouffroy, Théodore, ed. *Oeuvres complètes de Thomas Reid, chef de l'école*

écossaise, avec des fragments de M. Royer-Collard et une introduction de l'éditeur. 2 vols. Paris: Hachette, 1835.

105. Kant, Immanuel. *Critique of Pure Reason*, translated by N. K. Smith. London: Macmillan & Co. 1964.

106. — *Prolegomena to Any Future Metaphysics*, translated by Lewis White Beck. New York: Library of Liberal Arts, 1950.

107. Koyré, Alexandre, ed. *Newtonian Studies*. Chicago: University of Chicago Press, Phoenix Books, 1968.

108. Krolikowski, Walter P. "The Starting-Point in Scottish Common Sense Realism." *The Modern Schoolman* 33 (March 1956): 139–53.

109. Labrousse, Elizabeth. *Pierre Bayle et l'instrument critique*. Paris: Seghers 1965.

110. Laforêt, N. J. *La vie et les travaux d'Arnold Tits*. Brussels: H. Boemaere, 1853.

111. Laird, John A. *Study in Realism*. Cambridge: Cambridge University Press, 1920.

112. Lanson, Gustave. "Le rôle de l'expérience dans la formation de la philosophie du dix-huitième siècle en France." *Revue du Mois* 9 (1910): 5–28, 409–30.

113. Latimer, James F. *Immediate Perception as held by Reid and Hamilton considered as Refutation of the Skepticism of Hume*. Inaugural Dissertation. Leipzig. University of Leipzig, 1880.

114. Laurie, Henry. *Scottish Philosophy in its National Development*. Glasgow: James MacLehose and Sons, 1902.

115. Le Gendre, M. G. C. *Traité historique et critique de l'opinion*. 3rd ed. Paris: Briasson, 1741.

116. Lignac, Lelarge de (Abbé). *Le témoignage du sens intime et de l'expérience, opposé à la Foi profane & ridicule des Fatalistes modernes*. Auxerre: Fournier, 1760.

117. *Logique et Analyse*, nos. 41–42 (1968).

118. Lusignan, Serge. *Etude du "A Brief Account of Aristotle's Logic, with Remarks" de Thomas Reid*. Mémoire de maîtrise. Montreal: Université de Montréal, 1967.

119. Lyall, Alfred A. *A Review of the Principles of Necessary and Contingent Truth, in Reference Chiefly to the Doctrines of Hume and Reid*. London: Rivington, 1830.

120. Mabire, P. H. (Abbé). *Philosophie de Thomas Reid, extraite de ses ouvrages, avec une vie de l'auteur et un essai sur la philosophie écossaise*. 1st series, Paris: Périsse Frères, 1844. 2nd series, Paris: Jacques Lecoffre et Cie, 1846.

121. Maclaurin, Colin. *An Account of Sir Isaac Newton's Philosophical Discoveries in Four Books*. 2nd ed. London: A. Millar, 1750.

122. Marcil-Lacoste, Louise. "Dieu, garant de véracité ou Reid critique de Descartes." *Dialogue* 14, no. 4 (December 1975): 584–606.

123. – (in collaboration with Steven Burns). "Hume on Women." In *The Sexism of Social and Political Theory*, edited by Lorenne M. G. Clark and Lynda Lange. Toronto: University of Toronto Press, 1979.

124. – "La logique du paradoxe du Père Claude Buffier, S. J." *Dix-huitième siècle*, no. 8, "Les Jésuites" (1976), pp. 121–40.

125. – "La notion d'évidence et le sens commun: Fénelon et Reid." *Journal of the History of Philosophy* 15, no 3 (July 1977): 293–307.

126. – "Review of L. Turco's Dal sistema al senso comune." *ISIS* 69, no. 246 (March 1978): 135–37.

127. – "Sens commun et philosophie québécoise: trois exemples." *L'histoire de la philosophie au Québec de 1800 à 1950* ("Univers de la philosophie"), pp. 73–113. Montreal: Bellarmin, 1976.

128. – *"The Consistency of Hume's Position concerning Women."* *Dialogue* 15, no. 3 (September 1976): 425–41.

129. – "The Seriousness of Reid's Sceptical Admissions." *The Monist* 61, no. 2 (April 1978): 311–25.

130. – "Un philosophe du sens commun et la distinction kantienne des jugements a priori." *Actes du Congrès d'Ottawa sur Kant*, pp. 409–17. Ottawa: Presses de l'Université d'Ottawa, 1976.

131. – "Un scriptor, Voltaire et les Canadais." *Annales de l'ACFAS* 41, no. 3 (1974): 125–35.

132. Maréchal, Joseph. *Précis d'histoire de la philosophie moderne.* 2 vols. Paris: Desclée de Brouwer, 1951.

133. Marsak, Leonard M. "Bernard de Fontenelle, the Idea of Science in the French Enlightenment." *Transactions of the American Philosophical Society* 44, pt. 7 (December 1959): 3–40.

134. Mayor, Robert Grote. *Reason and Common Sense, An Inquiry into Some Problems of Philosophy.* London: Routledge & Kegan Paul, 1951.

135. McCormick, John F., S. J. "A Forerunner of the Scottish School." *The New Scholasticism* 5, no. 4 (October 1941): 299–317.

136. McCosh, James. *The Intuitions of the Mind Inductively Investigated.* New York: R. Carter and Brothers, 1860.

137. – *The Prevailing Types of Philosophy. Can They Logically Reach Reality?* New York: Charles Scribner's Sons, 1890.

138. – *The Scottish Philosophy, Biographical, Expository, Critical, from Hutcheson to Hamilton.* New York: Robert Carter and Brothers, 1875.

139. Mercier, Roger. *La réhabilitation de la nature humaine 1700–1750.* Villemonde: La Balance, 1960.

140. Molino, Jean. "Le bon sens du Marquis d'Argens. Un philosophie en 1740." Thesis, Sorbonne, 1972.

141. Monod, Albert (Abbé). *De Pascal à Chateaubriand, les défenseurs français du Christianisme de 1670 à 1802.* Paris: Alcan, 1916.

142. Montbas, Comte de. "Quelques encyclopédistes oubliés." *Revue des Travaux de l'Académie des Sciences morales et politiques* (1952), pp. 32–40.

143. Montesquieu, C. de S. *Essai sur le goût.* Introduction et notes par. C.-J. Beyer. Geneva: Droz, 1967.

144. Montgomery, Francis K. *La vie et l'oeuvre du Père Buffier.* Paris: Association du Doctorat, 1930.

145. Moore, G. E. *Philosophical Papers.* London: George Allen & Unwin, 1959.

146. Morgan, Betty Trebelle. *Histoire du Journal des Sçavans depuis 1665 jusqu'en 1701.* Paris: Presses Universitaires de France, 1928.

147. Norton, David F. "Francis Hutcheson in America." *Studies on Voltaire and the Eighteenth Century* 151–55 (1976): 1547–68.

148. – *From Moral Sense to Common Sense: An Essay on the Development of Scottish Common Sense Philosophy 1700–1765.* Ann Arbor, Mich.: University Microfilms, 1966.

149. – "George Turnbull and the Furniture of the Mind." *Journal of the History of Ideas* 35, no. 4 (October–December 1975): 701–16.

150. – "Hume and His Scottish Critics." In *McGill Hume Studies,* edited by D. F. Norton. San Diego: Austin Hill Press, 1978.

151. Palmer, Robert R. *Catholics and Unbelievers in Eighteenth Century France.* Princeton: Princeton University Press, 1939.

152. – "The French Jesuits in the Age of Enlightenment, A Statistical Study of the Journal of Trévous." *The American Historical Review* 45, no. 1 (October 1939): 44–50.

153. Pappas, John. "La rupture entre Voltaire et les Jésuites." *Les Lettres Romanes* 13, no. 4 (1959): 351–70.

154. Pascal, Blaise. *Pensées; The Provincial Letters.* New York: Random House, Modern Library, 1941.

155. Passmore, John. *A Hundred Years of Philosophy.* New ed. Harmondsworth: Penguin Books, 1968.

156. Peach, Bernard. "Common Sense and Practical Reason in Reid and Kant." *Sophia* 24, no. 1 (1956): 66–71.

157. Peirce, Charles Sanders. *Selected Writings. Values in a Universe of Chance.* New York: Dover Books, 1966.

158. – "Issues of Pragmatism." *The Monist* 15 (1905): 481–99.

159. Perrens, F. T. *Les libertins en France au dix-septième siècle.* Paris: Léon Chailley, 1896.

160. Petersen, R. *Scottish Common Sense in America 1768–1850. An Evaluation of Its Influence.* Ann Arbor, Mich.: University Microfilms 1972.

161. Picavet, Fr. *Les idéologues. Essai sur l'histoire des idées et des théories scientifiques, philosophiques, religieuses, etc. en France depuis 1789.* Paris: F. Alcan, 1891.

162. Pomeau, René. *La religion de Voltaire*. Paris: Nizet, 1956.
163. Popper, Karl R. *Objective Knowledge. An Evolutionary Approach*. Oxford: Clarendon Press, 1972.
164. Prévost, Abbé. *Le pour et contre, ouvrage périodique d'un goût nouveau*. No. xiv, vol. 10, no. 129. Paris: Didot, 1733.
165. Probst, D. K. "Francis Bacon and the Transformation of the Hermetic Tradition into the Rationalistic Church." Thesis, Université libre de Bruxelles, 1972.
166. Pust, Helga. *Common Sense bis zum Ende des 18. Jahrhunderts*. Europäische Schlüsselwörter. Vol. 2. Munich: Max Hueber Verlag, 1964.
167. – *Receuil de quelques pièces curieuses concernant la philosophie de Monsieur Descartes*. Amsterdam: Henry Desbordes, 1684.
168. Reid, Thomas. *Essays on the Intellectual Powers of Man*, edited and abridged by A. D. Woozley. London: Macmillan & Co., 1941.
169. – *Essays on the Intellectual Powers of Man*. Introduction by Baruch A. Brody. Cambridge, Mass.: M.I.T. Press, 1969.
170. – *Philosophical Orations of Thomas Reid*, edited with an introduction from the Birkwood Manuscripts by Walter Robson Humphries. Aberdeen: University Press, 1937.
171. – *Philosophical Works* with notes and supplementary dissertations by Sir William Hamilton and an introduction by Harry M. Bracken. 2 vols. Hildesheim: Georg Olms Verlagsbuchhandlung, 1967.
172. – *Sketch of the Character of the late Thomas Reid, D.D., Professor of Moral Philosophy in the University of Glasgow with Observations on the danger of political innovation*. From a Discourse delivered on 28th November 1794 by Dr. Reid, before The Literary Society in Glasgow College. [Rosebery Pamphlets, National Library, Ediburgh.] Reprinted in the Courier Office for J. McNayr & Co., 1796.
173. Rétat, Pierre. *Le dictionnaire de Bayle et la lutte philosophique au dix-huitième siècle*. Les Belles Lettres. Paris: Audin, 1971.
174. [Ripert de Montclar, M.] *Jésuites (Les) cités au Tribunal de la raison, ou opinions de nos plus célèbres écrivains et autres personnages les plus remarquables du compte rendu des constitutions des Jésuites*. Paris: F. Denn, 1826.
175. Robertson, J. C. "A Bacon-Facing Generation: Scottish Philosophy in the Early Nineteenth Century." *Journal of the History of Philosophy* 14, no. 14 (Jan. 1976): 37–49.
176. Rochemonteix, Camille de (Père). *Un collège de Jésuites aux dix-septième et dix-huitième siècles, le collège Henri IV de la Flèche*. 2 vols. Le Mans: Leguicheux, 1889.
177. Rome, Sydney. "Bishop Berkeley and Thomas Reid, a Study in the Origins of Scottish Realism." Thesis, Harvard University, 1940.
178. Rosmini-Serbati, Antonio. *The Origins of Ideas*. Translation. Vol. 1. London: Kegan Paul, 1883.

179. Ross, Ian [Simpson]. "Unpublished Letters of Thomas Reid to Lord Kames, 1762–1782." *Texas Studies in Literature and Language* 7, no. 1 (Spring 1965): 17–65.

180. Schalk, Fritz. *Praejudicium im Romanischen*. Frankfurt am Main: Vittorio Klostermann, 1971.

181. Schwarz, Stephen Dietrich. "Reid and the Justification of Perception." Thesis, Harvard University, 1966.

182. Sciacca, Michele Federico. *La filosofia di Tommaso Reid*. 3rd ed. Milan: Carlo Marzorati, 1963.

183. Segerstedt, Torgny T. *The Problem of Knowledge in Scottish Philosophy*. Lund: Gwd Gleerup, 1935.

184. Sicard, Augustin (Abbé). *Les études classiques avant la révolution*. Paris: Librarie académique Didier, 1887.

185. Sidgwick, Henry. "The Philosophy of Common Sense." *Mind* 14 (April 1895): 145–58.

186. Smout, T. C. *History of the Scottish People, 1560–1830*. London: Collins, 1969.

187. Snyders, Georges. *La pédagogie en France aux dix-septième et dix-huitième siècles*. Paris: Presses Universitaires de France, 1965.

188. Sommervogel, Carlos (Père). *Bibliothèque de la Compagnie de Jésus*. New ed., 2 vols. Paris: Picard, 1891.

189. – *Essai historique sur les Mémoires de Trévoux*. Paris: A Durand, 1864.

190. – *Table méthodique des Mémoires de Trévoux, 1701–1775*. 3 vols. Paris: A. Durand, 1864–65.

191. Sortais, Gaston. "Le Cartésianisme chez les Jésuites français aux dix-septième et dix-huitième siècles." *Archives de Philosophie* 6, no. 3 (1928): 1–93.

192. Souilhé, Joseph, S. J. *La Philosophie chrétienne de Descartes à nos jours*. Paris: Librairie Blond & Gay, 1934.

193. Stewart, Dugald, *Biographical Memoirs of A. Smith, W. Robertson, and T. Reid*, edited by Sir William Hamilton. Edinburgh: Thomas Constable & Co., 1868.

194. – *The Collected Works of Dugald Stewart*, edited by Sir William Hamilton. 13 vols. Edinburgh: Thomas Constable & Co., 1854.

195. Strasser, Johano. "Lumen naturale—sens commun—common sense: Zur Prinzipienlehre Descartes', Buffiers und Reids." *Zeitschrift für philosophische Forschung*, April–June 1969, pp. 177–98.

196. Tedechi, Paul. *Paradoxe de la pensée anglaise au XVIIIe siècle ou l'ambiguïté du sens commun*. Paris: A. G. Nizet, 1961.

197. Ueberweg, Friedrich. *History of Philosophy*. Vol. 2, *History of Modern Philosophy*, translated by G. S. Morris. New York: Charles Scribner's Sons, 1903.

198. Vernière, Paul. *Spinoza et la pensée française avant la révolution.* 2 vols. Paris: Presses Universitaires de France, 1954.

199. Wade, Iva O. *The Clandestine Organization and Diffusion of Philosophic Ideas in France from 1700–1750.* Princeton: Princeton University Press, 1938.

200. Waldman, Theodore. "Origins of the Legal Doctrine of Reasonable Doubt." *Journal of the History of Ideas* 20 (1959): 299–316.

201. Watson, R. A. *The Downfall of Cartesianism.* The Hague: Martinus Nijhoff, 1966.

202. Wiley, Margaret L. *The Subtle Knot, Creative Scepticism in the Seventeenth Century.* London: Allen & Unwin, 1952.

203. Wilkins, Kathleen S. *A Study of the Works of Claude Buffier.* Studies on Voltaire and the Eighteenth Century, No. 66. Geneva: Bestermann, 1969.

204. Zimmerman, J. P. "La morale laïque au commencement du dix-huitième siècle." *Revue d'histoire littéraire de France* 29, (1917): 42–64, 440–66.

Index

Abstraction, 31n, 84
Absurdity, 104; solipsism as, 50
Action, 91n, 113, 134; involuntary, 109n; voluntary, 109n, 126
Adequacy condition. *See* Newtonian rules, adequacy condition
Agnosticism, metaphysical, 41
Aguilar, Juan A. Ventosa, 6, 7n
Aguillon, François, *Opticorum*, 189-90
Alternatives, plausibility of, 40
Ambiguity, 20
Ambivalence, 20, 70, 71, 161
Analogies, 120, 140, 145; untested, 83
Antecedent, observable, 126–7; *latens processus*, 128
Apprehension, 89, 99, 100, 101, 102, 103, 105, 106, 108, 110, 119, 130, 132; conjunction with assent, 111, 114, 118; simple, 96, 138
A priori, 56
Arguments, 110–11n; *ad risum*, 1, 2, 169, 176; inductive, 119; methodological, 93; negative, 32; ontological, 47, 51; rational, 162, 163–64, 173, 176; rules of, 170; skeptical 3, 75, 172; transcendental, 118–19
Aristotle, 5, 189, 203; *Logic*, 8n
Arnauld, Antoine, 5, 98,
Assent, 23, 24, 27n, 62, 68, 99, 109, 110, 120, 128, 150; cause, 143; conjunction with apprehension, 111, 114–15, 118; to external objects, 60; generality, 105; immediate, 63, 102, 105, 106, 108, 110–11, 114, 117, 142–3, 154; irresistible, 107; laws, 103, 114, 118, 119, 125, 130, 132, 136–7,

138, 140, 144; necessity, 66; non-immediate causes, 168; particular, 105–6, 113; rationality, 147; real, 130
Assumptions, 129n, 145, 168–69; metaphysical, 111n
"Autorité générale," 21
Axioms, 117, 132, 184, 188; general, 132; induction, 131; self-evident, 83n

Bacon, Francis, 79, 83n 105n, 123–24; *Great Instauration*, 131; induction, 131; Reid's understanding of, 131-41; Table of Affirmation, 131; Table of Comparison, 131; Table of Investigation, 131, 163; Table of Negation, 132
Bayle, Pierre, 28, 31, 41
Beliefs, 7n, 16, 82, 89, 101, 112–13, 114, 115, 123, 136, 138, 164, 166, 167, 171, 175; *a priori* laws, 119; connection with conception, 107, 108, 109, 118n, 128, 132; corrigibility, 3; generalizations about, 115–16; immediacy, 86, 174; instinctive, 139; irresistible, 104–5, 132; justification, 2, 68; laws, 99n, 116n, 125, 136, 147, 173; levels, 111n, 159; natural, 139, 143, 172; ordinary, 93, 122, 144; real, 162; rehabilitation, 150, self-evident, 104, 169; signs, 103; skeptic's, 111–12; treatment, 148; variations, 110; versus arguments, 2
Benoist, Elie, 37
Berkeley, George, 1, 44, 94, 98, 119n, 136

Bouillier, F., 6, 37

Brutes, 180–206 *passim*

Buffier, Claude: acceptance of Locke, 18–19; agreement with Reid, 155; and introspection, 156–59; Cartesian influence on, 35; censorship of, 12n; common-sense doctrine, 14–15, 164–69; contrasted to Reid, 153–55; *Cours de sciences*, 12–13; *Elémens de métaphysique à la portée de tout le monde*, 14, 16; *Examen des préjugez vulgaires*, 14, 15; grammatical model, 57n; influences on, 5; interests, 11; as Jesuit, 11–13; *Mémoires de Trévoux*, 30; *Pratique de la mémoire artificielle*, 12n; *Principes du raisonnement*, 12, 14, 16, 23; *Traité des Premières Vérités*, 6n, 13, 14, 15, 16, 32

Cause, 62, 105, 114, 126–27; and effect, 87; efficient, 81, 102, 116n, 120, 126, 127, 128, 130, 133, 144, 147, 162, 171; intelligent, 39, 127; natural, 126; physical, 127, 130, 133, 162; self-sufficient, 103

Certainty, sources of, 66

Church, authority of, 39–40n

Cicero, 110; *De oratore*, 188n

Classes, grammatical, 204

Cogito, 49, 51, 53, 55–56, 62, 65, 66, 67, 68, 69, 98n, 161, 163, 167, 169, 170; Cartesian, 33, 44, 58n; conjunctive features, 172; elements, 58; enlarged, 44; limitations, 49; metaphysical side, 58n; philosophical understanding, 54; psychological side, 58n

Common sense: arousal, 198; as disposition, 34; as faculty, 74, 89n, 181, 184, 187, 189, 200; Buffier's defense, 40; Buffier's notion, 13, 14; caricatures of, 153, 169–77; common appeal, 97–98, 100, 181; connection with induction, 121–24; defining, 16–21, 21–32, 32–43, 65, 76, 82–83, 156–59; dictates, 134, 141, 149, 150, 188; epistemological status, 154; first principles, 33–34, 64, 65, 141, 167; justification, 73, 84, 158, 170; main foundation, 43; maxims of, 122; meaning, 143–44, 187; notion of, 80; philosophical notion of, 83; principles, 31, 33–34, 35, 43–44, 118n, 161;

Reid's definition, 88–94; Reid's use of, 73; role in conduct, 91; role in morals, 91n; as source of truth, 33; truths, 30; use as refutation, 75n. *See also* Philosophy, common-sense; Principles, first; Propositions, self-evident

– appeal to, 2, 67, 92, 97–98, 143, 146, 149, 156, 158, 188; Buffier's justification, 43–65; justification, 3, 9, 16, 17, 65, 153, 169; Reid's justification, 119–24, 160, 161; validity, 42–44, 143; value, 160

Comparisons, 200

Composition, notion of, 195, 196

Conceptions, 83, 84, 86, 88, 89, 95, 103, 110, 117, 118, 130, 173, 193–94; abstract, 95; characteristics, 110; connection with belief, 107, 108, 118n, 128, 132; in judgment, 107–8; reflection on, 131; test for truth, 109–11. *See also* Judgment; Reflection

Conclusions, 88, 89, 90, 112, 137; inductive, 121, 166; validity, 114

Connection, causal, 108

Consciousness, 45, 49, 56, 81, 113n, 114, 139, 154, 190; fallacious, 201; limits, 135–36n

Consent, universal, 35, 36, 37, 39, 132; appeal to, 104

Consistency, logical, 68, 161, 163

Contradiction, 29, 49n, 50, 53, 141, 154; law of, 51; principle of, 2

Contrariety: law of, 49n, 51; notion of, 203–4

Convictions, 86, 107–08, 109; fallacious, 201. *See also* Beliefs

Cooper, Anthony Ashley, Lord Shaftesbury, 3, 5, 92, 188–89; *Sensus Communis*, 91

Copula, 55

Countertruths, 28

Cousin, V., 5

Curâ primâ, dating, 179–80

Custom, 17, 105, 128, 143, 168

D'Holbach, Paul Henri Dietrich, Baron, 3

Deduction; principles, 74; logical, 52, 56. *See also* Reasoning, deductive

Definitions, 80

Demonstrations: logical, 61; metaphysical, 51; syllogistic, 131

Descartes, René, 3, 4, 5, 19, 20n, 44n, 45, 58n, 67, 77n, 98, 108n, 110, 148, 155

Description, 197–98; appeal to, 118

Designer, intelligent. *See* God

Dictionnaire de Trévoux, 11

Diogenes, 1

Discernment, 181, 204; direct, 24, 35; reflexive, 24, 57; uncommon, 187

Dispositions: common sense as, 65, 66, 68; rational, 160

Distinctions, making 59–60, 66–67, 206–7

Distinguishing, as operation of mind, 197–99

Dogmatism, 15, 29, 59–60, 140, 154, 170–71, 172, 173–74; of internality, 68

Education, 104, 181, 185, 187

Effects, 128, 167, 168, 196. *See also* Cause

Elitism, epistemological, 175

Empiricism: Lockean-Humean, 5; *reductio ad absurdum*, 119

Enthymeme, *cogito* as, 45, 46

Error juris, 139

Error personae, 139

Error(s), 29, 41, 104, 136, 137, 141, 157, 185; safe side, 147; valid, 50, 51, 52, 58–59, 81

Essence, metaphysical, 18–19

Evidence, 100–102; of first principles, 80; inductive, 129n; intuitive, 80; laws of, 118, 130, 134n; metaphysical, 48; natural, 110, 134; sources, 59; theories, 138. *See also* Self-evidence

Existence, 21, 34, 55–56; of bodies, 33, 38, 42, 46, 50, 62; continued, 200, 202; derivation, 138; external objects, 46, 49, 60, 64, 66, 107, 139, 165; future, 46; judgments about, 60, 66; knowledge, 61; notion of, 63; other beings, 38, 39, 48, 59, 60, 61, 65, 68, 112, 160, 166, 186; past, 46, 87; present, 87; real, 48, 110n; self-, 107; test for, 109; thinking beings, 103n; truths of, 63, 172

Experience, 41, 105, 106, 110n, 130, 143, 181, 191

Experimenta fructifera, 131

Experimenta lucifera, 131, 132

Experimental method. *See* Method, experimental

Experimentum crucis, 162

Extravagance, 28n

Facts, 103, 108, 115, 137; empirical, 111n, 113n; metaphysical, 113n

Faculties, 20, 21, 66, 94, 122, 123, 127n, 154, 156, 163; common sense as, 74, 89n, 181, 183, 184, 187, 189, 200; fallibility, 142; God-given, 145, 146–47; intellectual, 167, 189; of judgment, 82; natural, 146–47; rational, 191; reliability, 142, 168; spiritual, 22

Falsity, 24

Fénelon, 94n, 98n

Gallicanism, doctrine of, 12n

Generalizations, 118n, 120, 121–22, 166

God, 38, 145–49; Cartesian appeal to, 148; existence, 48, 116, 148, 149, 169; laws, 146; veracity, 33n, 47

Gregory, David, 126, 189n; *Astronomiae*, 190

Hamilton, Sir William, 7, 15

Horace, 19, 189

Human nature, 28n

Hume, David, 3, 4, 5, 91, 94n, 98, 99, 102n, 108n, 111–12, 119n, 123, 128, 148, 150, 163, 206; *Treatise*, 173

Hutcheson, Francis, 5

Hypotheses, 103, 108, 129, 138–39, 145, 168, 169; elimination, 129; form, 134; ambiguity, 128; use, 126

Hypotheses non fingo, 128, 129, 130, 147

Ideas, 107, 108; association, 138; clearness, 19, 67; comparison, 95; conformity, 53; defining, 19, 95–96; distinctness, 54, 67, 160; formation, 23, 24; innate, 21, 22, 23, 62, 66, 156; representative, 95, 107, 123n; similarities among, 159; of sensation, 205; truth, 102; way of, 138, 139

Identity, 170, 201–3; as first truth, 200; concept, 161; laws, 50, 70; logic, 68; notion of, 56; perfect, 31, 55, 200; personal, 200–201; reappraisal, 161; rules, 52, 54, 56, 66, 68, 159, 160, 168, 170

Idiots, 180, 181, 187–203 *passim*

Idols of the theater, 140
Imagination, 62, 138, 181, 190
Impossibility, evidence of, 110n
Impressions, 20, 24, 88, 102, 113n; natural, 32, 37
Induction, 105, 128–29, 142, 143, 145, 146, 147, 171, 180; aim, 168; appeal to, 120, 141, 149–51; connection with common sense, 121–23; importance, 111n; rules of, 173; use of, 164. *See also* Reasoning, inductive
Inductive method. *See* Method, inductive
Infants, 180–206 *passim*
Inferences, 57, 89, 107, 148; logic of, 26
Inquisition: philosophical, 173; tribunal of, 138–40
Introspection, 154, 155; Buffier on, 156–59, 164; Reid on, 156–59, 164

Jesuits, 13n, 49; philosophical role, 5n
Johnson, Samuel, 1
Judgment(s), 2, 22, 32–33, 83, 84, 112, 114, 120–21, 130, 136, 137, 138, 142, 173, 183, 188, 189; analyzing, 88; assent to, 86, 106; basis, 110–11, 116; common, 90, 93, 94, 121, 145; compatible, 161; conception as, 107; by consequence, 24–25; contingent, 96; definition, 95–96; discursive, 84n; elements, 107; faculty of, 82; formation, 21, 31, 92–93, 199; general law, 136; identical, 66; imperceptible, 23; inductive approach, 109; intuitive, 84n, 90n, 101, 110, 182; logical, 171; mechanism, 96; metaphysical theory, 74n; natural, 88, 116n, 120n, 145, 154, 182, 184; natural laws governing, 82, 136; necessary, 88, 96; ordinary, 78, 144; original, 102n; perceptual, 86, 115; by principle, 24, 25; *quod facti*, 119, 137; *quod juris*, 119, 137; reflections on, 84, 108, 109, 122, 144, 157, 158; self-evident, 68, 93; similar, 31–32; suspension, 42, 165; tests for, 109; truth, 16, 24, 60; ultimate laws, 118; uniform, 156; veracity, 39
Juvenal, 189

Kames, 126
Kant, Immanuel, 47, 119n, 173; *Prolegomena to Any Future Metaphysics*, 2
Knowledge, 62, 103n, 147, 154, 160,

163, 166, 183; conjunctive, 56, 60; first principles, 93, 117, 122, 166; general laws, 121–22; genuine, 96; ideal, 60–61, 67; intuitive, 60; limitations, 18–19, 63; metaphysical, 40, 67; principles, 65, 78, 100; real, 60, 67; through reason, 185

Lamennais, Félicité Robert de, 5, 21, 39n
Language, 80, 83n, 111n
Law: common, 135n; natural, 134n; ultimate, 133
Lignac Lelarge de, 30n
Likeness, epistemological, 52, 53, 54
Literary Society of Glasgow, 179–80
Locke, John, 4, 11, 18, 23, 31, 57n, 60, 98, 195, 196, 199n, 200, 201, 202, 205; *Essay concerning Human Understanding*, 5
Logic, 17; inductive, 159, 163

McCormick, J. F., 8
McCosh, J., 7
Malebranche, Nicolas de, 5, 98
Mémoires de Trévoux, 11, 30
Memory, 62, 87, 111, 181, 191, 192, 194, 201
Methods: analytical, 57, 84; Baconian-Newtonian, 83, 127n; Cartesian, 127n, 149; experimental, 100, 112, 118, 119, 120, 121–22, 123–24, 124–26, 131, 137, 140, 144, 145, 148, 149, 151, 158, 162, 163, 169, 171; inductive, 79, 127n, 131, 137, 144, 145, 161, 163, 168, 169; inductive-introspective, 119; *reductio*, 128, 129; reflexive, 127n; synthetical, 57, 84
Mind: affection of, 108; Buffier's views on, 157, 159–64; dispositions, 156; natural laws, 142, 145; operations of, 16, 22, 81, 98, 102n, 103n, 121, 123, 128, 129n, 135–36, 144, 182, 196–97; powers, 144, 171–72, 183, 190, 192; Reid's views on, 159–64; science of, 123, 126–28, 131, 134, 140, 143, 145, 148, 150, 151, 162, 163
Montgomery, F. K., 7–8
Moore, George Edward, 5

Nature: God-given order, 168; grammar of, 83, 131, 135; gifts of, 89n, 187; human, 28n, 171; interpreting, 146;

laws of, 103, 106, 118, 125, 126, 127n, 142, 149, 150; sentiment, 64; work of, 101

Necessity, 112, 116–17

Newton, Sir Isaac, 79, 83n, 103, 112, 149, 168; methodological rules, 105n, 122, 123–31; *New Organon*, 124; *Regulae philosophandi*, 81, 123, 124, 130, 133, 155

Newtonian rules, 134, 143, 171; adequacy condition, 124, 130, 161, 162, 170; reality condition, 124–25, 126, 129, 130, 147, 150, 161, 162, 170

Nolite judicare, 41

Noncontradiction: law of, 70; rules of, 50, 68, 170–71

Notions: Cartesian, 56n; false, 140

Objects: internal, 59; nature, 60; noninternal, 59; science of, 162

Observations, 121, 182, 199; field of, 121, 122, 126, 161; inductive, 121

Omissions, 112

Opinions, 104, 132, 170–71; absurdity, 188; analysis, 141; common, 154–55; fallacious, 201; judgment of, 188; public, 27, 29; relativity, 27, 28, 36, 94n, 155; vulgar, 27

Panic, 199

Paradoxes: Buffier's plea for, 14; defense, 29, 30, 41, 171; legitimate, 30, 165; logic of, 157

Passion, 199

Peirce, Charles Sanders, 5

Peisse, Louis, 11

Perceptions, 19, 20, 24, 33, 55, 83, 89, 91, 94, 95–96, 97, 115, 116n, 132, 136n, 143, 165, 171, 173, 182, 188, 190, 196; acquired, 190; elements of, 107; of external objects, 88; internal, 46–47; Reid's view of, 84–88, 107; sensory, 22, 29, 43, 85, 157, 186, 190, 193–94, 199

Petitio principii, 51

Phenomena: accounting for, 138n; consequent, 126, 127; general, 109; natural, 103, 113, 140, 181; observable, 126

Philosophies: ancient, 123; modern, 123

Philosophy: inductive, 133–34; natural, 140

— common sense: caricatures, 2, 3, 153,

169–77; counterexamples, 3; foundation, 43–44; institutionalization, 3; justification, 3, 4, 58–59; limitations, 70; perceptions about, 9; relevancy, 1; treatment of, 9

Plausibility, 25, 26

Possibility, knowledge of, 109n

Postulatum, 129n

Pouchard, M., 12n

Power(s), 87, 94, 116; existence, 144; intellectual, 120, 126, 171, 199, 207; relation to effects, 127

"Prearogativae instantiarium," 133

Prejudices, 69, 79, 81, 141, 157, 185; Buffier's analysis, 14; "legitimate," 28; vulgar, 15, 21, 27, 28, 29, 31, 66, 70, 98, 156, 170, 171

Principles: *a priori*, 119; common-sense, 23, 117, 123, 130, 160–61, 164–65; general, 113; self-evident, 68, 70, 98, 99, 100, 103, 105, 111, 113–14, 115, 118, 137, 142, 144, 146, 157, 173, 175; subordinate, 23; thinking, 201; truths of, 25

— first, 7n, 23, 26, 27n, 30, 41, 42, 43, 44, 56n, 65, 67, 69, 70, 80, 112, 113, 122, 130, 141, 144, 148, 151, 155, 183, 184, 185, 186, 188; agreement on, 99; analysis, 97–100; appeal to, 98n, 120, 158; assent to, 124, 141; belief in, 148; Buffier's, 165; clearness, 35, 38, 158; codification, 105, 111, 117–19, 123, 126, 165, 171; counterclaims, 38; determination, 15, 31; discernment, 34; discovery, 81, 100; distinction, 133; formulation, 165, 167; justification, 36; laws of, 104, 117–18; list, 33–34, 154; metaphysical, 113n; plausibility, 38, 157; Reid's, 97–100, 115–16, 119–20; rejection, 40; science, 124; status, 37, 133, 134, 164–67; theory, 126; truth, 16, 36, 47, 56n; unaccountability, 137; undemonstrability, 144

Procedures: eliminative, 105, 106, 114, 130, 144, 148; empirical, 38; inductive, 141; inductive-introspective, 76, 93

Propositions, 35, 42; certain, 2; conceptions of, 108, 110; conjunctive, 55; contrary, 203; contingent, 97; necessary, 97; self-contradictory, 109; universal, 31

– self-evident, 16, 17, 33, 36, 43, 69, 70, 71, 92, 94, 98n, 102, 103, 104, 105, 119, 121, 122, 123, 131, 132–33, 144, 150, 157, 158–59, 161, 163, 165, 168, 169, 171, 185; agreement on, 108, 136; assent to, 24, 105–6, 109, 128, 130, 140, 144, 154; codification, 93, 99, 100, 111–19, 126, 129, 131, 137, 142, 148; as hypotheses, 129; justification, 160, 174; as ultimate laws, 133

Rationalism, Cartesian-Malebranchian, 5
Rationality: limits, 173, 174; nature, 175
Realism, metaphysical, 17, 67
Reality, 31n, 138; of objects, 104, 162
Reality condition. *See* Newtonian rules, reality condition
Reason, human, 22, 75, 83, 99, 122, 175, 176; appeal to, 35; degree, 184; existence, 39; first principles, 20; highest tribunal, 94, 121; intuitive, 144; limits, 40, 43; natural, 154, 170; "practical," 171; unity, 69
Reasonableness, notion of, 40
Reasoning, 84, 89, 96, 105, 129, 130, 133, 141, 143, 147, 185; abstract, 109n; *ad absurdum*, 104, 132; *ad hominem*, 104, 132; analogical, 81, 123; . basis, 165; deductive, 104, 106, 107, 132, 155–56, 160, 162–63, 167, 173, 174; fallacious, 137; foundation, 188; hypothetical, 26; inductive, 107, 122, 131–32; limits, 137; logical, 20, 24, 25, 26, 52, 60, 67; mathematical, 25; reflection on, 131
Recollection, 192
Reductio ad absurdum, 1, 51, 109, 119, 150
Reductionism, 139, 170, 171
Reflection, 29, 30, 40, 81, 93, 113n, 119, 120, 121, 122, 125, 128, 131, 134, 135, 139, 143, 144, 145, 181, 190, 191, 192, 196, 202–3; experimental, 159; introspective, 102; on judgment, 157, 158; as sentiment, 24
Regress, infinite, 40
Reid, Thomas: accusations against, 6–9; *Active Powers*, 133n; agreement with Buffier, 155; and introspection, 156–59; appeal to induction, 150–51; commitment to experimental method, 76; commitment to induction, 140–41; common-sense doctrine, 164–69;

contrasted to Buffier, 153–55; *curâ primâ*, 179–208; eliminative procedure, 105–6, 129; epistemology, 78; "Essay on Conception," 96n; "Essay on Judgment," 78–79, 82; influences on, 5; *Inquiry*, 8n, 73, 75, 76, 77n, 78, 83, 84, 85, 93, 95, 107, 116n, 143, 180, 183; *Intellectual Powers*, 8n, 73, 75, 76, 78, 79, 83, 143, 183–84, 185, 186; methodology, 76–78, 79–82; "Of Common Sense," 187–208; originality, 6–9, 73–74, 153, 177; rational means, 132; reliance on Deity, 146
Relation, causal, 126–27
Relativism, philosophical, 30
Remembrance, 46
Revisionism, ambiguous, 140
Ridicule, 28n, 104, 132
Rudis indigestaque moles, 95n, 205

Sameness, notion of, 32, 56
Science, 107, 115, 151, 158; natural, 126–28; natural laws, 165
Segerstedt, T., 8
Self-evidence, 35, 39, 81, 99, 101, 110–11, 116, 120, 125–26, 130–31, 134, 136, 141, 150, 156, 158, 161, 171, 174–75, 183–84; approach to, 149; assent to, 138, 147; Buffier's notion, 157; inductive treatment, 107; laws of, 135, 138, 139, 140, 173; methodological model, 111; noninductivist systems, 135; nonobvious notion, 174; Reid's theory, 129, 130, 157
Sensations, 23, 85, 86, 87, 88, 94–95, 157, 192–93, 195, 196, 203
Senses, 111, 115; epistemological role, 96; evidence of, 134; external, 186; images of, 139; judgments using, 83–84; rules of, 37; testimony, 37, 39n, 42–43
Sensorium comune, 21, 66
Sensus communis, 91, 188n
Sentiment(s), 23, 25, 26; epistomological function, 24; natural, 38; noninternal, 53; rational, 167
– internal, 21, 24, 33, 39n, 44–65; *passim*, 66, 69, 156, 158, 160, 164, 166; appeal to, 53; Buffier's definition, 44–45; epistemological features, 47–48; unwarranted reduction, 54
Shaftesbury. *See* Cooper, Anthony Ashley, Lord Shaftesbury

Similarity, notion of, 56
Similitude, 202–3; perfect, 202
Simplicity, notion of, 195–96
Skepticism, 40, 41, 51, 52, 53, 67, 69, 75, 107, 111–12, 141, 154, 163, 165, 167, 169, 171, 172–73, 175
Socrates, 201
Solipsism, 45, 49–50, 51, 52, 60, 61, 63, 65, 66, 68, 69, 160, 163, 167, 170, 172; metaphysical, 44, 49
Spinoza, Baruch, 31
Stewart, D., 6
Syllogisms, 57, 102; chain-, 26; demonstrations, 131

Tautologies, 54, 56, 57, 68, 160, 162
Theories: *a priori*, 100; justification, 126
Things: contingent, 110–11; definitions, 18, 80; existence, 61, 64n, 69; knowledge of, 19, 63; intrinsic nature, 18, 20, 61, 62n, 63, 67, 69, 166; metaphysical essence, 18–19; necessary, 110; reality, 25
Thought, 55–56; act of, 110; conformity, 95; distinctions, 58; immediate, 57n; objects of, 67, 110, 138; particularity, 69; ultimate laws, 114, 141
Tolerance, intellectual, 30
Tradition, Cartesian, 47
Tribunal of justice, analogy of, 134–36, 137–38, 140, 154
Truth(s), 20, 24, 36, 99n, 126, 136, 167; abstract, 116–17; basis for, 163; Buffier's model of, 69, 70; conjunctive, 55–56, 58, 63, 66, 67, 68, 160; connections, 171; of consequences, 54, 57n, 60, 67; contingent, 7n, 86, 87, 111n, 112–13, 115, 116, 118, 119, 122, 133, 134, 146, 165, 166, 186;

criteria, 46, 67; defining, 52, 67–68, 130–31, 176; of existence, 54, 63; external, 13, 54, 60, 61; first, 14–15, 18; hypothetical, 67; impressions, 62, 63, 64, 69, 70, 159; internal, 51–52, 53, 54, 60, 61, 63–64, 71; of intrinsic nature, 54; intuitive, 56, 57, 58, 59, 63, 67, 68; logical, 25–26, 31n, 32, 44, 52, 56, 57; nature, 176; necessary, 86–87, 112–13, 115, 116–17, 118, 119, 132, 133, 165, 186; objective, 67; origin, 45; plausible, 25; of principles, 54, 56n, 66, 67, 68; rules, 39n; self-evident, 16, 33, 63, 65, 77n, 91, 92, 98n, 100, 116, 144, 172, 184; sources, 52, 59, 66; test for, 109; tribunal of, 90n, 144; undemonstrability, 78

Understanding, 108, 134, 189; common, 89, 90–91, 93, 100, 107, 115, 117, 144, 150, 158; limits, 40, 147; natural, 187; natural powers, 180, 181, 190
Unity, notion of, 55, 195–96
Universality, 175

Variety, principle of, 56–57n
Voltaire, *Le siècle de Louis XIV*, 11
Veracity, 166
Verification, 140

Will, 62, 87, 109n, 116
Wit, 28n
Words, use of, 17–18, 27, 80, 97; ambiguity in, 21

Yes-or-No rule, 28, 30, 64, 69, 70, 71, 171

Zeno, 3